The
Dorrance Fund

Tramways and Trolleys

Tramways and Trolleys

THE RISE OF URBAN MASS TRANSPORT IN EUROPE

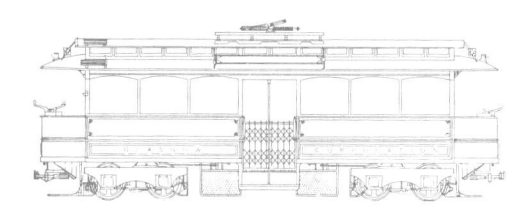

by John P. McKay

PRINCETON UNIVERSITY PRESS, PRINCETON, NEW JERSEY

COPYRIGHT © 1976 BY JOHN P. MC KAY
PUBLISHED BY PRINCETON UNIVERSITY PRESS, PRINCETON, NEW JERSEY
IN THE UNITED KINGDOM: PRINCETON UNIVERSITY PRESS, GUILDFORD, SURREY
ALL RIGHTS RESERVED

LIBRARY OF CONGRESS CATALOGING IN PUBLICATION DATA WILL
BE FOUND ON THE LAST PRINTED PAGE OF THIS BOOK

THIS BOOK HAS BEEN COMPOSED IN LINOTYPE BASKERVILLE
ON A FORMAT PLANNED BY BRUCE D. CAMPBELL
PRINTED IN THE UNITED STATES OF AMERICA
BY PRINCETON UNIVERSITY PRESS, PRINCETON, NEW JERSEY

To my parents

Preface

The last years of the nineteenth century witnessed a profound and many-sided transformation of European urban passenger transportation. Yet, in spite of its obvious importance from many points of view, there is not a single comprehensive study of this transformation and the electric streetcar revolution which made it possible. This book is an attempt to remedy that situation by means of a statistical and historical investigation of the growth of the European electric tramway industry between roughly 1890 and 1910, with primary focus on France, Germany, and Great Britain. (Considerable material relating to Russia and Belgian foreign investment will be presented separately in a subsequent publication.) At the very least this attempt, which has required the use of the very diverse and scattered materials discussed in the bibliography, will establish the basic trends and facts; it should therefore provide students in a variety of fields with new data which they may use for many different purposes.

This being said, I have no intention of waiting for others to grind my grain, and I have analyzed and evaluated my data on the rise of urban mass transport in Europe within the framework of certain basic problem areas studied by social scientists. Three of these were most important: the development, diffusion, and public management of technology and innovation; patterns of entrepreneurship and economic activity; and the impact of transportation changes —in this case the "transit take-off"—upon the urban environment and the lives of European city dwellers. In all three areas I believe I have reached some significant conclusions. These are summarized in the final chapter, where I also draw some lessons from the past and inferences for the future.

This problematic focus has facilitated the organization

of an almost infinitely expandable subject, since every city (or suburb, or company, etc.) could form the subject of a short monograph. A problematic focus also represents an attempt to move in new directions and to reduce what I believe have been fundamental deficiencies in the existing literature on the history of urban public transportation, deficiencies which must be overcome if the field is to come of age.

First, when a transit historian reads in a recent work the assertion that "The city, which is inherently cosmopolitan, has been treated with an exceptional provincialism," he can only smile.[1] How much more provincial the study of urban transport has been. Almost all investigation has remained resolutely local, has rarely even extended to the national boundaries the scholar quoted above deplores, and has almost never attempted to cross them. This atomistic approach has resulted in a great dearth of comparison, or comparable material, which would allow us to generalize and get at underlying processes. Yet these processes are almost certain to exist: not only because they pertain to a given class of events; but also because of the underlying unity of economic and social developments in the European civilization in this period, a unity the national approach of so much historical research has often obscured. This work has therefore adopted a broad European framework in an attempt to form and answer provisionally some of the basic questions, in order that future investigators and local historians will be encouraged to speak a common language and eventually reach more sophisticated syntheses.

The adoption of a problematic approach is related to what I feel has been a second deficiency. As with transportation history in general,[2] great stress has been placed on purely technical and mechanical details of vehicles and

---

[1] Leonard Reissman, *The Urban Process: Cities in Industrial Societies* (New York, 1964), p. vii.

[2] H. J. Dyos and D. H. Aldcroft, *British Transport: An Economic Survey from the Seventeenth Century to the Twentieth* (Leicester, 1969), p. 402.

traffic operations in studies of the development of urban public transportation. Not that I lack admiration for the expertise of local historians and transit enthusiasts in this area; yet it is clearly time to move beyond the enumeration of equipment and presentation of timetables to broader, less specialized concerns. We need to stress the forces and institutions which determined these purely technical developments and analyze consequences and implications of alternative technologies for economy and society. This I have tried to do. If others are stimulated to build upon these efforts, no one would be happier than I.

Many individuals and institutions have extended their aid to me in the preparation of this study, and I thank them all. A John Simon Guggenheim Foundation Fellowship permitted extended research in Europe and was greatly appreciated. Participation in a freewheeling, interdisciplinary investigation of the energy crisis and relationships between technology and society funded by the Sloan Foundation in the College of Engineering, University of Illinois, provided much stimulation. Indeed, this study can be seen as one man's contribution to such questions. In addition to helpful cooperation of librarians, archivists, and directors at the Bibliothèque Nationale, the Archives Nationales, the Crédit Lyonnais, and the Banque de l'Union Parisienne in Paris, the Bibliothèque Royale in Brussels, the Staatsbibliothek in Munich, and the John Crerar Library in Chicago, which also kindly permitted me to reproduce rare photographs, I wish to single out the invaluable support of the collection and staff at the Library of the University of Illinois, Urbana-Champaign. Its superlative collection of late nineteenth century technical periodicals and specialized monographs; its Special Languages Library; its indefatigable Interlibrary Loan Service; and other services too numerous to name: without such support this study, like countless others, would quite literally have been impossible. Let us hope that the people of Illinois and the nation will not permit the black magic of demagogic politicians to turn their great library into a mediocre one. I also wish to thank most sincerely the University of Illinois Research Board for summer grants and research assistants; the contribution of Dr. John Johnson, now of Macquarie University, Australia, was invaluable. The secretaries of the History Department and Mrs. Sharon Walter cheerfully typed the final manuscript. To my family I owe special debts: once again Jo Ann typed early drafts and generously gave her support and encouragement; Phil and Tom were enthusiastic and discerning companions on many explorations of European transportation. Finally, it is a pleasure to thank Professors Wallace D. Farnham, Charles P. Kindleberger, and Larry D. Neal, in addition to the two readers of the Princeton University Press, for being kind enough to read the entire manuscript and make numerous valuable comments and suggestions. In doing so they signally aided me, although I must claim sole responsibility for all remaining errors and shortcomings.

Contents

Preface	vii
Abbreviations	xiii
List of Tables	xiv
List of Illustrations	xv

I. Introduction: The Challenge
1. *Early Public Transportation*	3
2. *The Horsecar System*	13
3. *The Search for Alternatives*	25

II. Breakthrough and Development
1. *Electric Traction Experiments*	35
2. *American Innovation*	40
3. *The New Techno-Economic Matrix*	51
4. *Diffusion in Europe*	67

III. The Pattern of Adoption
1. *Aesthetic Values and Public Policy*	84
2. *The Development of Technological Alternatives*	95
3. *Negotiations and Agreements*	107

IV. Private Enterprise in France
	125
1. *The French Thomson-Houston Company*	126
2. *Followers and Competitors*	144
3. *The Mature Industry After 1900*	154

V. Municipal Enterprise in Great Britain
1. *Early Efforts*	163
2. *The Glasgow Model*	173
3. *The New Institutional Framework*	184

VI. The Impact on Society
1. *The Riding Public*	192
2. *Suburbs and Cities*	205
3. *Leisure and Recreation*	225
4. *The Tramway Workers*	229

VII. Conclusions
	239
Bibliography	247
Index	257

Abbreviations

AAA	*Annals of the American Academy of Political and Social Sciences*
AN	Archives Nationales, Paris
ASRA	American Street-Railway Association. *Proceedings.*
BUP	Archives de la Banque de l'Union Parisienne, Paris
CL	Archives du Crédit Lyonnais, Paris
EE	*Electrical Engineer* (London)
ERTJ	*Electric Railway and Tramway Journal* (London)
EZ	*Elektrotechnische Zeitschrift*
HC	House of Commons. Sessional Papers.
IE	*Industrie Electrique*
JTH	*Journal of Transport History*
MA	*Municipal Affairs* (New York)
MTA	Municipal Tramways Association of Great Britain. *Proceedings.*
SRJ	*Street Railway Journal*
TH	*Transport History*
ZGLSW	*Zeitschrift für das gesamte Local- und Strassenbahn-Wesen*
ZK	*Zeitschrift für Kleinbahnen*
ZOIAV	*Zeitschrift des Oesterreichischen Ingenieur- und Architekten-Vereines*
ZTS	*Zeitschrift für Transportwesen und Strassenbau*
ZVDI	*Zeitschrift des Vereines deutscher Ingenieure*

List of Tables

1.	Tramway and Railroad Passengers in 1886-1887	22
2.	Omnibus and Tramway Passengers in Berlin	25
3.	Total and per Rider Costs of Tramway Service	60
4.	Total Capital Invested in All Tramways in France and the United Kingdom, 1890-1912	68
5.	Electric Tramways in Europe	72
6.	Systems of Electric Traction on European Tramways	76
7.	Growth of Tramway Lines and Tramway Riders	82
8.	The Rouen Tramways Company, 1882-1913	136
9.	Streetcar Rides per Capita in Large German Cities	194
10.	Annual Rides per Capita on Public Transit	197
11.	Growth of Population in Metropolitan Brussels	212
12.	Tramway Development in Greater Manchester	217

List of Illustrations

1. Santiago de Chile. Railway station. A scene from the horsecar era. (A.E.G. [1899?]; courtesy John Crerar Library.)   28
2. Inauguration of steam tramways on Palmer Harding's concession for Paris and southern suburbs, 1876. (*L'Illustration*, 19 August 1876.)   28
3. Stuttgart. Motor-car with 2 trail-cars. Rush-hour traffic and capacity. (A.E.G. [1899?]; courtesy John Crerar Library.)   56
4. Kiev. Steep hills and the first city with electric tramways in Russia, May 1892. (A.E.G. [1899?]; courtesy John Crerar Library.)   56
5. Genoa. Upper and lower entrances of the S. Ugo spiral tunnel. (A.E.G. [1899?]; courtesy John Crerar Library.)   57
6. Halle a. S. Horsecars and electric cars; note the converted trailer. (A.E.G. [1899?]; courtesy John Crerar Library.)   64
7. Duisberg. Overhead wiring on draw-bridges. (A.E.G. [1899?]; courtesy John Crerar Library.)   64
8. Halle a. S. Central railway station. Laying new rails for electrification. (A.E.G. [1899?]; courtesy John Crerar Library.)   65
9. Berlin. Conduit traction in front of the Brandenburg Gate. (*Die Grosse Berliner Strassenbahn, 1871-1902*.)   103
10. Breslau. Wires and poles skillfully arranged. (A.E.G. [1899?]; courtesy John Crerar Library.)   103
11. Examples of Mannesmann steel poles, widely used in Europe.   104
12. Heilbronn. A typically festive inauguration of electric traction. (A.E.G. [1899?]; courtesy John Crerar Library.)   105
13. Hamburg. View on Jungferstieg, showing row of handsome double bracket poles. (*SRJ*, 1902.)   122
14. Various types of waiting stations used in Hamburg. (*SRJ*, 1902.)   122

15. Brussels. The built-up and surrounding area in 1880. (Alfred Mabille, *Les environs de Bruxelles* [Brussels, 1880].) 211
16. Manchester. Distribution of population and transport, circa 1913. (Manchester, *The Passenger Transportation Problem* [Manchester, 1914].) 218

Tramways and Trolleys

I. Introduction: The Challenge

1. *Early Public Transportation*

For centuries the peoples of Europe moved through their cities in a simple and effective manner as old as all mankind. They walked. For though the great majority of European urban centers were in existence by 1500, and had been exercising sophisticated economic, administrative, and cultural functions essential to the surge of medieval civilization from the eleventh century on, the populations and areas involved were very small by modern standards. Only the very largest centers reached 50,000 and most were far less. Of the estimated 3,000 towns in the Holy Roman Empire at the end of the Middle Ages, for example, only a dozen or so had populations of 10,000 or above, while another fifteen to twenty had between 2,000 and 10,000 inhabitants.[1]

These urban dwellers, crowded around the original cathedral or fortress, or bridge or port, as the case might be, and tightly restricted by protective walls, used space with great economy. Even in a great city like Bruges hardly any point was more than one kilometer from the city center. In most towns the most distant points within the walls were not more than a kilometer apart—a fifteen-minute stroll through the narrow streets. To this must be added the fact that the average urban resident lived on or very near his place of work. Little wonder, then, that within the city transportation facilities concentrated on moving goods rather than men.

The baroque city of the centralizing state expanded the urban horizon both spatially and functionally. Such a city

[1] Robert E. Dickinson, *The West European City* (London, 1951), p. 290. This excellent work, which has an extensive bibliography, provides capsule histories, maps, and analyses of a number of European cities before the Industrial Revolution; see especially pp. 251-445.

also expanded somewhat the means of transit, primarily for the rich and the powerful. The keeping of a coach and livery spread from royalty to nobility and then to wealthy bourgeoisie in the course of the late sixteenth and seventeenth centuries in the larger cities. London led the way, as it so often did in the early modern period. By 1617 Fynes Morison could write, "Sixty or seventy years ago coaches were very rare in England, but at this day pride is so increased, as there be few gentlemen of any account who have not their coaches, so as the streets of London are almost stopped up with them."[2] By the 1630s there were an estimated 6,000 coaches in the capital.

In Paris the number of coaches grew from only three in 1550 to three hundred ten in 1658. Thereafter the increase was extremely rapid, to perhaps 12,000 at the beginning of the eighteenth century, as the earlier restrictions on carriage ownership were dropped and a private coach became a social necessity for all who could afford one. "Coaches are so numerous in Paris that several houses have two or three," wrote a contemporary observer in 1717. "Many lawyers, merchants and ordinary bourgeois use them as a matter of course, and there is even some hesitation about going on horseback or on foot through the streets, where the common people are very insolent and disrespectful to gentlemen."[3] The privately owned vehicle, a symbol of status and an object of emulation, was well established.

It was quite the contrary with urban public transportation. Indeed, there is no evidence of a successful service transporting passengers along a predetermined itinerary for fares within cities before the nineteenth century, although overland stagecoaches carried passengers between

[2] Quoted by J. Joyce, *The Story of Passenger Transport in Britain* (London, 1967), p. 115.
[3] Alfred Martin, *Etude historique et statistique sur les moyens de transport dans Paris* (Paris, 1894), p. 14; see also Octave Uzanne, *La locomotion à travers le temps, les mœurs et l'espace* (Paris, n.d.), pp. 67-86.

towns from the seventeenth century on.[4] True, the great thinker Blaise Pascal is generally credited with the establishment of just such an urban service in Paris in 1662. The company proposed to establish "public coaches on the model of the stagecoaches," clearly the forerunner of the nineteenth-century omnibus. The petitioners argued that their coaches would be greatly appreciated by all those who could afford a modest fare of five sols, but who were unable to stand the expense of hiring a hackney carriage. Nonetheless only "bourgeois and people of merit" were permitted to use Pascal's coaches, as the monopoly was granted on condition that "soldiers, pages, lackeys, and other servants, as well as workers and laborers, will not be able to enter these coaches." This unpopular measure excluded much of the Parisian population and no doubt contributed to the company's demise within a few years.[5]

As the foregoing suggests, various forerunners of modern taxi service did develop more successfully in early modern Europe. After 1634 hackney carriages could be hired in London by anyone who did not have his own conveyance; by 1700 the city had about 600 such vehicles.[6] As for similar growth in Paris, which has been examined carefully by Martin, two points stand out. First, hackney service was granted to a monopoly whose fares and service were thoroughly regulated. Second, there were apparently about 300 coaches for hire in 1711 in Paris and about 350 in 1786.[7] This lack of growth suggests that demand for hired vehicles was limited and static, because of the expense involved. Demand came mainly from the same group that owned private coaches, whose number also failed to increase in Paris throughout the eighteenth century.

[4] See, for example, J. Crofts, *Packhorse, Waggon and Post; Land Carriage and Communications under the Tudors and Stuarts* (London, 1967), pp. 109-32.
[5] Martin, *Etude historique*, pp. 68-79.
[6] Joyce, *Passenger Transport*, p. 115.
[7] Martin, *Etude historique*, pp. 27-36.

One might also mention transport by hired sedan chair, which appeared in several cities like London, Paris, Berlin, and Dresden in the seventeenth century. Since the passenger was carried by two strong men and therefore arrived no sooner than if he had walked himself, the sedan chair was primarily a way for the wealthy, especially wealthy women, to escape mud and filth in the streets. Not surprisingly, in at least two German capitals officials saw sedan chair service more in terms of providing the poor with employment than in terms of responding to a genuine transportation need.[8]

It is of course a commonplace that the Industrial Revolution, beginning in England toward the end of the eighteenth century and spreading across the continent in the course of the nineteenth, initiated a series of changes and transformations of unprecedented proportions in almost every aspect of human endeavor. One might reason that European urban transportation witnessed similar great changes at an early date. Such was not the case. Indeed, in spite of new services and other innovations, the scope and content of change in European urban transport long lagged behind burgeoning industrialization and urbanization. Well into the 1860s the use of vehicles for urban transit was restricted to a small clientele, and it was not until the 1870s that a "public" transportation system worthy of the name developed in cities. Even then the impact was limited, and it was only in the 1890s that a mass transit system as revolutionary as early industrialization and urbanization finally emerged.

The reasons for the lag in urban transit are complex. In the first place, as Dickinson points out, "the economic forces of the nineteenth century resulted in a great concentration of inhabitants in compact urban agglomerations. Factories, offices and houses had to be crammed into the smallest pos-

[8] Hermann Grossmann, *Die kommunale Bedeutung des Strassenbahnwesens beleuchet am Werdegange der Dresdner Strassenbahnen* (Dresden, 1903), pp. 4-6.

sible area." Thus even when a continental city experienced rapid growth of total population, the urbanized area spread slowly beyond the historic walls, and "builders sought to erect houses as close as possible to the existing town and its factories, and with the highest possible density."[9] Such a crushing together of people may have been due in large part to a lack of adequate urban transportation. Certainly the rudimentary urban transport which did exist remained an expendable luxury for the great bulk of the population. That population continued to live and move in what Sam B. Warner has graphically described as the "walking city."[10]

Take Lille, France, for example. Growing hardly at all in the eighteenth century, it emerged as a leading textile and industrial center in the first half of the nineteenth century. Population jumped from 59,000 in 1804 to about 100,000 in 1860. Yet all this increase was crowded into the already inhabited area within the city walls, an area of less than three square kilometers. There one found the horrors of overcrowding and congestion, cellar living, filth, and disease, as well as a rapidly growing working-class population living within walking distance of the mills and factories.[11]

Perhaps English cities provided the best indication of the still modest dimensions of the urban area in the middle of the nineteenth century, since industrial growth began earlier there and crumbling town walls were less of a barrier to outward expansion. In a major city like Liverpool the main area of new building between 1830 and 1870 was no more than two miles from the center of the city. In Birmingham it was not more than two and one-half.[12] In 1870 a city like Kingston-upon-Hull, which had a population of 121,000

[9] Dickinson, *West European City*, pp. 446, 463. I found Dickinson's discussion of urban growth since the Industrial Revolution, pp. 446-544, very useful. There is a good bibliography.

[10] Sam B. Warner, Jr., *Streetcar Suburbs: The Process of Growth in Boston, 1870-1900* (Cambridge, Mass., 1962), pp. 15-21.

[11] Dickinson, *West European City*, pp. 135-36.

[12] John R. Kellett, *The Impact of Railways on Victorian Cities* (London, 1969), pp. 355-57, 360-62.

and was the twelfth largest city in England, had a "built-up" area of only about two square miles. Industrial and commercial establishments were concentrated in a relatively small area and working-class housing was nearby, so that the men and women could walk to work.[13]

The framework of power and energy contributed mightily to this urban concentration. The energy in coal could easily be transported by barge and then rail to any of a vast number of locations, where steam engines could then convert it into power. But that power could be transmitted only short distances by elaborate shafts and belts: hence the multistoried factories, where all divisions were as close as possible to the central power source. And the advantages of locating an individual factory near other factories—what economists term complementarities—fostered groups of land-saving vertical factories to cluster together in those industrial cities like Birmingham and Lille mentioned above.

Urban concentration was also promoted by the railroad. Ideal for linking major points, like cities or mines or ports, this fundamental transport innovation gave existing agglomerations further advantages in cost, reliability, and centrality. This applied not only to the location of industry but to the expansion of administrative and cultural functions, which almost invariably built on existing centers. Indeed, the greatest urban concentrations developed in the national and regional capitals, where increased administrative, commercial, and cultural functions resulted in urban growth linked only indirectly to industry.

Of crucial importance in moving goods and passengers long distances *between* cities, railroads were nonetheless of very little significance in moving people *within* cities. More surprisingly, until the end of the century railroads also carried few commuters toward the edge of the urban

[13] G. A. Lee, "The Tramways of Kingston-upon-Hull: A Study in Municipal Enterprise" (unpublished Ph.D. thesis, Sheffield University, 1968), pp. 1-5.

area. Therefore they did very little to develop suburbs which might have relieved congestion and overcrowding at the center. Kellett's masterful study on the impact of railroads on Victorian cities leaves no doubt that this was the British case. In four of the five cities he studied—Glasgow, Liverpool, Manchester, and Birmingham—there were few if any suburbs or "bedroom communities" which developed because of the railway link to the city center.[14]

Suburban railway travel was far greater in London, but then that megalopolis was eight times as large as any other British city. Yet only in the last two decades of the century did railway commuter traffic expand rapidly there, reaching perhaps 250,000 commuters in 1906, or one out of every four persons in the London labor force.[15] In the mid-1850s, however, the careful historians of London transport estimate that no more than 6,000 to 10,000 persons commuted to the city by rail, as opposed to perhaps 244,000 commuting by foot or omnibus.[16] There is nothing to compare with Kellett's study for continental cities, but the fragmentary data suggest that generally the railway played the same limited role in suburban expansion.[17] In short, railroads were expensive and few, as well as relatively inaccessible and inflexible because of few stations and special fixed rights of way. Thus they did little to alleviate the urban transport problem they certainly helped to create.

In fact, the old transportation technology of animate power—the horse—proved more adaptable to the needs of weary pedestrians than the new one of steam and iron. In addition to a growing number of private coaches and hired

[14] Kellett, *Impact of Railways*, pp. 354-65. Railroads may have played a more positive role in early suburban development in America. See Charles J. Kennedy, "Commuter Services in the Boston Area, 1835-1860," *Business History Review* 36 (1962): 153-70.

[15] *Ibid.*, pp. 365-82.

[16] T. C. Barker and Michael Robbins, *A History of London Transport: Passenger Travel and the Development of the Metropolis*, vol. 1, *The Nineteenth Century* (London, 1963), p. 58.

[17] For example, Martin, *Etude historique*, particularly pp. 175-79; *40 Jahre Essener Strassenbahnen, 1893-1933* (Essen, 1933), p. 13.

cabs for the well-to-do, omnibuses were horse-drawn. And these omnibuses provided not only the first means of urban public transit, but the dominant form in Europe until the beginning of the 1870s as well. Yet had Pascal reappeared he would have found his basic concept little altered, for the omnibus was hardly more than the overland stagecoach and its cousin, the "short stage," successfully adapted to the urban environment.

The omnibus originated in 1826, in Nantes, of all places, near which a retired French army officer named Baudry had built some baths. These baths were to use the condensed steam (hot water) which was produced by a steam engine that powered his grain mill. To attract patrons Baudry then initiated a coach line from the center of Nantes out to his baths. Interest in the baths failed to grow, but the coaches became popular as passengers boarded them for various destinations along the route, leading Baudry to close his baths and concentrate his "omnibus" service within the city. He had abandoned his original name of Richebourg Baths Coach after being struck by the aptness of a sign over the door of a hatmaker named Omnes—"Omnes Omnibus," or "Omnes for all." And when Baudry received permission to establish a similar service in Paris two years later, in 1828, the new vehicles were indeed "for all"—who could pay a fare averaging 25 centimes.[18]

Omnibus service was well received by the Parisian population, and this success induced imitation in other large cities. An English coachmaker established in Paris was so impressed that he returned home to introduce the French innovation to London in 1829. Abraham Bower copied in turn in 1831, and four years later there were more than a hundred omnibuses running through the streets of New

[18] Martin, *Etude historique*, pp. 80-85; John A. Miller, *Fares, Please!: From Horse-cars to Streamliners* (New York, 1941), pp. 3-4; Wolfgang Hendlmeier, *Von der Pferde-Eisenbahn zur Schnell-Strassenbahn* (Munich, 1968), p. 9.

York.[19] In the next thirty years most large European and American cities followed, though it would be difficult if not impossible to say when in every case. Bordeaux (1827) actually preceded Paris, and Lyons had various omnibus types of services in the 1820s before regular and successful operation began in 1837.[20] In the 1830s and 1840s omnibuses were widely used in American cities such as Philadelphia (1831), Boston (1835), and Baltimore (1844).[21] German cities lagged behind somewhat, but regular service began in Dresden in 1838, in Berlin in 1846, in Hanover in 1852, in Leipzig in 1860, and Munich in 1861. Once omnibus service began, new lines were quickly demanded and added. In Dresden, for example, there were fifteen lines crossing and crisscrossing the city by the late 1860s.[22]

Omnibus service had many technical limitations, however. With an average speed of perhaps five miles per hour the omnibus beat walking, but not by much. This was especially true in the historic center of the European city, which omnibuses traversed with great difficulty before large thoroughfares modeled on Haussmann's rebuilding of Paris began to be cut through the medieval undergrowth in the 1850s and 1860s. Service also responded poorly to the predictable wide fluctuations in demand. Thus omnibuses were all too often full in the morning, noon, and evening rush hours, or on rainy days, precisely when they were needed most. Holding extra coaches, teams, and drivers in reserve for such peak loads was uneconomical, and for safety reasons standing was generally forbidden in European cities. Finally, there was the problem of the quality of the roadway. If the pavement were fairly smooth and all-weather—preferably good granite block—vehicles could move satis-

[19] See Miller, *Fares, Please!*, p. 508, for a description of New York's omnibuses.
[20] Jean Arrivetz, *Histoire des transports à Lyon* (Lyon, 1966), p. 10.
[21] Miller, *Fares, Please!*, pp. 8-9; George Rogers Taylor, *The Transportation Revolution, 1815-1860* (New York, 1951), pp. 390-91.
[22] Grossmann, *Die kommunale Bedeutung*, pp. 13-15.

factorily. But if the surface were cobblestone or dirt, as it frequently was, then the ride was rough at best or a struggle through mud at worst.[23]

Scattered materials on the economic and social side of omnibus development are harder to piece together and evaluate properly. On the one hand, passenger traffic grew substantially before the advent of horse tramways. In Paris, for example, the number of omnibus passengers increased threefold from 40,000,000 in 1855, when the General Omnibus Company was founded, to 120,000,000 in 1867.[24] London followed a similar pattern. The number of omnibuses increased from about 620 in 1839 to about 1,300 in 1850, and by 1859 the London General Omnibus Company Ltd. was carrying 39,000,000 riders annually.[25] These and other examples clearly suggest that the humble omnibus played a substantial if neglected role in urban living from roughly the 1830s to the end of the 1860s. And, at least in England, the omnibus contributed to the growth of new middle-class residential areas one to two miles from the city center, as the railroad did not.[26]

At the same time, it seems clear that fares were quite high and that the regular clientele was restricted to the reasonably well-to-do.[27] True, fares tended to decline with time. Companies might add top decks to increase capacity and attract economy-minded passengers, as when Paris adopted the London double decker in 1855. Buses drawn by two horses and carrying seventeen passengers for a fare of 30 centimes were then replaced by double deckers carrying fourteen down and twelve on top, at 30 centimes and 15

[23] In addition to the works cited above, particularly those by Miller, Barker and Robbins, and Grossmann, see G. C. Dickinson, "The Development of Suburban Road Transport in Leeds, 1840-95," *JTH* 4 (1960): 214-23; G. A. Sekon, *Locomotion in Victorian London* (London, 1938).
[24] Martin, *Etude historique*, Appendix, Diagram no. 2.
[25] Barker and Robbins, *London Transport*, 1:59, 98.
[26] Kellett, *Impact of Railways*, pp. 355-71.
[27] Dickinson, "Leeds," p. 219; Barker and Robbins, *London Transport*, 1:35-36; Grossmann, *Die kommunale Bedeutung*, pp. 13-15.

centimes respectively.[28] But even though the fare from a Victorian suburb like Camberwell to London might fall from 1s. 6d. in 1851 to a range of 3d. to 6d. in the 1860s, it was at most within the financial reach of the better-paid clerk or artisan.[29] In short, neither fare reductions nor non-middle-class patronage should be exaggerated. As the historian of public transit in Dresden states, "Omnibus travel had many inconveniences attached to it which limited its use by the wealthy, and it was not cheap enough to be used to even the same extent by the poorer classes."[30] The development of suitable mass transit for the emerging urban civilization had scarcely begun.

2. *The Horsecar System*

The tramcar, like the railroad, had its origins in the coal industry. There it was used to move coal through the underground tunnels, as well as from the pit head to the nearest navigable waterway. The first such trams rode on planks, which were soon superseded by oak rails connected by cross-timbers. The wheels of the tram wore slots in the rails, which were replaced as needed. This resulted in a remarkable improvement, since the reduction in friction enabled a horse to pull about forty-two hundredweight of coal as opposed to only seventeen on an ordinary road.[31] When the steam engine on rails—the locomotive—replaced horses at the surface, the economies were so great that inland surface transportation was revolutionized in the decades after 1830.

It was logical therefore to experiment with the same friction-reducing rails in urban transit. One of the first such

[28] Martin, *Etude historique*, pp. 87, 95, 102. Those on top were not entitled to the free transfer of those on the bottom.
[29] H. J. Dyos, *Victorian Suburb: A Study of the Growth of Camberwell* (Leicester, 1961), p. 69.
[30] Grossmann, *Die kommunale Bedeutung*, p. 15.
[31] D. Kinnear Clark, *Tramways: Their Construction and Working* (London, 2nd ed., 1894), pp. 2-3.

attempts to put a coach on a track was made by John Mason on the New York and Harlem Railroad Company in 1832. First conceived of as a means of linking the projected Harlem River terminal of the railroad to Albany with New York proper, this horse-drawn railway soon focused on moving passengers within the city. This venture was followed by another in New Orleans two years later.[32] Little further progress was made until the early 1850s, however—the date sometimes erroneously given as the birth of the street railway, or urban tramway.

In 1852 a French engineer living in New York named Alphonse Loubat laid down a line using rolled wrought-iron rails, which were grooved and lay flush with the pavement. This was a significant innovation because the first tramcars had used step rails, that is, rails which protruded above street level, like iron barriers. Such rails had seriously interfered with coach and wagon traffic and created public hostility, which limited rapid diffusion. With the new rail the situation changed, and by 1860 horsecars were generally replacing omnibuses in American cities.[33]

The greatest advantage of the horsecar over the omnibus was the reduced friction and the correspondingly more efficient use of horse-power. Thus if a force of about thirty kilos was necessary to move a ton on cobblestones and twenty kilos on a well-paved street (and of course enormously more through muddy ones), the grooved rail required only about eight kilos for that same ton. A team of horses could therefore pull vehicles of two tons or more with up to fifty passengers—double the weight and number of most omnibuses.[34] This advantage became all the greater when streets were poorly paved, or dirt, and one English authority felt that it was the primitive character of Ameri-

[32] Miller, *Fares, Please!*, pp. 16-21.
[33] Taylor, *Transportation Revolution*, pp. 390-91.
[34] Barker and Robbins, *London Transport*, 1:179; Charles Dollfus and Edgar de Geoffroy, *Histoire de la locomotion terrestre: Les Chemins de fer* (Paris, 1935), p. 250.

can streets which made development of the horsecar an absolute necessity in the New World.[35] Even with adequate paving horsecars did noticeably better on hills and grades, which almost every tramway network contained at some point. It is interesting to note in this connection that at Kingston-upon-Hull small one-horse wagonettes seating eight to ten passengers were able to negotiate the streets of the flattest town in England so well that they bankrupted the tramway whose lines they followed and whose passengers they stole.[36]

There were other advantages. The horsecar was faster, smoother, and less noisy. There was also more room inside, easier entry and exit, and somewhat greater safety due to the brake, which increased control.[37] Finally, since the investment in rails paid for itself handsomely in the reduction of expenses per passenger, the operator could reduce fares and tap a new clientele.

Developed in part to deal with peculiarities of the North American urban environment, not the least of which was the need for spatial expansion due to extraordinary population growth (New York's population, for example, increased more than eight times to more than 1,000,000 between 1820 and 1860), street railways were adopted more cautiously in Europe. True, Loubat returned to France and in 1853 received permission to experiment with his system in the Paris streets. The trials were promising and Loubat was then granted the right to establish a twenty-nine-kilometer line to link Sèvres on the southwest and Vincennes on the east, passing by way of the Place de la Concorde and the Louvre in the center of the city.

The first of its kind in Europe, Loubat's "American rail-

[35] Clark, *Tramways*, pp. 5-10.
[36] Lee, "Tramways of Hull," pp. 49-50; also his "Wagonettes of Kingston-upon-Hull: A Transport Curiosity," *TH* 2 (1969): 136-54.
[37] Barker and Robbins, *London Transport*, 1:178-79; Alexander Easton, *A Practical Treatise on Street or Horse-Power Railways* (Philadelphia, 1859), pp. 4-8.

road" was not very successful, in large part because of the wary attitude of public officials. For, in spite of his pleas, Loubat was never authorized to finish laying rails through the center of the city. This meant that he and his successor, the General Omnibus Company, were forced to dubious expedients. They had to build cars that could leave the rails at will and then roll on the pavement, or they were compelled to switch the rear axles at the Place de la Concorde so that the tramcar could continue into the city center as an omnibus. This obviously destroyed the unity of the service, and it was only after a pause of twenty years that a whole series of concessions finally marked the real beginnings of Parisian tramway development.[38]

When a brash thirty-year-old American, George Francis Train, introduced the first real horse railways into England in 1859 he also met strong opposition. The step rails stood above the level of the road, and although such an arrangement was sometimes grudgingly tolerated in the United States, local authorities were quick to order that they be torn up and removed when they saw the consequences.[39] Some lines were saved by substituting flat grooved rails, which were roomy enough for the free play of the flanges, yet narrow enough to prevent the wheels of common road vehicles from entering them. Thus horse-drawn streetcars, a fundamental American innovation in public transit, were accepted only after they had been modified to suit English conditions, but not before creating "the aura of public enmity which they so often had to bear with in England."[40]

There could be no doubt of the superiority of tramways over omnibuses, however, and Europe followed America after a lag of ten to fifteen years. As late as 1869, only a very few larger cities had streetcar service, usually confined to a small number of lines. By the end of the next decade of

[38] Martin, *Etude statistique*, pp. 90-91, 148-49.
[39] Clark, *Tramways*, pp. 12-14.
[40] Charles Klapper, *The Golden Age of Tramways* (London, 1961), p. 24. Klapper's interesting book has a good chapter on Train's well-publicized efforts.

economic boom and company promotion, tramways were working in most medium-sized cities, and with many lines. In England, for example, the successful passing of a bill to permit tramways in Liverpool in 1868 broke a legislative deadlock and quickly led to a "mild tramway mania."[41] In France tramway concessions for Le Havre, Marseille, Nancy, Orléans, Paris, and Tours—to name only a few— were granted between 1873 and 1875. All of these concessions (Paris excepted) were combined by the Banque Française et Italienne in 1875 into the General French Tramways Company, the largest French holding company of its kind and long the bellwether of the industry in France.[42] As for Germany, prior to the Franco-Prussian war tramway service had begun in only three cities: Berlin (1865), Hamburg (1866) and Stuttgart (1868). Then in 1872 tramways were opened in Leipzig, Frankfurt on the Main, Hanover, and Dresden, followed by Danzig, Uetersen, and Wuppertal in 1873, and then Wiesbaden, Bremen, Metz, Munich, Dusseldorf, Karlsruhe, Cologne, Breslau, and Magdeburg by the end of 1877.[43] The European tramway had overcome inertial friction and was rolling along.

In spite of great variation from city to city it seems possible to distinguish a typical pattern of lines and service. Almost invariably one of the first lines used a main thoroughfare to link the railroad station, originally on the edge of the city but now surrounded by buildings, with central points in the old town and from there on across to a new industrial or recreational area on the opposite fringe. Subsequent crosstown lines through the center to the nearby villages, industrial suburbs, parks, etc. would then create the opened or half-opened fan of radial urban transport familiar to all.[44]

[41] Klapper, *Golden Age*, p. 31.
[42] A complete list of all tramways operating in France in 1895, including the years service began, may be found in AN, F 14, 8588.
[43] Hendlmeier, *Von der Pferde-Eisenbahn*, pp. 10-12.
[44] Dresden's early lines were a perfect example. Grossmann, *Die kommunale Bedeutung*, pp. 20-24.

Continental cities, as opposed to most of their English counterparts, were also able to add streetcar lines on the circular boulevards, many of them constructed from the 1850s on, when the most recent of the long-standing walled fortifications were razed. Since fortifications had required large open spaces on both sides of the wall, cities like Brussels, Paris, and Vienna, to name only three of the most famous examples, could build spacious "ring streets" around what became the heart of the greatly expanded urban area. These "ring streets" were extremely useful for the tramway, as for the automobile today, for they linked all the major spokes radiating from the center and permitted crosstown traffic to skirt the already over-congested core.[45]

But the tramway was not all-conquering. In the largest cities, like London (where horse tramways never penetrated the heart of the capital), Paris, and Berlin, omnibus service did not disappear completely until the twentieth century. Not that the companies wanted it that way. The company in Brussels was typical when it stated in 1881 that it wished to substitute tramways for omnibuses on all its principal routes. The request was long denied, however, for certain narrow, highly congested streets which connected the Grande Place of the historic city with the new administrative and commercial city on the heights to the west. The authorities felt that tramways lacked the necessary maneuverability, and would block traffic and present a safety hazard.[46]

The foregoing suggests two institutional forces shaping European street railway development in addition to technological change and urban population growth. The first of these was public authority, both national and local, which regulated tramways but did not operate them. The second was private enterprise, which sought the permission of public authority to build and operate tramways in the public

[45] Dickinson, *West European City*, pp. 463-69; August Boshart, *Strassenbahnen* (Berlin, 1920), p. 21.
[46] AN, 65 AQ, Q 508, Tramways Bruxellois, Annual Report, 1881.

streets for private profit. Let us look briefly at each of these.

Since railroad construction had been regulated from the beginning on the continent, it was natural that similar treatment should be extended to the so-called "American railroads" used for urban transit. Thus the national state would establish a general juridical framework within which it granted tramway concessions to petitioning entrepreneurs, who worked out specific terms with the local governments concerned. One key to continental legislation was that all such concessions were for long but precisely defined periods, normally forty to fifty years. Upon expiration of the concession all the immovable property—mainly tracks— was to revert to the city without any payment of any kind. Generally the city also had the option but not the obligation to purchase all of the movable property, primarily cars and horses, at its fair market value as determined by impartial experts. The rights of property were thus circumscribed at the very outset by this built-in mechanism for eventual municipal ownership.

Nor was an ultimate judgment day the only limitation by any means. There were normally provisions for purchase of a concession before expiration, a fixing of routes, fares, and frequency of service, and penalties for nonfulfillment of contract. In addition to these and other contractual arrangements spelled out in the concession, national and local authorities had extensive police powers to maintain order and safety in the streets. This allowed them to regulate the speed and capacity of cars, or require or reject modifications of equipment, as a matter of course. Naturally, specific concessions differed in their details, especially in the early 1870s. After all, each concession represented a negotiated agreement between one of several competing entrepreneurs and a city council. But practical experience and basically similar national acts, like the French law on tramways of the 11th of June 1880, meant these were minor variations on a common regulatory theme.

One should note that across the channel in Great Britain,

the supposed home of laissez-faire capitalism, regulation was equally rigorous. The State Carriage Act of 1832, recognizing omnibus service and simultaneously licensing and regulating it, set a precedent that was extended in the Tramways Act of 1870. The 1870 Act established clearcut procedures for introducing streetcar service. The promoter was first to get the consent of the local government involved and was then to apply for a Provisional Order from the Board of Trade, which had to be ratified by an act of Parliament. Although the local government could construct the tramway lines, it was required to lease them to a private operating company, and for not more than twenty-one years. This meant that British tramway leases to private companies were coming to an end in the 1890s, when continental tramway concessions also dating from the 1870s still had years to run. The Tramway Act also laid down general rules—rails flush with road, animal power unless specified to the contrary, maintenance by the company of the street between the rails as well as an additional eighteen inches outside the track, etc.[47]

Horse tramways in Europe were regulated but they were generally owned and operated by private companies. These companies accepted the risks and expenses involved in their operations, and received neither subsidies nor aids from the government. Nor were concessions exclusive for a given city, normally, though they perhaps might be for a given line. Thus there was the threat of future competition from other companies.

Entrepreneurs were willing to take these very real risks because they hoped to tap two quite different sources of profit. The more obvious source was from normal operation after the lines were built. Perhaps more important in the initial considerations of the typical entrepreneur, who was often a general contractor, was the prospect of the normal or inflated profits which he might derive from laying track

---

[47] Lee, "Tramways of Hull," p. 14; Klapper, *Golden Age*, pp. 31-33.

and providing equipment. Palmer Harding's undertaking at Rouen in the late 1870s was probably fairly typical, although the data are poor in spite of various vague allusions to the inflated capital of early European tramway companies. Harding, an English contractor, apparently received 3,500,000 francs in shares for tracks and equipment costing 2,000,000 francs, leaving a nominal profit of 1,500,000 francs.[48] The French tramway law of 1880 subsequently called for the state's engineers to verify the amount of capital actually expended and thereby limit the inflation of capital. But construction profits remained a primary incentive for streetcar investment in France as elsewhere.

This, then, was the institutional framework for the development of horsecar railways in Europe from the early seventies to the early nineties. That horsecar development is obviously very important for this study because it provided the point of departure—the "initial conditions"—for change in the 1890s.[49] Similarly, without a clear and unbiased summary of what European horse railways did and did not do, it is impossible to appraise the extent of that subsequent change and my contention that the technical revolution of electric traction had a profound and even revolutionary impact. Unfortunately, that would first require a book-length investigation of its own, since existing material on horse tramways is often picturesque but seldom complete, with the exception of a very few monographs on transport in individual cities. Therefore the following can be no more than an introduction to certain key problems.

One certainty that immediately emerges is that there was considerable development of European horse tramways before they began to disappear in the 1890s. How considerable is another question, since much of the early data are very incomplete. Nonetheless, an interesting study by an

[48] AN, F 14, 13528, Notes on bonds, 1881.
[49] See the stimulating discussion of J.R.T. Hughes, "Fact and Theory in Economic History," in Ralph Andreano, ed., *The New Economic History* (New York, 1970), pp. 53 ff.

Austrian statistician managed to estimate the aggregate number of passengers carried during 1886 in a number of leading countries. To give some idea of what this "very neglected development" meant, he compared it with the "well-studied" railroad traffic, as may be seen in Table 1.

Table 1

TRAMWAY AND RAILROAD PASSENGERS IN 1886-87
(*in millions*)

	Tramways	Railroads
Austria-Hungary (1887)	83.9	66.4
Belgium (1885-86)	31.3	65.9
Great Britain (1886)	416.5	725.6
Germany (1887)	245.7	295.8
Holland (1886)	83.9	66.4
Switzerland (1886)	6.7	24.8
Total	868.0	1244.9

SOURCE: Wilhelm von Lindheim, *Strassenbahnen in Belgien, Deutschland, Grossbritannien und Irland, Frankreich, Italien, Oesterreich-Ungarn, den Niederlanden, Niederländisch-Indien, der Schweiz und den verschiedenen Staaten von Amerika: Statistisches und Finanzielles unter Besondere Berücksichtigung der Wiener Verhältnisse* (Vienna, 1888), p. 9.

Thus from almost nothing tramway traffic in these countries grew in twenty years to 70 percent of the number carried by railroads in 1886-87.

In accounting for this rapid rise it is customary to point first of all to urban population growth and the spatial expansion of cities, to the point where walking was not always a pleasant prospect and public transit began to be a necessity. What is seldom mentioned is that lower operating costs most probably allowed tramways to gain not only existing, predominantly middle-class omnibus traffic, but to create new and additional traffic from less comfortable classes as well.

In London, one of the most carefully studied cases, lower fares permitted tramway companies to add "to existing transport users a section of the community hitherto little catered for by public transport."[50] Specifically, London tramways were not only carrying the middle classes, but they were focusing especially on sections of the working classes who had previously been unable to afford a ride.[51] According to one late-Victorian observer in the *Cornhill Magazine*, "the working man is rarely seen on the upholstered cushions [of London omnibuses]; he feels himself uncomfortable and *de trop*. The tramcar is *his* familiar vehicle and he can ensconce himself there in his mortar-splashed clothes without restraint."[52] Scanty continental data tend to confirm the tramway's more democratic character. The Reims Tramways Company of France, for example, stated in 1886 that the bulk of its riders came from the working class and that this justified the company's low-fares policy.[53]

It seems clear, however, that the number of streetcar passengers in typical cities generally grew rapidly only in the first decade or so after their establishment, and that they increased much more slowly thereafter. Furthermore, much of the growth at the reduced rate of increase was due to larger total population, as rides per urban dweller per year stagnated in city after city. Thus whatever expansion of the market among the poorer social classes there was, it had run its course by the 1880s. Nor was the level of per capita use at all high, but rather quite the contrary. (This point is discussed in detail in chapter VI.) European mass transit was a case of prematurely arrested development.

Take Paris, for example. In 1874 omnibuses carried 113,000,000 riders in Paris and its suburbs, as opposed to 93,000,000 in 1864 and 36,000,000 in 1855. Tramways carried only 2,600,000. Four years later, in 1878, omnibuses

[50] Barker and Robbins, *London Transport*, 1:179.
[51] *Ibid.*, 196.
[52] Quoted in Barker and Robbins, *London Transport*, 1:263.
[53] AN, F 14, 13517, Annual Report, 1886.

had dropped slightly to 103,000,000 passengers, and the host of new tramways transported 123,000,000 passengers. After that awesome surge, however, tramway traffic grew very modestly to 160,000,000 passengers in 1892 (when almost all lines were horse-powered), as did the number of omnibus passengers, which reached 128,000,000 in 1892.[54] Thus the number of people using first omnibuses and then tramways grew very rapidly for a short period, as new users were attracted, and then stagnated after having saturated the market.

The Vienna Streetcar Company provides a similar example. Beginning in 1868 with twelve kilometers of lines, of which the Ring Boulevard was the most important, and 3,300,000 passengers, the company had forty-three kilometers of lines in 1874 and carried 23,000,000 riders. Twenty years later, on the eve of electrification, the company had eighty kilometers of lines and carried 54,000,000 passengers annually. Yet this growth was due almost entirely to the increase in population, as usage per capita remained almost constant. Thus each Viennese resident averaged riding the tramways thirty-four times per year in 1873 and only forty times per year twenty years later.[55] Leipzig was similar. The number of riders more than doubled between 1885 and 1895, but then so did population. The average annual number of rides per urban inhabitant stayed almost constant (forty-nine in 1885, fifty-three in 1895). The trams carried more people, but individuals did not use them more often.[56]

The city of Berlin provides a final example of the possibilities of horse streetcar development. (See Table 2.)
As may be seen in this skeletal summary, the growth of traffic was constant and very substantial, and despite the technical limitations of horse traction the company was clearly

[54] Martin, *Etude statistique*, pp. 274-77, and diagram no. 2.
[55] "40 jähriger Bestand der Strassenbahnen in Wien," *ZOIAV* 57 (1905): 648; CL, Tramways de Vienne, Résultats Statistiques.
[56] Wilhelm Sternberg, *Das Verkehrsgewerbe Leipzigs* (Jena, 1904), pp. 90-91.

Table 2

OMNIBUS AND TRAMWAY PASSENGERS IN BERLIN

(in millions)

Year	Omnibus	Tramways	Population[a]	Tramway Rides per Capita	Dividends[b] (percent)
1873	14.3	3.7	.90	4	6.25
1875	14.1	18.3	1.04	18	6.25
1880	10.7	51.6	1.23	42	9.0
1885	16.1	87.3	1.45	60	11.0
1890	27.8	140.9	1.82	77	12.5
1895	37.4	164.3	2.13	77	12.5

SOURCE: Edward Buchmann, *Die Entwickelung der Grossen Berliner Strassenbahn und ihre Bedeutung für die Verkehrsentwickelung Berlins* (Berlin, 1910), pp. 83, 96-97, appendix.

[a] Berlin and its suburbs.
[b] For the Great Berlin Street Railway Company.

profitable and securely established. At the same time one notes that between 1890 and 1895 per capita use of tramways failed to increase and the growth of traffic was due solely to the greater population. Thus the stagnation in horsecar traffic, which set in earlier in smaller cities like Leipzig, or less rapidly growing cities like Paris, was eventually found in a Gargantua like Berlin.

3. *The Search for Alternatives*

This stagnation reflected the many limitations inherent in a system of urban passenger transport based upon animate traction. For it the horse was unquestionably more efficient pulling cars mounted on rails than on ordinary pavement, the noble beast remained ill-suited for the grueling task to which it had been assigned. Constantly straining to start up from dead stops and to pull up grades, horses had a working life on street railways of only four or five years. Even so, five to seven horses were required for each tramcar, which helped account for the fact that costs attributable to traction—the horses—normally accounted for fully fifty percent of total operating expenses.[57]

There was also the problem of illness and disease, which might range from the catastrophic dimensions of the Great Epizootic of 1872 in the United States to that which the Keighley Tramways Company experienced soon after it was founded in 1888. There the horses got pinkeye and all service was discontinued for two months until they recovered. A negligible compensation was that there were no droppings to be swept up twice a day, as was usually the case.[58] Horse droppings posed a serious hygiene problem for municipal governments and were a source of unpleasant odors.

There was also the problem of tramway horses causing an uneven wearing of the streets, which resulted in companies being required to maintain the pavement between the tracks and a certain distance beyond the outside rail. This paving requirement, a standard clause in tramway concessions, was resented by the companies, as being unfair. "As soon as the condition of the pavement between or along our rails deteriorates slightly, we are required to repair it completely. Yet we are not the only one responsible, for, as opposed to the railroads, our tracks are run over and run along by everyone, and our rails must endure all possible shocks and support all weights."[59] The problem was compounded because coachmen very often drove their left wheels over the smooth surface of the right rail, leaving the right wheels of their carriages to trace a narrow band that

[57] Among others, see Frank Rowsome, Jr., *Trolley Car Treasury: A Century of American Streetcars—Horsecars, Cable Cars, Interurbans, and Trolleys* (New York, 1956), pp. 27-29; George Hilton, "Transport Technology and the Urban Pattern," *Journal of Contemporary History* 4 (1969): 123-24; *EE* 6 (1891): 26-27.

[58] J. S. King, *Keighley Corporation Transport* (Huddersfield, 1964), pp. 14-19.

[59] AN, 65 AQ, Q 1381, Cie Générale Française de Tramways, Annual Report, 1877.

soon cut and ruined even the best stone pavement, much to the dismay of public officials.[60]

The result of these limitations was a broad effort to develop suitable alternatives to horse traction from the early 1870s onward. Specifically, this attempt first centered on efforts to adapt the proven technology of the steam locomotive, so effective on main railroad lines, to the needs of urban transit. A whole series of steam tram experiments, inventions, and models followed, of which only a few need be noted.

One leading steam tram producer was Merryweather and Sons of London, which had considerable experience building light steam engines used for pumping on fire wagons, and which built the first steam locomotive for urban tramways in England in 1872.[61] This led to equipping Palmer Harding's South Paris Tramways concession, beginning in 1875. By 1877 Merryweather had supplied various Paris tramways with forty-six locomotives, or almost one-third of the 176 steam trams the firm built between 1875 and 1892. As figure 2 shows, Merryweather followed the general practice of pulling passenger cars by means of a separate "dummy" locomotive—so named because its boxy little body was supposed to deceive horses into thinking it was an ordinary tramcar. Merryweather's locomotive had a typical small vertical boiler and two horizontal cylinders, and it was fired by coke to reduce smoke and cinders discharged into the air through the smokestack.[62] Exported throughout Europe, these locomotives were also widely used on an experimental basis by street railway companies which did not adopt steam traction permanently.

Another leading producer was the Swiss Engineering

[60] AN, F 14, 15005, Report, 25 April 1890.
[61] H. A. Whitcombe, *History of the Steam Tram* (South Godstone, Surrey, 1954), pp. 12-14.
[62] *Ibid.*; Dollfus and de Geoffroy, *Histoire de la locomotion terrestre*, pp. 254-55; Rowsome, *Trolley Car Treasury*, 35-36; Klapper, *Golden Age*, 40-44.

1. Santiago de Chile. Railway station. A scene from the horsecar era.

2. Inauguration of steam tramways on Palmer Harding's concession for Paris and southern suburbs, 1876.

Works of Winterthur, which began building tram locomotives in 1877 and eventually produced about 300 of them. Kitson and Company of Leeds, a leading builder of mainline locomotives, also produced some 300 steam tramway locomotives between 1878 and 1901. The steam tram was also adopted for street use by placing the engine upon the passenger car, although this method was less frequently used than the dummy locomotive. Here the design of the Englishman W. R. Rowan seems to have been most widely used by a number of builders, not only in Great Britain but also in Austria, France, Germany, and Switzerland. With tubular boilers arranged to cool the gases, the little engine gave off no disagreeable odors if the coke was of high quality and no steam if the effort required was moderate.[63] In France, Serpollet, then Purrey locomotives—the latter with compact tubular boilers and a reduced total weight—met with some success, particularly in the late 1880s.

Generally speaking, however, neither the steam tram locomotive nor the self-propelled car containing its own steam engine and boiler was a success as far as urban transit was concerned. Rather the normal pattern saw many companies conducting many experiments with many systems over a period of years. But the usual result of such experiments was to discontinue or restrict severely the use of the steam tram after a short time, or revert entirely to horse traction. The North Metropolitan Tramways of London, for example, used a Merryweather locomotive on one line for a month in 1877, and investigated and used Wilkinson steam trams in 1883 and 1884, along with Beaumont and Mekarski compressed-air engines.[64] Almost identical were the experiments of the Great Berlin Street Railway, which employed seven locomotives on one line for three weeks in 1880, and the Brussels Tramways Company, which used

[63] Klapper, *Golden Age*, 42-43; AN, F 14, 15006, Report on experimental use of Rowan engines on Pigalle-Trocadéro line, 22 October 1890.

[64] V. E. Burrows, *Tramways in Metropolitan Essex* (Huddersfield, 1967), pp. 23-45; Barker and Robbins, *London Transport*, 1:294-95.

three locomotives on the Uccle line for a brief period in 1879.[65]

One of the several companies founded in the 1870s to serve suburban Paris, the North Paris Tramways Company, used both steam trams on the line from Etoile to Courbevoie and Mekarski compressed air cars (see below) on the Boulevard Haussmann. The results were poor and contributed to the company's bankruptcy in 1881, after which all lines returned to less expensive horse traction.[66] The list of such brief and unsuccessful experiments with steam trams for urban transit could be greatly extended. Thus the maximum of 500 steam trams operating in Great Britain in the mid-1890s, or the 700 operating in the United States in the late 1880s, must be seen primarily as serving light or local railways in sparsely populated rural areas that would not support the heavy investment of standard main-line railroad construction.[67] Only on a very few purely suburban lines did steam trams have any real urban significance in Europe.

Two interrelated factors largely account for this failure of steam tramways as a mode of urban transportation. The first of these was the strict anti-pollution requirements which public authorities imposed in order to limit the obnoxious smoke, sparks, cinders, and noise associated with steam engines. Such measures were taken not only to preserve safety in the streets, and particularly to guard against frightening horses, but also to preserve the amenities of the city from a smoke-belching, ear-splitting inconvenience. The provisions of the Use of Mechanical Power on Tramways Act of 11 August 1879, which set very stringent condi-

[65] Eduard Buchmann, *Die Entwickelung der Grossen Berliner Strassenbahn und ihre Bedeutung für die Verkehrsentwickelung Berlins* (Berlin, 1910), p. 16; AN, 65 AQ, Q 508, Tramways Bruxellois, Annual Report, 1879.

[66] CL, Cie des Tramways de Paris et du Département de la Seine, Etude, 1909.

[67] Klapper, *Golden Age*, p. 47. For a brief chronology of adoption and subsequent abandonment of steam streetcars in major cities of the United States, see *ASRA*, 1887-88, pp. 68-70.

THE SEARCH FOR ALTERNATIVES 31

tions to be enforced by the Board of Trade for all British tramways, were typical. Steam tramways could emit no visible smoke or steam; the engine had to operate without noise produced by blast or from the clatter of machinery; all working parts had to be concealed; and the tram had to be governed automatically to a top speed of ten miles per hour.[68] In short, the steam tramway in Europe had to overcome the environmental liabilities of steam locomotives, which had helped to make railroads of such limited significance for urban transportation throughout the nineteenth century.

Although the evidence is somewhat fragmentary, there is strong reason to believe that such strict constraints reflected the views and desires of society as a whole. In Hamburg a quickly discontinued steam tram was contemptuously nicknamed "the smoking flatiron" and was very little appreciated. The officials of Leipzig never permitted even experimental use of steam tramways in their city.[69] Other cities, such as Paris, reflected the same pattern.

In order to try to meet the demanding specifications for a clean, non-polluting steam engine, inventors and engineers resorted to a number of ingenious and costly expedients. They burned the best-quality coke, enclosed the locomotive, and developed special devices to handle the exhaust. Among British builders "the exhaust was passed into a nest of thin copper tubes on the cab roof and was condensed by air cooling in Kitson engines; Burrell of Thetfort put an air tube through each steam tube so that cold air penetrated the steam; Wilkinson favored a steam chest on the roof, through which air was conducted by a system of tubes."[70] (All this added unwanted weight to the seven- to eight-ton steam tram locomotives, which proceeded to wear out the light rails and roadbeds which had been adequate for horse traction.) Yet in spite of the costly concessions to

[68] Whitcombe, *History of the Steam Tram*, p. 18.
[69] Erich Staisch, *Die elektrische S-Bahn in Hamburg* (Hamburg, 1964), pp. 58-59; Sternberg, *Das Verkehrsgewerbe Leipzigs*, p. 48.
[70] Klapper, *Golden Age*, pp. 45-46.

environmental concerns, steam tram engines were only partly successful in eliminating pollution and were rarely permitted in the city proper.

This leads to the second cause for the failure of steam tramways for urban transportation: their inability to achieve a definite economic advantage over horse tramways, given the expensive but highly desirable environmental restraints placed upon them. A shareholder's report of the General French Tramways Company correctly summed up the two-sided nature of the challenge in 1876. "The problem of mechanical traction does not consist solely in eliminating the serious drawbacks of locomotives—smoke, noise, etc.—but above all in obtaining an economical engine." And after examining and experimenting with the various mechanical systems, the company had reluctantly decided that they simply cost more than horse traction with all its inconveniences, at least for the time being.[71] As the various examples discussed above show, this was the typical experience, and the steam locomotives that managed to win approval did not result in increased profits.

One indication of this very limited acceptability of the steam tram locomotive was the fireless steam engine, an engine developed exclusively to meet the tough regulations designed to protect the quality of the urban environment. The idea was ingenious. Instead of generating steam and the unwanted smoke and ash in boilers and locomotives moving through the streets, pressurized steam for the locomotive was generated in a stationary boiler at a depot at the end of the line. The locomotive would then run on that stored energy, as the steam was released from the "fireless boiler" to move the piston. In this way smoke, sparks, and cinders were eliminated, and the dead weight of the locomotive was greatly reduced.[72]

[71] AN, 65 AQ, Q 1381, Annual Report, 1876.
[72] Dollfus and de Geoffroy, *Histoire de la locomotion terrestre*, pp. 254-55; AN, F 14, 15005, including Léon Francq, "La locomotion sans foyer . . . système Francq et Lamm" (1878).

First used by Emile Lamm in New Orleans in 1873, the engine was perfected by a French engineer, Léon Francq, who bought the European rights to Lamm's invention. Francq fireless locomotives were used experimentally on the St. Augustin-Neuilly line in 1876, then regularly on the suburban line from Rueil to Marly from 1878, and in Lille, Roubaix, and Lyons, among other places, thereafter. There was no question that these locomotives worked—the system was in use in Lyons as late as 1905—and the elimination of the fireman on the locomotive clearly reduced labor costs. But such locomotives could not go more than fifteen kilometers without recharging with steam, while unusual effort might use up steam and leave the locomotive stranded somewhere along the line. Again, there was no real advantage over horse traction.

Another interesting French response to the problem was the Mekarski compressed-air system. This resembled the fireless steam engine in that energy was accumulated at a depot and then utilized along the line, except that compressed air as opposed to steam was used to drive the pistons of the motor. That motor was generally placed on the tramcar and did not require a separate locomotive. Mekarski's system was used from 1878 to 1913 at Nantes, where Mekarski was able to convince the city that his method would represent a great improvement over the horse tramways the General French Tramways Company sought to install.[73] Mekarski's system and variations of it were also used on a number of Paris lines, particularly from the Hôtel de Ville to the fashionable western quarters of Passy, Auteuil, and Versailles well into the twentieth century.

The great advantage of this system was its absolute cleanliness. Its great disadvantages were the large amount of coal required to run the stationary compressors and its lack of dependability. The line from the Hôtel de Ville to Versailles was popularly known by the Parisian public as the

[73] AN, 65 AQ, Q 138¹, Cie Générale Française de Tramways, Annual Report, 1876; CL, Tramways de Nantes, Etude, November 1913.

"Out-of-order" (*Reste-en-panne*), according to one account.[74] Operating costs were high and there was no economic incentive for companies to adopt the system. The Nantes Tramways Company, which was the only sizable network to adopt the system and of which Mekarski remained the manager until 1913, was close to bankruptcy throughout the 1880s. In 1913 passenger traffic at Nantes was judged to be quite underdeveloped, "mainly because the system of traction is slow and not in favor."[75] Mekarski had met the environmental and aesthetic requirements of clean, quiet, and unobtrusive traction, but his technology failed to achieve an economic advantage over common horse traction.

This leads to a preliminary conclusion and a hypothesis. Steam tram locomotives, fireless engines, and compressed-air engines, not to mention other attempts which remained only historical curiosities, failed because at best they could not meet either the environmental-aesthetic-cultural requirements, on the one hand, or the technical-economic requirements on the other. To meet one without the other meant limited application, as either municipal officials or private tramway owners failed to accept the given method. Our hypothesis therefore is that both of these requirements —economic and non-economic—would have to be met before European urban transportation might be fundamentally altered.

[74] *Le Radical*, 12 September 1896, in AN, F 14, 15012.
[75] CL, Tramways de Nantes, February 1913.

II. Breakthrough and Development

1. *Electric Traction Experiments*

As the limitations of horse traction became increasingly evident, the creative response that led men to grapple with steam, compressed air, and cables led them to investigate electricity as a motive force for urban public transportation. Thus a whole series of pioneers and inventors made important technical contributions before the decisive breakthrough, a familiar pattern in the process of strategic innovation. These technical contributions depended in turn upon basic scientific discoveries in electricity and the development of electrical engineering capability. Indeed, without the rapid emergence of the electric industry, the fascinating object of a number of studies,[1] the commercial development of electric street railways would have been impossible. For electric traction was only one of the more remarkable electrical applications, even if it did create a whole new system of public transportation.

Attempts to use electricity in transportation began very early. One of the first of these was that of Thomas Davenport, a blacksmith in Rutland, Vermont. Davenport constructed more than one hundred electric motors between 1835 and 1841, and he grasped the fundamental concept of combining fixed and rotating electromagnets, the one reversible and the other non-reversible, which later characterized commercially successful electric motors. One of his motors drove a model electric railway.[2] In Russia, Profes-

[1] See the articles and bibliography in Charles Singer et al., *A History of Technology*, 5 vols. (Oxford, 1958), 5;177-234; also Malcolm MacLaren, *The Rise of the Electrical Industry* (Princeton, N.J., 1943) and the discussion and bibliography in David S. Landes, *The Unbound Prometheus: Technological Change and Industrial Development in Western Europe from 1750 to the Present* (Cambridge, 1969), pp. 281-90.

[2] On this and other early experiments see, in particular, F. L. Pope, "Notes on the Electric Railway," *EE* 7 (1891): 168-69, 186-87, 210-11. Also Klapper, *Golden Age*, pp. 55 ff.

sor H. M. Jacobi of St. Petersburg used an electric motor to drive a paddlewheel on a small boat on the Neva River in 1839. In Scotland, Robert Davidson reached the speed of four miles per hour with an electric motor on a railway car, and a Page motor propelled a Baltimore and Ohio Railroad locomotive at nineteen miles per hour in 1854.[3] All such applications were experimental and evanescent.

According to Dr. Passer in his excellent study of the American electrical manufacturers, the reason was simple. With the primary battery the only source of electric current, power from that source was fully twenty times as costly as equivalent power from a steam engine. "Until a more economical source of current was available, there was no possibility of electric power's coming into general use."[4]

That fundamental step forward was taken in the 1870s with the development of the dynamo, which provided the previously missing source of cheap current. The work of many men—Pacinotti, Siemens, Gramme and others—the dynamo found many uses, most notably in arc and then incandescent bulb lighting. By providing a cheap source of current, the dynamo also reawakened interest in electricity as a means of furnishing power to move vehicles. The mechanical energy of the steam engine was to be converted by the electric generator—the dynamo—into electricity, and then reconverted into mechanical energy by a motor—basically a dynamo running in reverse—on the car. The great appeal of electrical energy was thus its transmissibility and its divisibility: generated efficiently at a single point it would then be parceled out to vehicles, as needed, all over town. The vision was simple and seductive, but it required a full decade of many-sided experiments to make it a reality.

The most basic technical problem was to find an effective

[3] Harold C. Passer, *The Electrical Manufacturers, 1875-1900: A Study in Competition, Entrepreneurship, Technical Change, and Economic Growth* (Cambridge, Mass., 1953), pp. 211-12.
[4] *Ibid.*

way to provide the motor on the moving vehicle with current.[5] Siemens and Halske of Berlin, the preeminent continental enterprise built both on early successes in the telegraph industry and on Werner von Siemens' development of the dynamo, was the pathbreaker. Indeed, the firm provided a series of models for electric traction which others could build upon.[6] In 1879 Siemens built a small line to carry visitors around the grounds of the Berlin Industrial Exhibition. Current at 150 volts was carried from the generator to the three-horsepower motor on the moving car by means of an isolated center rail. After passing through the motor, the current passed through the wheels and returned to the generator by means of the running rails. This return completed the circuit, a necessity in an electric system using any sort of conductor to supply current. The third-rail method functioned well, and more than 86,000 visitors rode the tiny train during the five months of the exhibition. A remarkable achievement—the first practical electric train in the world with current taken from a stationary generator —Siemens' demonstration served primarily as a curiosity to draw visitors.

Werner von Siemens saw electric traction as more than an exposition toy. Rather it was to provide a means to improve urban transit radically, and nowhere was the need for such improvement greater than in Siemens' own Berlin. His formulation of the problem was revealing, however. Precisely because of the intense congestion—with private and commercial lorries, omnibuses, tramways, carriages, and pedestrians all competing for precious street space— Siemens reasoned that electric vehicles in the streets would

[5] *Ibid.*, pp. 216 ff.; Barker and Robbins, *London Transport*, 1:296-98.
[6] This discussion of Siemens' early efforts is based primarily upon Hendlmeier, *Von der Pferde-Eisenbahn*, pp. 16-22; Georg Siemens, *Geschichte des Hauses Siemens*, 3 vols. (Munich, 1947-52), 1:127-28; Julius Weil, *Die Entstehung und Entwicklung unserer elektrischen Strassenbahnen* (Leipzig, 1899), pp. 3-6; Karl Hochenegg, "Ueber die Entwicklung der elektrischen Bahnen," *ZOIAV* 54 (1902), supplement, 54-56.

scarcely exceed the pace of a horse and would have little utility. Therefore he proposed construction of two elevated urban railroads, powered by electricity. The electric trains would then zoom along their own unencumbered right of way ten meters above the street, at top speeds of thirty to forty kilometers per hour. But the opposition of adjoining property owners was intense. Arguing that both property values and the quality of the environment would decline drastically, and pointing to New York's experience with steam-driven elevateds to drive their case home, they eventually convinced the king and his officials to reject the entire project.

Other initiatives were more successful. While waiting for approval on the elevated electric, Siemens built and opened the world's first electric tramway, taking current generated outside the car and successfully serving a fare-paying public on a regular basis in 1881. This 2.5-kilometer line replaced an old horse-drawn service previously used to transport materials to build the Officer's School at Gross-Lichterfelde, in the suburbs of Berlin. Instead of using a third rail, he connected one of the running rails directly to the positive pole of the dynamo and the other rail to the negative, so that one provided the outward path to the motor and the other the homeward course. Although the rails were placed to the side of the road and raised six inches above the surface, shocks to horses and inattentive pedestrians touching both rails simultaneously did occur.

Obviously such live rails capable of giving shocks could not be used in public streets. And only on short lines could the difference in potential between the open rails be low enough so that shocks were disagreeable but not dangerous. Such lines might amuse at beaches and resorts as well as at expositions, however. Thus Magnus Volk opened a one-mile, third-rail line at Brighton for the pleasure of vacationers in 1884, the fourth passenger-carrying electric line in the United Kingdom. (Siemens had scored another first, this time for an electric tramway from Portrush to Bushmills, Northern Ireland, in 1882; in 1883 amusement lines were also opened at Blackpool and Ryde Pier.)[7] Volk's operation was sometimes stopped, and literally so, by English children who made the same discovery of their German counterparts at Gross-Lichterfelde. "The children playing on the beach soon learnt by sundry practical demonstrations *in corpore vili* to avoid those rails, though the more mischievous took their revenge by surreptitiously placing conductors across them, often thereby affording the electrical energy an easier path back to the stationary dynamo than that provided by Mr. Volk through the motor on the car, so bringing the same to a standstill."[8]

Siemens also experimented with the first overhead conductors, the method that was subsequently to win the day. At the Paris Exposition of 1881 a copper wire was placed inside a small overhead pipe, which was split open so that the underriding contact apparatus could take current down a cable to the motor. In 1884 this system was introduced on the Frankfurt-Offenbach Tramway, the first overhead electric service for public transportation in Germany. Siemens also successfully used small eight-wheeled contact carriages running atop two copper-wire conductors (one positive and one negative) on an experimental line in Charlottenburg in 1881.[9]

European inventors also experimented with self-contained, battery-powered cars from at least 1880 on. The French early exhibited a fondness for this device; at the beginning of 1882 two different battery cars, one by Philippart, Faure and Reynier of Paris and one by Trouvé using a Siemens coil motor, were in experimental use. With the Siemens carriages mentioned above, they were apparently

[7] Klapper, *Golden Age*, 57-59.   [8] *EE* 14 (1894): 19.
[9] These different methods are well illustrated by Hendlmeier with photos and drawings. Also see the handsome photo album by P. H. Prasuhn, *Chronik der Strassenbahn* (Hanover, 1969), pp. 15-17, 63-64.

the only electric tramways in operation in the world at the beginning of 1882.[10]

Such efforts, and particularly those of Siemens—probably the world's single largest and most advanced electrical manufacturer at the beginning of the 1880s—show that Europeans were the early leaders in electric traction research and development. Yet in spite of some undeniable technical successes, these efforts remained isolated curiosities and the horsecar system of urban transport still reigned supreme in Europe in 1890, as we have seen. Interest in electric traction did not result in continued improvement after Siemens' firsts, and Europeans failed to make the decisive entrepreneurial innovation fostering a new industry. Rather the scene must now shift to North America, even if the primary focus of this study is European. For the electric streetcar, which completely transformed European urban transportation in the late 1890s, was an American innovation like the horsecar it superannuated. And in view of Europe's early lead, one must ask what special factors and differences caused the United States to overtake and temporarily surpass Europe in this field.

2. *American Innovation*

When American experiments with electric traction began in the 1880s there was already a considerable network of mechanized urban transportation in the United States. The cable car, first perfected by Andrew Hallidie in San Francisco in 1873, had spread to a number of cities. By 1890, when cable-car transport was at its zenith, there were 283 miles of track over which 373,000,000 passengers traveled per year.[11] Initial investment costs were high, but the cable

[10] *Electrician* (New York) 1 (1882): 10-11.
[11] U.S., Census Office, *Report on Transportation Business in the United States, 1890.* Part I. *Transportation By Land* (Washington, D.C., 1895), p. 682; *SRJ* 24 (1904): 600. The definitive work is George W. Hilton, *The Cable Car in America* (Berkeley, Cal., 1971).

AMERICAN INNOVATION 41

car traveled two or three times as fast as the horsecar and could ascend grades impossibly steep for its equestrian competitor. America's broad straight thoroughfares also facilitated use of the endless chain, whereas in the sinuosities of the European urban landscape the cable car was little more than a rare curiosity.

Steam street railways, normally of the dummy type, were also present in force in the United States, particularly on suburban lines. In 1890 they were carrying 287,000,000 passengers over 527 miles of line. Thus on the eve of electrification steam and cable power combined were transporting about one-half as many passengers as the 1.23 billion who were being carried by horse power alone.[12] Further mechanization was logical. Interestingly enough, America never experimented with fireless steam engines, compressed-air engines, and electric-battery cars to anything like the extent Europe did. Instead, American efforts in the 1880s focused on the model Siemens had provided, that is, the direct transmission of electricity by means of a conductor to the moving vehicle. The result was a revolutionary technical and economic breakthrough, the dependable electric streetcar.

The story of this remarkable achievement is an exciting one in the best tradition of pioneering entrepreneurial innovation.[13] More importantly, an examination of the American origins of the innovation is essential to an understanding of its subsequent diffusion and modification in Europe. For both reasons, then, a brief look at the American background is warranted.

The first significant efforts were those of the masterful

[12] U.S., Census, *Transportation, 1890*, 1, 682.
[13] Useful and well-illustrated discussions may be found in Miller, *Fares, Please!*, pp. 54-69, and Frank Rowsome, Jr., *Trolley Car Treasury: A Century of American Streetcars—Horsecars, Cablecars, Interurbans, and Trolleys* (New York, 1956), pp. 65-95. The most penetrating treatment by far is Passer, *Electrical Manufacturers*, pp. 213-55, and I have relied heavily upon it in my discussion of American electric railways.

Thomas Edison. Concentrating on the application of electricity for lighting, Edison also found time to experiment with electric power for transportation at Menlo Park, beginning in January 1880. Edison thought of electric traction in terms of inexpensive light railways for thinly populated agricultural regions. Such electric lines could serve as feeders to the conventional and expensive steam railroads, toward which farmers struggled to cart their produce. He hired a mechanical engineer to build an electric locomotive, with an ordinary Edison generator running in reverse serving as the motor. Current was picked up by the wheels of the locomotive.

The locomotive worked well, and Henry Villard of the Northern Pacific Railroad decided to back further experiments on a three-mile line constructed at Menlo Park. Villard agreed to pay expenses and construct fifty miles of electric railway in the plains states if Edison's locomotive attained lower operating costs per ton-mile than those of steam railroads. In his tests Edison was able to meet these conditions successfully, but the bankruptcy of the Northern Pacific aborted the project. Uninterested in going further without his financial backers, Edison then combined with S. D. Field to form a separate company to develop the traction patents of both inventors. (Field's patents resembled Siemens', which were later denied by American courts.)[14] Field decided to focus on developing an electric locomotive drawing current from a third rail to replace the steam-driven elevated railroads of New York. These efforts went unrewarded, although Field did build a tiny demonstration line to haul visitors at the Chicago Railway Exposition of 1883. The result was that Edison did not return to electric traction until 1890, considerably after the success of others.

In his analysis of Edison's electric traction efforts, Passer concludes that the reason for Edison's failure to become the pioneering innovator in electric railways is far from obvi-

[14] "Electric Railway Work in America Prior to 1888," *SRJ* 24 (1904): 559.

ous.[15] Here comparison with Siemens' similarly puzzling failure adds support to Passer's explanation. For Siemens was also an inventor of unusual ability. He was also well-equipped, and he even operated isolated commercial as well as experimental lines. He also had the capacity to make the pioneering breakthrough. Clearly, the limited time available for electric transport problems was one factor in both cases. As Edison said later, "I had too many things to attend to, especially in connection with electric lighting."[16] Once the cost-conscious Edison invented the incandescent lamp in 1879, there were innumerable problems associated with the mass-marketing of the light for home and office. Electric railways were bound to suffer. As for Siemens, whose firm held a near monopoly position in the German electrical industry at this time, he was skeptical of Edison's light bulb and turned down an offer to manufacture Edison's invention under a licensing agreement in 1881.[17] It was precisely at that moment that Siemens was heart and soul for electric traction, and electric lighting was something of an intrusion. Yet after new firms—primarily Rathenau's A.E.G. (Allgemeine Elektricitäts-Gesellschaft)—arose to manufacture light bulbs, there naturally developed an enormously increased demand for central power stations and the indispensable Siemens dynamo to generate current. In responding to these opportunities Siemens and his firm were also diverted from traction to lighting.[18] Opportunities in electrical manufacturing were so great and many-sided from about 1875 to 1900 that even the most gifted participants lacked the time to respond to more than a portion of them.

A second factor was that neither Edison nor Siemens accurately foresaw the nature of the demand for electric transportation in the immediate future. As Passer points

[15] Passer, *Electrical Manufacturers*, p. 221.
[16] *Electric World* 4 (1884): 42, as quoted by Passer, p. 221.
[17] Passer, *Electrical Manufacturers*, p. 80.
[18] Siemens, *Geschichte*, 1:128-42.

out, Edison envisioned electric railways as feeders for main lines in agricultural areas, not as substitutes for existing horse railways in cities. Siemens' concern with urban uses was more perceptive. Yet because he underestimated the contribution electric traction could make to already clogged surface traffic in almost any city, and because he was well aware of the administrative difficulties involved in securing approval for his still experimental overhead electric methods of tramway traction,[19] he concentrated on rapid elevated railways. Such elevated railways, with their expensive, independent rights of way would, he thought, answer the needs of the megalopolis. This was a special and atypical problem, however, whose solution would have limited influence on the general public-transportation problem. Thus there was little reason to continue experimentation with electric power conveyed by both surface and overhead conductors, as at exhibitions or on the Gross-Lichterfelde line, once permission for the new Berlin elevated had been denied.[20] No other German city could seriously consider elevated railways (or subways) because no other German city was populous enough to generate the traffic necessary to pay for a system so expensive in fixed investment. In this way the quest for dependable electric traction passed to newcomers on the American side of the Atlantic, of which only three of the most significant will be considered.

The first commercial electric street railway in the United States began operation in Cleveland in July 1884. Built by Edward Bentley and Walter Knight, the car drew current from an underground wooden conduit carrying two copper-wire conductors placed in a trench between the rails, by means of a small plow attached to the moving car.[21] One

[19] Hochenegg, "Entwicklung," *ZOIAV* 54 (1902), supplement, p. 55; Hendlmeier, *Von der Pferde-Eisenbahn*, p. 22.

[20] As Siemens said at the opening of the Lichterfelde line, the track was to be envisaged as standing on columns and as providing a model for the elevated railroad which had been rejected, not as a model for surface electric traction. Weil, *Entstehung*, p. 6.

[21] See Knight's own optimistic description in *ASRA* 3 (1884-85): 131-33.

of the first of many attempts to use a protected slotted conduit to hold the live conductor, the mile-long section encountered many technical difficulties. Successive experiments with wire belts, friction wheels, and paper gears (to lessen the noise) pointed up the general and unresolved problem of connecting the motor shaft to the car axle on any electric streetcar.[22] And the unevenness of the existing track caused the electric cars to jump the track and thereby damage the plow.

The cars functioned, but they were costly and unreliable. As a representative of the East Cleveland Company asked the annual meeting of the American Street-Railway Association in October 1885, how could his company "present an accurate statement in dollars and cents of the running of a thing that will not run at all?"[23] No wonder the East Cleveland discontinued use of the cars after a year, and it was not until 1886 that the Bentley-Knight Company received contracts for three small lines. Although improvements were made, the firm failed to develop a satisfactory streetcar motor and remained wedded to the expensive conduit method, as opposed to the cheaper overhead conductor they also used. Progressively unable to compete after 1887, Bentley and Knight were nonetheless able to sell out in 1888 to the Thomson-Houston Company, which believed that some of the conduit patents might prove useful.[24]

A Belgian-born Detroit furniture manufacturer named Charles Van Depoele, who was fascinated by electricity, had greater success. His first experiments resembled Edison's in that he built an electric locomotive capable of reliably pulling three large passenger cars on a demonstration line at the Toronto Exhibition of 1884. The next year, following the path of Siemens, he substituted an overhead wire for the underground conductor. There was a significant improvement, however. Whereas Siemens had used either slotted gas piping in which the under-running shut-

[22] Passer, *Electrical Manufacturers*, p. 225.
[23] *ASRA* 4 (1885-86): 95.
[24] Passer, *Electrical Manufacturers*, pp. 227-30.

tle-shaped lugs and carriage slid (as at the Paris Exposition of 1881 and on the Frankfurt-Offenbach line in 1884), or an over-running carriage rolling atop two parallel wires and attached to the car by cable (on the experimental line at Charlottenburg),[25] Van Depoele conceived of an under-running wheel contact—a trolley—attached to the end of a pole mounted on the roof of the motor car. That pole was in turn pressed into continuous contact with a single overhead wire by means of a strong spring. This was an important step forward because it kept the under-running trolley from losing contact with the conductor. In the fall of 1885 Van Depoele temporarily equipped four cars with motors and overhead conductor at South Bend, Indiana, and in 1886 he began to make permanent electric street railway installations. By the end of the year he had equipped twenty-eight cars and thirty miles of track, and by February 1888 seven of the eleven different electric lines in the United States used his equipment.[26] This placed him far ahead of his American competitors.

Although Van Depoele practically abandoned his under-running, spring-loaded trolley for the potentially less satisfactory over-running trolley, a dependable electric motor was his Achilles' heel.[27] The heavy motor was placed on the front platform, which was not capable of supporting it for more than a few weeks before the little converted horsecars began to break apart. The clumsy chain drive connecting the motor to the car axle collected dirt and required frequent repair, as did the motors themselves, which sparked badly with their primitive metal brushes. Van Depoele's idea of using the rails for the return portion of the electrical circuit was excellent, but because the rails were not bonded the current often jumped to buried gas and water

[25] Hendlmeier, *Von der Pferde-Eisenbahn*, pp. 20-25.
[26] Charles Harte, "Boom Days of the Electric Railways," *ERTJ* 78 (1938): 329; *SRJ* 24 (1904): 559-61; Passer, *Electrical Manufacturers*, p. 232.
[27] *Ibid.*, p. 234.

pipes. These would then begin to corrode electrolytically and could eventually burst dramatically.[28]

In the face of such problems Van Depoele's principal financial backer refused to provide the capital necessary to expand Van Depoele's manufacturing facilities. Unable to sell the company to Sprague, who was by then dangerously extended with his project at Richmond, Virginia (see below), Van Depoele and his backer accepted the offer of the Thomson-Houston Company in March 1888. Van Depoele himself also joined Thomson-Houston, where he and his new associates hoped to refine his pioneering efforts into a really workable system suitable for mass adoption. But before that occurred a brilliant young ex-naval officer named Frank J. Sprague broke through to dramatic success and launched the electric streetcar revolution.

European experience played its part in Sprague's development. At the age of twenty-five the young American naval officer, temporarily stationed in Europe, was the secretary of an award jury at the London Crystal Palace Electrical Exhibition of 1882. There he was able to study the state of the electrical art in Europe at first hand. He also rode several times on the London underground, which employed steam railroad locomotives to pull its cars through its narrow tunnels. The smoke, gas, cinders, and sparks, which had of course necessitated placing the train underground in the first place, were most offensive. Sprague thought an improved electric motor might provide clean power. Because of the difficulties switching tracks would present for a surface conductor, he envisioned an overhead conductor with an under-running contact atop the car. At the Crystal Palace Exhibition Sprague also met with an impressed Edison representative, E. H. Johnson. Returning to the United States, Sprague resigned his commission and went to work for Edison in May 1883.[29]

[28] Rowsome, *Trolley Car Treasury*, pp. 79-80.
[29] In addition to Passer, *Electrical Manufacturers*, pp. 237-49, see Frank J. Sprague, "Some Personal Experiences," *SRJ* 24 (1904): 566-76.

Sprague stayed with Edison only one year. Experimenting on his own with an improved electric motor, in which Edison showed little interest, the independent Sprague set up his own company in late 1884. The actual manufacturing of the motors was farmed out to the Edison group, and in 1885 the Edison Electric Light Company was recommending it to its customers "as the only practical and economic motor existing today."[30] In 1886 Sprague leased a factory to establish his own manufacturing plant, and by the beginning of 1887 250 Sprague motors had been sold, most of them to industrial users.

Success in designing and selling large motors went hand in hand with railway work. Like Siemens, he first looked in the direction of elevated lines with private rights of way. After two years of experiments with a third-rail system on the four elevated lines of New York City Sprague had developed a good demonstration car. Unfortunately, when he demonstrated his car a fuse blew with an explosive flash and this so impressed Jay Gould, one of the capitalists controlling the New York elevated company, that he panicked and tried to jump off the train he had come to inspect. Gould subsequently refused to have anything to do with electric traction, and Sprague was thus forced to turn to surface street railways. In early 1887 he received his first contracts.

Sprague provided motors for some experiments with battery cars, but he focused on overhead conductors. As he told a group of street railway men in October 1887 before he had completed any major installation, "the overhead line is the cheapest." It is significant that he realized that the overhead system "may be unsightly in its appearance, and perhaps be somewhat in the way." That was very much in line with common opinion, which the streetcar operators had heard on other occasions and which had influenced both Siemens and Edison to some extent. And Sprague admitted that overhead lines "perhaps would not be tolerated

[30] Quoted by Passer, *Electrical Manufacturers*, p. 239.

in twenty large cities in the country." Nonetheless, its possibilities were enormous: it would do well "in a great many cases, where other systems would not pay."[31] A brilliant, innovative American engineer, Sprague instinctively grasped that in his environment strong incentives for private decision-makers could almost always be trusted to override non-economic considerations and "impractical" aesthetic principles.

The most important of Sprague's 1887 contracts was to equip a new streetcar company at Richmond, Virginia. There Sprague made an audacious gamble bordering on the foolhardy. A group of New York investors had received a franchise to build and operate a second street railway company at Richmond. They realized from the start, however, that the steep hills and primitive, unpaved clay streets their line was to run over made animal traction unusually expensive and potentially unprofitable. Sprague's well-publicized efforts seemed an answer, and although certain basic conditions of the new line were still undecided, Sprague jumped at the opportunity to prove his system. With forty cars and twelve miles of track this would be the world's largest electric street railway by far.

Sprague's experience and expertise with motors was perhaps the key to his success. The problem of sparking metallic brushes on the commutator, the problem whose solution had eluded Van Depoele, was solved by substituting carbon brushes. Each car was equipped with two motors, which "were mounted beneath the car and suspended by what was called the wheelbarrow suspension. Each motor was mounted by three points, two on the car axle and one on the car. This permitted the car to move relative to the axle and motor without misaligning the gearing."[32] Sprague also perfected the overhead method by designing a universal swiveling, under-running trolley to pick up current from a sin-

[31] "Remarks of Mr. F. J. Sprague on Electricity as a Motive Power," *ASRA* 6 (1887-88): 60-68.
[32] Passer, *Electrical Manufacturers*, p. 245.

gle copper-wire conductor attached to poles installed for that purpose. The rails were used for the return circuit. Here then was the remarkably successful synthesis of features that "became standard on American street railways."[33]

Because Sprague was racing the clock to fulfill his contract and because the contractor did a poor job of laying track and roadbed under admittedly adverse conditions, Sprague lost heavily on the Richmond installation. Initial difficulties of continuous service after the grand opening in February 1888 added to total expenses, so that Sprague eventually spent $160,000 for the $90,000 he received. Yet the streetcar company reported operating costs which it estimated were only 40 percent of what they would have been with animal power. Richmond temporarily became the mecca for railway operators and investors, and a vast profitable market for equipment opened up before Sprague. The gamble had paid off. Shortly thereafter the Thomson-Houston Company succeeded in perfecting Van Depoele's methods of overhead electric traction and emerged as a very tough competitor, as Sprague himself was quick to admit.[34]

In the next two years electrification shot through the American street railway industry like current through a copper wire. By July 1, 1890, the transportation census showed that of a total of 5,783 miles of American street railway line one-sixth (914 miles) was already electrified, which was almost twice the length of all steam street railways (524 miles) and more than three times the length of all cable lines (283 miles).[35] By the end of 1893 total street railway track in the United States had soared to 12,200 miles; ten years later it had reached roughly 30,000 miles. Of this greatly increased total, fully 60 percent was electric by the

[33] *Ibid*. For a good contemporary account of the Richmond installation see *EE* 1 (1888): 560-63.
[34] *SRJ* 24 (1904): 570-71. See Passer, *Electrical Manufacturers*, pp. 249-55, for Thomson-Houston in the United States and chapter IV of this study for some of its European activities.
[35] U.S., Census, *Transportation, 1890*, 1, 681-82.

end of 1893, and 98 percent was electric by the end of 1903.[36] The horsecar was already a memory and the electric streetcar, now affectionately known as "the trolley" in fitting recognition of the small trolley wheel pressing upward against the overhead wire, rolled through the cities of the nation. In the words of one distinguished historian, the electric streetcar in America "was one of the most rapidly accepted innovations in the history of technology."[37] It brought a revolution in urban transport, a revolution that spread to Europe and around the world.

3. The New Techno-Economic Matrix

Before delving into problems of diffusion it is well to understand something more of what was being diffused, and why it was such an improvement. For the owners and managers of first American and then European horse tramways generally adopted overhead electric traction for the same reason that privately owned, capitalist industry generally adopts technological innovations: anticipated greater profits. In the simplest terms, these decision-makers concluded that this type of electric traction would cut their per unit operating costs markedly and also substantially increase total revenues. The result would then be a large increase in profits. In the best of circumstances, the result might even equal the reported 200 percent gain in net income reported in 1889 for one line in Boston, Mass., which, as the *Street Railway Journal* rhapsodized, "is something marvelous."[38] What then were the characteristics of the new system, and what were the sources of those gains from technology which might be translated into larger private profits?

[36] See below, note 62. Also *SRJ* 24 (1904): 598-600 for slightly different figures for the years 1884-1903.
[37] George W. Hilton, "Transport Technology and the Urban Pattern," *Journal of Contemporary History*, 4 (1969): 126.
[38] *SRJ* 5 (1889): 342.

In the first place, overhead electric traction broke the bottleneck of supply of urban transit by permitting tramway companies to increase enormously their capacity to carry passengers. There is strong reason to believe that this increase in supply capability was perhaps even more important than the reduction in operating costs, which was constantly trumpeted and sometimes exaggerated by the electrical producers and tramway promoters ever keen to sell their equipment and their shares. This judgment is due in part to the conception of the horsecar system developed in chapter 1. In city after city European horsecar traffic had expanded rapidly for a time and then stagnated, as surface congestion and widely fluctuating demand prevented expansion of service on "saturated" lines and networks. And though tramway managers certainly worried about their expenses, the real challenge from the point of view of society as a whole was not so much to cut costs on the existing output—imagine a new breed of horse that consumed garbage and waste instead of hay and oats—as to increase output rapidly without raising per unit costs unduly. One may think of Eric Lampard's formulation of the problem of economic growth, of which the growth of transport is an important component. In both cases "growth depends on increasing the supply capacity" and thereby raising, as rapidly as possible, the upper limit on potential output.[39]

Overhead electric traction resulted in just such a large and rapid increase in the supply capacity of public transport, for a number of reasons. First of all, the electric car went a minimum of 25 to 50 percent faster than the horsecar—even in highly congested European cities.[40] Faster both on level ground and in mounting grades, the electric streetcar could also run *downhill* faster and with greater

[39] Eric Lampard, "The Social Impact of the Industrial Revolution," in Melvin Kranzberg and Carroll Pursell, Jr., eds., *Technology in Western Civilization*, 2 vols. (New York, 1967), 1:305-06.

[40] For example, *60 Jahre Städtische elektrische Strassenbahn in Frankfurt am Main* (Frankfurt am Main[?], 1959), pp. 7-8; *SRJ* 5 (1889): 3; 6 (1890): 128; Boshart, *Strassenbahnen*, pp. 14-16.

safety, for it could be stopped suddenly in an emergency by putting the motor in reverse. This ability to reverse directions quickly, coupled with the elimination of horse space, also contributed to greater maneuverability and faster running.[41] Thus even where the total number of cars in operation could not be increased because of intense congestion in central thoroughfares, each car could run more kilometers per day and increase its capacity by that amount.

Imagine, for example, a typical horse tram running an average of eight kilometers per hour. This would result in a round trip on a typical four-kilometer line each hour and eighteen such trips in the course of its eighteen hours of service. A typical electric tram traveling twelve kilometers per hour would make the same round trip in forty minutes and offer twenty-seven round trips each day, while running 216 kilometers as opposed to 144. Put another way, trams that used to pass every nine minutes on a given line would now pass every six, while one that came every six would come every four, even if the number of cars in service remained the same.

Capacity for supply was also increased because each tramcar could be enlarged to carry more passengers. That, at least, was the pattern in the United States, where ever larger and heavier electric cars were built, and in Great Britain, where the traditional double-decker of the horsecar era was retained and enlarged. On the continent a different method was generally adopted. The electric motorcar long remained fairly small and single-decked, very much like the horsecar it replaced. But to the motorcar one or even two trailer cars would be attached, to be pulled easily by the motorcar as a train pulls its caboose. (See figure 3.)

This use of the trailer, which has remained almost universal to this day wherever the electric tramway is alive and well, as in West Germany or the Soviet Union, provided more than the obvious increase in carrying capacity. It also provided great flexibility, since it permitted the traf-

[41] *SRJ* 6 (1890): 151-52.

fic manager to add or subtract trailers to meet the fluctuating needs of rush-hour crowds or mid-morning slack. This was particularly important on the continent because police safety regulations severely limited standing and "straphanging": with the trailer almost everyone could find the required seat.[42] In Vienna in 1898, for example, trams drawn by two horses carried a maximum of 32 passengers at an average speed of 8 to 8.5 kilometers per hour. In 1905 electric motorcars with two trailers had a capacity of 130 passengers and averaged 10 to 10.5 kilometers per hour.[43]

Two other aspects of increased supply potential may be mentioned briefly. First, electric traction permitted easy ascent of moderate grades—which had previously required extra effort or double teams—as well as steep grades of 10 percent or more, which would never have been conquered by horse trams under any circumstances. In addition to those of Kiev, Russia (see figure 4), the electric tramways of Remscheid, Germany, provided an interesting and widely noted example of this aspect of improvement. These handled the steepest grades of any tramways in Europe when they were opened in 1895, grades which people had previously considered impossible on a friction roadway.

The heart of this old fortress town of about 43,000 inhabitants, with its residential area and commercial-administrative center, was on the top of a small mountain. This mountain rose fifty to sixty meters above the surrounding flatland, where the railroad station and a number of factories had risen. Thus the population was continually engaged in the wearisome task of moving up and down the steep incline. No wonder, then, that a wealthy local industrialist secured permission to establish an electric tramway company in Remscheid in 1892, which was then fitted out with Thomson-Houston equipment. The steep grades,

[42] F. Ross, "Die elektrischen Strassenbahnen und ihre Bedeutung für den Verkehr der Stadte," *Schweizerische Bauzeitung* 25 (1895): 158 ff; *SRJ* 21 (1903): 18.
[43] "Vienna Tramway Statistics," *SRJ* 26 (1905): 846-47.

exceeding 10 percent on one stretch of the Bismarck Strasse, required special safety brakes and sand on the rails on rainy days, but the new street railway was an indisputable technical and commercial success.[44] The lesson was clear: that bane of the horsecar manager and his horses—those steep and moderate grades almost invariably found somewhere in his city—was no more.

Second, in time of ice and snow the extra force required to move the cars could be delivered and normal service more easily maintained. And in the event of severe storms special electric snowplow cars could be called up to clean the track and get the trams running. In short, for all these reasons overhead electric traction dramatically increased the capacity to supply urban transit, and one could have predicted major consequences even if other aspects had remained constant.

Not only was supply of transport greatly expanded—a remarkable enough achievement—but the transport so supplied was of much better quality. Indeed, so great was the improvement that it is hardly an exaggeration to say that a new and different good was placed before the riding public. The greater speed meant a longer trip in the same length of time, for example; a regular commuter might therefore be willing to live farther from work, thereby fostering suburban expansion and dispersion from the city center. (See chapter VI.) Alternatively, there were substantial savings in time for rides going the same old distance, an advantage widely noted and appreciated.[45]

More frequent service, extension of old lines, building of new ones, and the absence of the "full-up" sign at peak hours were all aspects of this improved quality. But there were others, too. The electric tram was much more comfortable: it rode more smoothly; started and stopped with less

[44] "Die elektrische Strassenbahn im Remscheid," *ZK* 2 (1895): 71-76; *EE* 19 (1897): 306-07.
[45] For example, C. Klein-Bader, *75 Jahre Münchner Strassenbahn, 1876-1951* (Munich, 1951), p. 7.

3. Stuttgart. Motor-car with 2 trail-cars. Rush-hour traffic and capacity.

4. Kiev. Steep hills and the first city with electric tramways in Russia, May 1892.

5. Genoa. Upper and lower entrances of the S. Ugo spiral tunnel.

of a lurch; and did not oscillate from side to side like a ship in heavy seas. It was also cleaner, well-lighted electrically and thereby devoid of the offensive odor found previously when using oil, as well as much better heated, again electrically.[46]

Nor was this all. Fares were substantially lower on the trolley car than on the horse tram. A short ride might cost only half as much as it had before, for example. Or a much longer ride on extended lines to outlying suburbs would be possible at no increase in price. Thus the quality of urban transport was improved while the price fell, and sometimes drastically so, as we shall see.

Lower fares for the public reflected the reduction in the cost of providing service for tramway companies. Although variations were great and the data are somewhat contradictory, the basic reason was fairly obvious: the cost of power—of traction—fell by about 50 percent. And since, it will be remembered, the cost of horses had accounted for roughly half of total tramway expenses, and since there was some saving on labor because each driver now covered a greater distance each day, electric traction did indeed result in the immediate average reduction of at least 30 to 40 percent in total operating expenses that one of the leading German producers quite typically claimed for it.[47]

These are, of course, only estimates of the illusive "average" pattern. Actual results and estimates varied considerably. On the one hand, claims and examples of considerably higher savings on both power and total expenses are not hard to find. A writer in the prestigious American journal, *Scientific American*, stated in 1897 that "the old horse-car road in large cities operated at a total of 18 to 25 cents per car mile." Of this, 8 to 11 cents represented the cost of pow-

[46] *SRJ* 6 (1890): 152.
[47] Book published by Allgemeine Elektricitäts-Gesellschaft, Berlin, no title, no date [Berlin, 1899?], p. 13. See also *SRJ* 6 (1890): 29, 524-25; *EE* 8 (1891): 473-74; and Wilhelm Mattersdorf, "An Analysis of Street Railway Operation in Germany," *SRJ* 19 (1902): 439-43.

er—"that is, the care and maintenance of the horses, their feeding, and the depreciation of the same." And indeed, one knowledgeable street railway executive believed that "the cost of horse power for drawing cars has been found by long experience to vary from 10 to 11 cents per car mile."[48] With overhead electric power, however, the *Scientific American* writer found, "this item is reduced today to a cost, under general condition, ranging from 1 to 1½ cents per car mile. Is this not a marvelous gain in a few years . . . ?"[49] Indeed, perhaps a bit too marvelous, as other data would show electric traction expenses in the United States averaging 3 to 4 cents per car mile. Similarly, confidential reports on the tramways of Rouen, France, showed the cost of power declining by 75 percent, while total costs per car kilometer fell by 55 percent after the introduction of electric tramways.[50] On the other hand, one detailed German comparison, which carefully weighed all the tricky depreciation costs that electric enthusiasts sometimes glossed over, concluded that a decline of only 35 percent in the cost of traction was a reasonable expectation.[51]

Probably the best general indication of the extent of the cost reduction may be obtained by analysis of official statistics. Such statistics, compiled by the Board of Trade, were quite complete for Great Britain from the early 1870s. They are similarly so for France from 1896 on. Therefore a comparison of costs per tramway rider in these two countries in 1896 and 1910 gives a fairly suitable "before-and-after" picture of the savings that overhead electric traction actually produced over time.

These data, presented in table 3, should be read in the light of three qualifying comments. First, some electrification had already occurred in France by the end of 1895.

[48] Franklin Pope, "Notes on the Electric Railway," *EE* 7 (1891): 258.
[49] *Scientific American*, Supplement, No. 1064 (May 23, 1896), p. 17012.
[50] CL, Tramways de Rouen, Etude, September 1901.
[51] ZTS, as discussed in *EE* 14 (1894): 75-76.

Table 3

TOTAL AND PER RIDER COSTS OF TRAMWAY SERVICE

	France[a]			United Kingdom[b]		
Year	Riders Carried (millions)	Total Costs (millions of francs)	Cost per Rider (centimes)	Riders Carried (millions)	Total Costs (millions of £)	Cost per Rider (pence)
1896	356.2	44.8	12.6	759	3.1	.98
1910	1,066.9	75.5	7.1	2,907	8.5	.70

SOURCE: France. Ministère des Travaux Publics. Direction des Chemins de fer. *Statistique des chemins de fer français*, 1906, II, 655, 667; 1912, II, 895, 909. Great Britain. House of Commons, Sessional Papers. Board of Trade. Return of Street and Road Tramways, various years. (See *Alphabetical Index to the Bills . . . of the House of Commons*, 1852-1899 [London, 1909], p. 1395, and *Index to Bills . . . 1900 to 1948-49* [London, 1960], p. 671, for precise location.)

[a] Includes "tramways for passengers only" and "tramways for passengers, baggage and messages"; omits "tramways for passengers and freight," which were generally rural in nature.

[b] Great Britain and Ireland; includes tramways and light railways, which often served rural areas.

Second, the figures are for all urban and suburban tramways in France, but they include the interurban or rural light railways for the United Kingdom. This means that although horse power predominated in 1896 and overhead electric traction in 1910, other methods were also in use at both dates. Since steam, which was widely used on light railways, was slightly cheaper than horse power in 1896, and since other methods employed in 1910 were more expensive than the overhead trolley, there is thus a tendency to understate the savings in the substitution of overhead electric for animal traction. Finally, the data for both countries is for total expenses. This included depreciation expenses, which were believed to be adequate but which in fact were probably inadequate at both times. Thus this bias, which would overstate the savings resulting from electricity since there was now more capital to depreciate, tends to offset the other one.

Total costs per rider carried declined by more than 40 percent in France and by slightly less than 30 percent in the United Kingdom. One should note that the rise in general price levels in both countries approached 30 percent from 1895 to 1910.[52] The real decline in costs, adjusted for inflation, was therefore about 50 percent in the United Kingdom and 60 percent in France—a tremendous reduction. As for comparative costs at pre-1914 gold exchange ratios, the cost per passenger carried in both France and the United Kingdom equaled about 1.4 American cents.

The reduction in costs per passenger had to be purchased at the price of a great increase in capital invested. Old equipment had to be sold or scrapped, and then replaced by the new and much more expensive electrical apparatus. Indeed, again on the basis of French and British statistics, it seems clear that investment per kilometer of tramway track roughly doubled with electrification. The 175,000 francs invested by tramway companies per kilometer of line in France in 1890 had risen to 322,000 francs per kilometer in 1900, when electrification was largely completed.[53] In the United Kingdom investment per mile of line went from £9,000 in 1890, to £11,500 in 1900, and to £18,100 in 1910.[54]

Here, then, were needs for capital far in excess of the cash flow (profits plus depreciation) or borrowing power of all but the most profitable tramway companies. Such capital needs could have important consequences for the financial organization of individual companies and the whole industry, as we shall see, particularly in chapter IV. Another factor making for financial organization was that only a few powerful producers of equipment controlled the new and

[52] See Paul Rousseaux, *Les mouvements de fonds de l'économie anglaise* (Louvain, 1938).
[53] Edouard Fuster, ed., *Annuaire Général des Tramways de France* (Paris, 1901), pp. 13, 27.
[54] Great Britain, HC, Tramway Reports.

complicated technology. This contrasted sharply with the old framework, where the widely known methods of horse-car operations were fully understood by a host of independent operators.

Perhaps a more graphic way to show the change which the increase in investment summed up is to sketch briefly some aspects of the wholesale transformation of the enterprise which the new technology demanded. At the outset there was the question of power. It would be a mistake to suppose that in most cases a tramway company could simply plug into an existing electric power network. Quite the contrary: in the majority of cases streetcar electrification in Europe meant constructing a large central power station, complete with coal storage, steam engines, and electric generators, on a strategically situated site purchased for the purpose. Then there was the question of tearing down stables and constructing the very different electric car barns. This substitution might end up by being advantageous from a financial point of view, since the electric car barns and repair sheds could be located away from expensive land near the city center, where the slow-moving horses were normally kept. (In any event the combined area required for power station and car barns was less than that for stables, and this gave many companies a surplus of land which could eventually be sold in order to free up some capital.)

As for the overhead apparatus, it normally represented about 20 percent of the cost of electrification. It comprised not only the fine copper wire conductor and the support system of poles and house brackets, but also the "feeders"— the heavier wire used to carry current to the different sections of the overhead trolley wire. Originally placed overhead with the trolley wire in America, the European feeders were put underground with a connection to the overhead wire every 500 meters or so. There was thus a costly and vexatious tearing up of the street to lay the feeder cable, as well as setting of poles and overhead wires. Then there was the need to establish shops and train men for the daily inspection and maintenance of the cars, as well as for the periodic overhaul of motors, gears, trucks, and so forth. The old horsecars were often found in such shops on the continent, where they were refurbished to serve as trailers until they wore out. (See figure 6.) But the best indication of the need to redo almost everything, and all at the same time, was the relaying of track and roadbed. One might suppose that a tramway track is a tramway track, and that the adoption of electric traction would at least spare the rails in the street. In fact, the light and imperfectly aligned horse-tram track was totally inappropriate for electric cars. In order to get the most economical service it was necessary to rebuild the roadbed completely, even though this generally *doubled* the total cost of electrification.[55] Then the alignment could be made as nearly perfect as possible, and the heavier rails—thirty-six to forty-four kilograms per meter as opposed to the eighteen to twenty-four kilos used previously—would provide the desired smoother ride and longer wear, and the rails could be properly bonded together to insure a reliable return for the current to the power station. "This [rebuilding of the roadbed] is no doubt the most important step after deciding to adopt electricity; by this means you reduce the amount of wear and tear on your cars to a minimum, and prevent to a certain extent the damage to your motors. . . . It will also enable a faster and more even rate of speed."[56] Thus the indisputable gains from technology, which might be translated into large increases in profits for tramway companies, first required heavy new investment and a complete organization of service. (See figures 7 and 8.)

Total investment in urban tramways increased dramatically with electrification. This increase reflected not only greater investment per kilometer of line, but also the rapid

[55] CL, "Etude sur les résultats de la substitution de la traction électrique à traction animale sur les principaux réseaux de tramways en France," December 1900.
[56] *SRJ* 5 (1889): 340.

6. Halle a. S. Horsecars and electric cars; note the converted trailer.

7. Duisberg. Overhead wiring on draw-bridges.

8. Halle a. S. Central railway station. Laying new rails for electrification.

increase of the network. In order to get some idea of the large implications of this increase for European economies, it is useful to analyze briefly the fairly complete data on total investment for France and the United Kingdom over time. These data were collected in somewhat different ways, however, and they are not comparable without certain comments and adjustments.

The British data combine tramways and light railways, some of which were essentially rural, although 95 percent of the total trackage was worked electrically by 1912. There is therefore no breakdown as to urban, suburban, interurban, and rural lines. However, British figures do distinguish between the capital invested by local public authorities, primarily municipalities, and the capital invested by private companies. On the other hand, the French had no municipal ownership, but they did distinguish by tramway type.

Thus the first column of table 4 follows the official French data and combines those tramways authorized to carry passengers, baggage, and messages—usually suburban in character—with those strictly urban-suburban tramways authorized to carry passengers only. In order to permit comparison with Great Britain I have added in the second column, "tramways for passengers and freight," which were the lightest of the French light railways, often interurban or rural and sometimes steam-driven. The French "local interest railways," in which half a billion francs were invested in 1912, have been omitted; most of them were rural and more closely related to first- and second-class railroads than to tramways. In short, the totals for France and Great Britain are roughly comparable: they represent the total capital invested in urban, suburban, and some rural tramways in the two countries.

It is clear from table 4 that annual investment in French and British horse tramways was minimal in the early 1890s. The surge of new investment began in France in the mid 1890s and the high was in 1899, when 235,000,000 francs were invested in a single year. Thereafter total capital in the industry grew at about 6 percent per annum, with the purely suburban or interurban portion growing more rapidly than the urban. In the United Kingdom the surge came later, peaking in 1904, when more than £10,000,000 was invested in a single year. This increase went hand in hand with the growth of capital invested by local authorities. In both countries total capital invested in all tramways, as defined above, was substantial by the end of 1912: at the existing gold exchange ratios the French industry had taken $232,000,000; the British had absorbed $385,000,000.

It seems that new investment in electric tramways was large enough to make some real contribution to the return of fairly general prosperity throughout industrialized Europe, which began in the mid 1890s and continued with fluctuations to 1914. In the United Kingdom an average of £5,540,000 was expended annually on tramways (and light railways) in the first decade of the twentieth century. This amounted to about 3.5 percent of the £161,000,000 estimated to have gone into gross domestic investment each year in the same period.[57] Electric tramway investment was, of course, highly concentrated: at the 1904 high point for the United Kingdom, electric tramways and light railways took £11,000,000 and accounted for something like 6 percent of gross domestic investment in that year. In France, as in Germany and other continental countries, investment in electric tramways was earlier and even more concentrated. Such investment clearly played its part in the great European industrial boom at the very end of the nineteenth century.

4. *Diffusion in Europe*

If overhead electric traction swept across the United States of America with great speed immediately after 1888, it did no such thing in Europe. There was little emulation,

[57] Phyllis Deane and W. A. Cole, *British Economic Growth, 1688-1959* (Cambridge, 1964), pp. 264-67, 332-33.

though great discussion, in Europe for about five years, and electric traction was adopted rapidly only in the last years of the century. There was also considerable variation in the speed with which it was adopted in different countries. Finally, the overhead method of electric traction continued to have many rivals in Europe, long after it was univer-

Table 4

TOTAL CAPITAL INVESTED IN ALL TRAMWAYS
IN FRANCE AND THE UNITED KINGDOM,
1890-1912

	France (millions of francs)		
Year[a]	Urban Tramways	Tramways for Passengers and Freight	Total Capital
1890	115.2	40.5	155.7
1891	122.8	50.4	173.2
1892	147.5	43.4	191.0
1893	139.6	54.2	193.8
1894	165.2	70.1	235.3
1895	172.6	86.1	258.7
1896	198.3	98.2	296.5
1897	222.8	118.2	341.0
1898	251.1	137.3	388.4
1899	290.8	129.9	420.7
1900	502.7	153.0	655.7
1901	556.3	179.8	736.1
1902	591.2	207.6	798.8
1903	611.2	221.3	832.5
1904	618.6	241.5	860.1
1905	638.6	258.0	896.6
1906	650.4	277.2	927.6
1907	678.0	290.7	968.7
1908	707.4	300.0	1,007.4
1909	745.8	312.6	1,058.4
1910	730.4	335.0	1,065.4
1911	755.2	352.1	1,107.3
1912	800.8	402.7	1,203.5

Table 4—*Continued*

United Kingdom
(millions of £)

Year[a]	Local Authorities	Private Companies	Total Capital
1890	2.9	10.8	13.7
1891	2.9	11.3	14.2
1892	3.0	10.9	13.9
1893	3.1	11.0	14.1
1894	3.9	10.5	14.4
1895	3.2	11.8	15.0
1896	4.3	10.9	15.2
1897	4.5	10.4	14.9
1898	6.1	10.4	16.5
1899	8.1	10.5	18.6
1900	10.2	11.5	21.7
1901	14.1	12.7	26.8
1902	18.9	12.7	31.6
1903	24.5	17.2	41.7
1904	33.0	19.7	52.7
1905	37.2	21.0	58.2
1906	41.7	22.4	64.1
1907	44.9	23.3	68.2
1908	47.1	23.9	71.0
1909	49.6	24.4	74.0
1910	51.1	24.5	75.6
1911	52.7	24.7	77.4
1912	54.5	24.9	79.4

SOURCE: France, 1890-1898: Edouard Fuster, ed. *Annuaire Général des Tramways de France* (Paris, 1900), p. 27. 1899-1912: Ministère des Travaux Publics, Direction des Chemins de fer français. *Statistique des chemins de fer français*, 1906, II, 632, 654; 1912, II, 870, 894. United Kingdom: see source table 3.

NOTE: See text for discussion of tramway groupings.

[a] Year ending December 31 for France; year ending June 30 for United Kingdom through 1902, and on December 31 for private companies and March 31 of the following year for public authorities beginning in 1903.

sally accepted in the United States. In short, the process of diffusion and adoption was less smooth, more complex, and yes, more interesting, in the Old World than in the New. But before turning to detailed analysis of some of the forces shaping the European pattern and trying to relate that to our hypotheses and conceptual framework, an overview of the whole movement is necessary.

At the beginning of 1888, while Sprague was laboring at Richmond and when there were thirteen electric street railways of all types and sizes of less than fifty miles of track in the United States, Europe could boast fully eighteen electric tramways of all kinds.[58] Eight of these European lines, totalling perhaps twenty-two miles, were in Great Britain, where five employed either the running rails or a third rail as a surface conductor (Blackpool, Brighton, Newry-Bessbrook, Portrush, and Ryde Pier). Of the remaining ten tramways with approximately twelve miles of track located on the continent, seven had been built by Siemens from 1881 onward. The remaining three consisted of trials with Julien battery cars at Brussels and with Hüber battery cars at Cologne and Hamburg.[59] By 1888, then, Europe's early lead had disappeared and America had pulled even.

Five years later America had sped ahead, far ahead. Just how far is somewhat difficult to establish, however. Annual American figures as given by the authoritative *Street Railway Journal* (as opposed to government census reports at ten-year intervals) normally refer to miles of track—with double-tracked sections of given lines counted twice. European data are normally for kilometers of line—irrespective of whether the line was single-tracked or double-tracked—so estimates and adjustments are necessary.[60] Neverthe-

[58] *EE* 1 (1888): 178-79; 9 (1892): 186.
[59] *Ibid.*
[60] I have followed the lead of *Street Railway Journal* in a similar comparison (21 [1903]: 17) and assumed that 60 percent of American line was double-tracked, as *SRJ* believed 60 percent was double-tracked in Europe. I have also converted estimates of American line figures into kilometers to give some idea of the relative absolute figures.

less, it appears that 305 kilometers of line, or 3 to 4 percent of all lines, were electrified in Europe by the end of 1893, and that 902 kilometers, or 7.5 percent of the European total of 11,900 kilometers, were electrified by the end of 1895.[61] In the United States, on the other hand, about 2,500 kilometers of line, or 28 percent of the total, were electrified by the end of 1890; 7,500 kilometers, or 61 percent of the total, by the end of 1893; and 12,100 kilometers, or 84 percent of the total, by the end of 1895.[62] As one of many European observers put it in 1892, the development of the electric street railways had been prodigious in America since it became a "practical commercial success in 1888, while Europe has shown scarcely any improvement."[63]

After this initial lag European electrification began to move forward rapidly by the end of 1893. In five years the length of electric line increased more than tenfold, to almost 3,000 kilometers at the end of 1898. By that date the electric tramway boom was in full swing. It is even possible to make precise comparisons regarding the speed of adoption in different European countries between 1893 and 1898 because of the unique, country-by-country, annual surveys published by the excellent French journal, *L'Industrie Electrique*. These data are presented in table 5.[64] Unfortunately, *L'Industrie Electrique* discontinued its annual survey in 1899, except for France, and most official statistics on street railways—those of Austria and Great Britain were exceptions—failed to distinguish what modes of traction were being used. Thus there are only scattered data on the rapid electrification which continued throughout 1899 and 1900.

[61] *IE*, as cited in table 5, for electric line, and Gerard, *Bulletin de la commission internationale du congrès des chemins de fer*, December 1896, as quoted by *ZK* 4 (1897): 252-55, for the total of European tramway lines. Some lines which were essentially light railways may have been included by Gerard.

[62] Calculated (see note 60) on the basis of *SRJ* 8 (1892): 213; 10 (1894): 33; 12 (1896): 502.

[63] *EE* 9 (1892): 186.

[64] The *Industrie Electrique* surveys probably included electrification of a few tramways which were really light railways for rural areas.

Table 5

ELECTRIC TRAMWAYS IN EUROPE
(in kms. of line on Dec. 31)

Year	Austria	Belgium	France	Germany	Great Britain	Italy	Russia	Spain	Switzerland	All Other	TOTAL
1890											96
1891											
1892			37								
1893	33	3	41	102	71	13	3	14	24	1	305
1894	45	22	96	366	69	19	10	14	37	22	700
1895	71	25	132	406	94	40	10	29	47	48	902
1896	84	35	279	643	109	116	15	47	79	52	1459
1897	107	69	397	1138	134	133	31	61	146	74	2290
1898	113	69	488	1403	211	147	41	105	201	98	2876
1899			753	2048[a]							
1900	225		1486	2868							
1901				3099[b]							
1902			1995	3388	1401[c]						
1903				3692	2354[d]						
1904					2867						
1905	472				3209						
1910	586				3972						

SOURCE: 1890, *EE* 16 (1895): 368; 1893-98, for all countries, *IE*, supplements to no. 77 (1895), no. 101 (1896), no. 125 (1897), no. 149 (1898), no. 173 (1899); Austria, 1900-10, Austria, Eisenbahn Ministerium, *Österreichische Eisenbahnstatistik für das Jahr 1913*, II, xvi; France, 1892, 1899, 1900, 1902, *IE* 10 (1901): 127; 12 (1903): 456; Germany, 1899-1903, *EZ* 29 (1904): 636; Great Britain (and Ireland), 1902-1910, House of Commons, Tramway Reports.

[a] For September 1, 1899-1900.   [c] For June 30, 1902.
[b] For October 1, 1901-1903.
[d] December 31 for companies; March 31 of the following year for public authorities: 1903-1910.

Yet by the time the depression of 1901 arrived, electric systems were either in operation or in construction in almost all European cities. After 1903 or 1904 only a few mavericks clung to animal traction, and the electric tramways industry moved into the period of normal operation and more moderate growth.

The statistical data on streetcar electrification show that there were significant national differences within the general European development. Among the major European nations, Germany clearly led in adopting electric traction. Accounting for roughly one-third of all electric line at the end of 1893, Germany jumped to one-half of the European total the following year and continued to hold that position through 1898. Nor did this commanding position result from simply having more horse trams in the first place: in 1895 Germany accounted for only an estimated 15 percent of all streetcar lines in Europe.[65] Indeed, 23 percent of all German streetcar lines were already electrified by the end of 1895, when a British observer could state correctly that "by far the greater proportion of European electric tramway installations are to be found in Germany."[66] By the end of 1902 virtually all German lines were electrified.

Compare this with Great Britain, on the other extreme. There electric traction was accepted slowly and grudgingly, especially in view of the fact that in early 1888 Great Britain had approximately twice the electric lines of all the continental countries combined. Yet by the end of 1895 only 6 percent of the British total was electrified, rising to 12 percent by the end of 1898, and 38 percent by the end of 1902.[67] Thus, electrification in Britain was concentrated in the early years of the twentieth century and lagged behind Germany's by almost a decade. At first glance, we see a striking example of that hardening of British entrepreneurial arteries before 1914 that economic historians have

[65] Gerard, *ZK* 4 (1897): 252-55.   [66] Dawson, *EE* 16 (1895): 368.
[67] *IE* (per table 5) for electric lines and Board of Trade Tramway Reports for total lines.

traditionally contrasted with German dynamism.[68] That France and indeed most continental countries occupied the middle ground, leaning more toward the German than the British extreme, is less expectable. These questions of comparative European economic history will require further consideration.

To speak of the coming of electric traction in this way, as if there were only one basic kind, clearly distinct from earlier types (primarily animal and steam), is quite legitimate for the United States. There electric traction did mean the standard overhead trolley-wire conductor, of which the Sprague, Thomson-Houston, and Westinghouse varieties accounted for perhaps 85 percent circa 1894. Other types of electric traction were virtually unknown, and they were quickly abandoned when occasionally tried.[69]

In Europe, however, there was electric traction and then there was electric traction. That is, although the overhead-wire method dominated, it was challenged by a number of competing electric methods well into the twentieth century. These challengers may be grouped into two basic groups, although there were as many variations as there were inventors. First, there was storage-battery electric traction. Large batteries were charged at the central power station and then placed on the car, often under the seats. The batteries drove the car until they needed recharging, which was done at the power station. With this method the tramway had its own mobile power source and there was no need for any kind of wire conductor. The second method utilized an underground (as opposed to overhead) conductor—normally a wire conductor placed in an enclosed and carefully insulated conduit laid in the roadbed between the rails, or under one of them. Some form of plow connected

[68] For example, Landes, *Unbound Prometheus*, pp. 326-58. Some revisionist discussion may be found in Donald N. McCloskey, ed., *Essays on a Mature Economy: Britain after 1840* (Princeton, N.J., 1971).

[69] *ZK* 1 (1894): 587; Oscar T. Crosby and Louis Bell, *The Electric Railway in Theory and Practice* (New York, 1892), pp. 235, 253.

to the motor then extended into the conduit's slot to pick up the electric current.

But this was not all. In addition to the "pure" types—overhead-wire conductor, surface-conduit conductor, and independent portable batteries—there were many "mixed" types, which incorporated two or even three different kinds of traction on a given car or a given line. And these "mixed" types might even be joined with non-electric forms of mechanical traction—principally fireless steam engines or compressed air. Finally, within given cities there was the less impressive but nonetheless slow-to-die pattern of electric traction on some lines and straight animal traction on others, or animal traction past a certain point on a given line. Some of the many examples of European transit systems which did not follow the American pattern of "pure" overhead-wire conductor will be examined in this study. But the basic point is clear enough: Europe developed and used a wide variety of technological alternatives to complement the dominant overhead method, the method America developed and did not go beyond.

It is difficult to present any reliable figures on the relative weights of overhead and non-overhead methods. Companies changed and experimented considerably, and methods of reporting varied. Nonetheless, the annual electric tramways censuses conducted by *L'Industrie Electrique* were complete through 1898, and those data are presented in table 6. We should note that only electric systems are considered and that generally each city is considered as one line, although some of the largest cities had multiple lines. "Other" also includes "mixed" systems in which the overhead conductor was one part of the mixture. An example of this would be a line equipped with cars that drew current from the overhead wire over one stretch of line and then from its batteries over another. In any event the problem of European technological diversity is posed, and it will be analyzed in the following chapter.

In any overview of electric tramway development Ger-

Table 6

SYSTEMS OF ELECTRIC TRACTION ON EUROPEAN TRAMWAYS
(December 31 of year)

Year	France Over-head	France Other	France Total	Germany Over head	Germany Other	Germany Total	Great Britain Over-head	Great Britain Other	Great Britain Total	All Europe[a] Over-head	All Europe[a] Other	All Europe[a] Total	Year
1893	7	4	11	21	1	22							1893
1894	11	5	16	33	3	36	4	9	13	31	12	43	1894
1895	19	7	26	45	6	51	7	10	17	55	15	70	1895
1896	36	8	44	56	9	65	10	8	18	91	20	111	1896
1897	42	14	56	63	10	73	14	8	22	122	28	150	1897
1898	56	16	72				19	10	29	172	32	204	1898
1899	76	30	106							206	42	248	1899
1900	85	64	149										1900
1902													1902

SOURCE: *IE*, as given in table 5.

[a] In addition to France, Germany, and Great Britain, includes Austria-Hungary, Belgium, Bosnia, Holland, Italy, Ireland, Portugal, Rumania, Russia, Serbia, Spain, Sweden and Norway, and Switzerland.

many deserves special consideration. Not only did Germany electrify most rapidly and provide a first-hand example for other European countries, but her great electrical producers played a key role in spreading the innovation. The first electric line on the American pattern in Germany, and indeed in all Europe, opened in Bremen on June 22, 1890. As was so often the case in late nineteenth-century urban transport history, a large exposition which would place exceptional demands upon transit facilities was an important initiating factor. It was in this connection that the Bremen Tramways Company requested and received permission to equip one of its routes with Thomson-Houston cars and overhead-wire conductors. The line began at the center of town, near the city hall, passed by the new railway station, and terminated at the Exposition Grounds, where a major industrial exhibition was scheduled for that summer.[70] This meant that not only ordinary visitors but many business leaders would be introduced to the new method of traction as they shuttled between the railroad station, the fairgrounds, and the center of town.

According to contemporary reports this overhead trolley line, with its cluster of five incandescent lamps suspended from every other support pole to light the night, was a great success. In the first ten weeks 331,000 passengers rode the electric cars. No wonder that shortly after the opening of the first line, construction began on a second. Both worked so satisfactorily that by April 1891 the street railway company decided to remove all its horsecars and substitute electric trams of the Thomson-Houston type on its whole service.[71]

Before Bremen's tramways were totally electrified in 1892, the Allgemeine Elektricitäts-Gesellschaft, popularly known as A.E.G., installed its overhead system over a network of eight kilometers at Halle. Service began in May 1891, and Halle became the first town in Europe to have a

[70] *SRJ* 6 (1890): 47, 433-34, 474-75; *EE* 6 (1890): 165-66, 233.
[71] *EE* 6 (1890): 328; 7 (1891): 354-55.

major electric traction network in operation.[72] A.E.G. had entered into an agreement with the city in 1890 to equip Halle's municipally sponsored network with electric traction. This line presented various difficulties because the Halle Tramway Company, which had been established earlier, had previously preempted the best routes. Thus the city had to operate its cars over secondary thoroughfares which were extremely narrow and quite steep at points. The success of the installation was considerable, and not the least from a financial point of view: whereas the city-sponsored network had been losing 7 to 8 percent of its capital per year with horse traction, it paid an annual dividend of 5.1 percent in its first year and a greater amount every year thereafter until 1900.[73]

A.E.G. had already profited enormously from American innovation. As its guiding spirit, Emil Rathenau had lead the firm to a strong position as one of the chief European licensees of the Edison incandescent light bulb in the 1880s. So it was natural that A.E.G. should acquire the European rights to Sprague's patents, which were acquired by Edison's company by 1890. Thus beginning with the Halle installation A.E.G. stood as a major competitor of the Union Elektricitäts-Gesellschaft, the German firm formed to use Thomson-Houston patents in Germany. In 1892 A.E.G. completed its second major installation, equipping twelve kilometers of overhead line and eighteen cars at Gera.

The year 1892 also marked an impressive resurgence of the Siemens and Halske Company. In July 1889 the firm had successfully equipped an experimental electric line with the underground conduit method in Budapest.[74] Then, unlike its two principal competitors, Siemens and Halske did not simply copy the American wheel trolley but developed its own unique overhead contact method. As one expert put it,

[72] Hochenegg, *ZOIAV* 54 (1902): 55-56.
[73] Allgemeine Elektricitäts-Gesellschaft (1899?), pp. 7-8.
[74] Hochenegg, *ZOIAV* 54 (1902): 55-56; Heinrich Vellguth, "Electric Railway Practice on the Continent of Europe," *SRJ* 21 (1903): 354-56.

"Siemens and Halske, true to the traditions of a firm which laid the very foundations of the electrical industry half a century ago, refused to stake its ancient reputation on the vagaries of the trolley-wheel, and started on the modern phase of its career in street railway work with its broad bow or stirrup contact piece."[75] This type of moving contact-piece, first used commercially in 1893 to equip lines in Hanover and Dresden, had some definite advantages. The bow ("Bügel") was about 1.6 meters wide at the top, and therefore there was no problem of it jumping the overhead wire it pressed against. Nor did the bow trolley require the conducting wire to conform so precisely to the line of the track, although competitors alleged that the overhead wire wore out more quickly because of the bow's side to side sliding on the wire.[76]

From 1893 onward so many German cities introduced electric streetcars that any listing—much less any description—would try the patience of all but the most dedicated streetcar enthusiast. Suffice it to say that by the end of 1898 sixty-nine cities were equipped with electric tramways and that the vast majority had been installed by the three early leaders. A.E.G. took the lion's share and equipped twenty-seven cities with the Sprague system; Thomson-Houston methods installed by the Union Elektricitäts-Gesellschaft (U.E.G.) prevailed in sixteen; and Siemens and Halske accounted for ten. In five instances Siemens and Halske combined with U.E.G. to share installations, while U.E.G. and A.E.G. joined forces once, at Leipzig. Another large firm, Schukert and Company, was first of the also-rans with five installations, followed by Singer with two, and Krummer, Oerlikon, and Tudor-Hagen with one each.[77] The concentration of skill and initiative in the hands of a very few firms was striking.

Electrification produced profits not only for the equip-

[75] Louis Magee, "Electric Railway Practice in Germany," *SRJ* 15 (1899): 647.
[76] Hendlmeier, *Von der Pferde-Eisenbahn*, pp. 23-25.
[77] *IE* 8 (1899): Supplement to March 10, 1899, pp. 1-20.

ment producers (see chapter IV), but also for the German operating companies. In most cases these companies increased their earnings per share and were able to raise their dividends after electrification.[78] The few very profitable horse tramways, like that in Berlin, may have registered modest per-share increases, but the smaller and previously less successful companies were often able to make great gains. Therefore, when we construct an unweighted average of dividends paid by the twenty-odd street railway companies listed on the Berlin Stock Exchange in the crucial period, we find them paying an average dividend of 5.34 percent on their capital stock in 1894, 5.68 percent in 1895, 6.86 percent in 1896, 8.21 percent in 1897 and 8.12 percent in 1898.[79]

Unfortunately, there were simply no good statistics for German street railways at the national level until the Imperial Government began collecting them in 1902—after the most dramatic changes had taken place. It is therefore difficult to establish the extent of the electric streetcar revolution at the national level with reliable before-and-after pictures. Here, however, comparative history stands us in good stead, for though the timing of the adoption of electric traction varied significantly, the final results in different countries seem to have been quite similar. Not only were all lines in all countries electrified sooner or later (with the rarest of exceptions), but the length of those lines increased substantially—perhaps three times in twenty years on average, at the national level.

The number of riders increased more dramatically in the same period. In Great Britain, which began late but finished strong, the number of tramway (and light railway) passen-

[78] F. Hermes, *Finanzierung und Rentabilität deutscher Strassenbahnen* (Jena, 1909), pp. 84-86.

[79] Based on Max Meyer, "Die an der Berliner Börse vertretenen Strassenbahnen," *ZGLSW* 19 (1900): 31-32. (I have excluded the completely atypical Hamburg-Altonaer Zentralbahn.) I agree with the *Value Line Investment Survey* and others that such broad, unweighted indexes are generally the best measure of the ordinary investor's fortunes and interest.

gers rose fivefold between 1895, when British electric traction was largely a gleam in the technician's eye, and 1913. Similarly, whereas the horse railways of Austria-Hungary, France, Germany, and Great Britain were carrying about 920,000,000 passengers in 1886, electric tramways were carrying 6.7 billion passengers in 1910, when electric traction reigned supreme.[80] Thus the stagnating traffic patterns of the later part of the horsecar era were decisively broken as usage surged ahead. This may be seen in table 7, which has been extended backward as far as possible since to my knowledge the data on the leading nations have never been assembled.

It must be remembered that such global figures, useful as they are for seeing the sweep of the entire development, give a rather inadequate view of the change in individual cities. In city after city the number of passengers carried would double or triple in a very few years, while the length of line was increased by 50 to 75 percent. The passenger traffic in Mulhouse doubled with electrification between 1891 and 1894.[81] In Berlin, horsecars carried 164,000,000 passengers in 1895, and electric cars carried 330,000,000 in 1901.[82] In Lyons electrification doubled the traffic on some lines in a few months.[83] In 1908 insiders at the French Banque de l'Union Parisienne, preparing to float shares for the General Paris Tramways Company in connection with the long-delayed electrification of the four lines from Châtelet, projected an immediate doubling of revenues for these lines as a minimum, "since this is significantly less than the increase obtained on other lines [in Paris]."[84] The list could go on and on.

[80] Table 1 (with an estimate of 175,000,000 for France) and table 6. Hungary, which kept its own railway statistics, is included in the 6.7 billion figure. Hungarian urban and communal railroads carried 192,000,000 riders in 1910. Hungary, *Annuaire Statistique Hongrois: 1910* (Budapest, 1912), p. 211.
[81] *ZK* 3 (1896): 477.
[82] Buchmann, *Entwickelung*, p. 96.
[83] Arrivetz, *Histoire*, p. 21.
[84] BUP, Cie Gle Parisienne de Tramways, No. 216, Note, February 1908.

Table 7

GROWTH OF TRAMWAY LINES AND TRAMWAY RIDERS
(in kilometers of line and millions of riders)

Year	Austria[a] Line	Austria[a] Riders	France[b] Line	France[b] Riders	Germany[c] Line	Germany[c] Riders	United Kingdom[d] Line	United Kingdom[d] Riders
1872			24					
1876	56		140					
1880	84		411				254	173
1885	145		530				592	365
1890	182		661				1306	526
1895	222	92	842	356[e]	1835		1526	662
1900	417	164	1401	602	3006	1134[g]	1581	1065
1905	555	271	2003	872	3399	1501	1895	2236
1910	697	427	2229	1067	4387	2107	3606	2907
1913	785	512	2313[f]	1133[f]	5110		4181	3246
							4352	

[a] Includes local and certain light railways.
[b] Includes tramways for passengers, baggage, and messages, does not include local or light railways.
[c] For urban street railways only; does not include local or light railways.
[d] Includes light railways.
[e] 1896.
[f] 1912.
[g] 1901.

SOURCES: Austria, Eisenbahn Ministerium. Österreichische Eisenbahnstatistik für das Jahr 1913, II, xi, xvi, xxii. France, Ministère des Travaux Publics. Direction des Chemins de Fer. Statistique des Chemins de Fer, 1906, II, 6, 667; 1912, II, 7, 909; Annuaire Statistique 17 (1897): 239. Germany, Statistisches Reichsamt. Statistisches Jahrbuch für das Deutsche Reich, 1902-1914; N. Neefe, ed., Statistisches Jahrbuch Deutscher Städte 19 (1913): 265. Great Britain, House of Commons, Board of Trade, Returns for Street and Road Tramways.

These dramatic increases lead to an important conclusion. We have seen that the electric streetcar constituted a great technical and economic advance over horsecar service. This new system increased the supply potential of urban transport, met unsatisfied demand, and stimulated additional usage. The stagnation of the later horsecar era was overcome, and the growth of European urban public transport was little short of phenomenal.

Moreover, the traffic patterns of city after city show a very clear and quick break between old and new—a discontinuity which appears as a step function when graphed. This is a discontinuity which the national figures tend to smooth and obscure into a normal growth curve, since electrification hit different cities at different times all through the 1890s and early 1900s. It is the jump from one whole system of urban transport to another that causes the sharp discontinuity. And it is this sharp discontinuity—this sharp break with the past—that allows us to speak without exaggeration of an electric streetcar revolution in Europe.

In recognizing this transport revolution we have raised a whole series of problems, however. In the first place, there is the problem of timing and comparative economic development. Why did Europe lag behind America in its adoption of the new technology? And why was Great Britain the worst laggard of all? Then there is the problem of technological alternatives. Why did Europeans continue to investigate and install technological alternatives to the simple and very effective overhead method that satisfied Americans completely? Perhaps some of the answers to both questions are related to European institutional arrangements and cultural and aesthetic perceptions, which we hypothesized would play a key role in any transport solution in chapter 1. It is to this hypothesis we now turn, reserving other problems of the streetcar revolution for subsequent chapters.

III. The Pattern of Adoption

1. *Aesthetic Values and Public Policy*

Had European society chosen to regard the mechanization of urban transit primarily from a technical and economic viewpoint, there can be no doubt that the adoption of overhead electric traction would have been almost as rapid in Europe as in the United States. Certainly all the basic ingredients—the public transit challenge, the emerging urban civilization, industrial capacity, technical expertise, and reserves of human and financial capital—were present, and abundantly so.

In fact, European society as a whole refused any such narrow techno-economic view. Rather, many people asked themselves what would be the total impact of adopting the American trolley system upon their cities. Certainly the trolley system was technically and economically feasible, but did it also contain serious consequences and harmful side effects? That, for many, was the real question. And for many the answer was a resounding yes.

The fundamental criticism involved the essence of the American innovation—the overhead wires and their support poles. Indeed, the aesthetic and artistic drawbacks of "ugly wires" and "hideous poles" were so great that some European critics demanded that the American innovation be banned completely, if possible. Better, they argued, to put up with inadequate animal traction and send the inventors and technicians back to the drawing boards than to desecrate the traditional charm and beauty of the city with such "visual pollution."

This aesthetic reaction was most pronounced in large cities, where poles and wires along great boulevards and through historic squares seemed most offensive. In Munich many important people "gave the city council hell with their protests against defacing the general aspect of the city with overhead wires," and for several years "the rescued kings, poets, and lions on their stone pedestals in the center of the city continued to look down upon splendid, wire-free squares."[1] And it was a dreary town indeed that did not find a broad boulevard or an historic square worth saving. In Nancy, France, for example—hardly a picture-book city—the alderman absolutely refused to permit overhead wires through the historic Stanislas and Carrière Squares, which had long been traversed by horse trams.[2] Therefore, even if opposition was slight against certain suburban lines, or lines through working-class and industrial districts, the refusal to use strategic squares and boulevards at the center was a minimal demand.

The idea that substantial numbers of Europeans strenuously opposed overhead electric traction for aesthetic reasons may be supported by countless statements and actions. Indeed, the problem is one of avoiding scholarly overkill at this point, since this theme will appear again and again.

The comment of an English engineer in 1892 was both typical and correct. "Our American cousins . . . do not stick at forming a network of wires over their streets, so long as it facilitates locomotion, but in Europe we proceed more cautiously, and there is little doubt that these objectionable overhead wires have considerably interfered with the progress of electric traction on this side of the Atlantic."[3] Non-technical people were normally more intense on the subject. In 1897 the Birmingham city councillors of the subcommittee on tramways made a special tour of various continental streetcar systems, partly to get the facts and partly to strengthen their opposition to overhead methods. "Your subcommittee would point out that the unsightliness and

[1] Klein-Bader, 75 Jahre Münchner Strassenbahn, p. 13.
[2] AN, F 14, 13507, Tramways de Nancy, 24 April 1901.
[3] J. H. Cox, "Street Tramways and Electric Traction," *EE* 10 (1892): 86. Note the almost identical views of M. Walckenaer, *Note sur la traction électrique à prise de courant aérienne* (Paris, 1897), pp. 5-6.

otherwise objectionable features of the overhead wire are recognized in many of the places they have visited. The municipal authorities at Paris, Vienna, and Berlin stated that in no case would they permit overhead wires in the central portion of those cities. At Brussels several miles of conduit are being laid to avoid them; at Dresden and Budapest they are not allowed in the principal streets, and even in some of the outer districts, where permission has been given, it is conditional, and the wires have to be removed upon notice being given." And the list of cities went on, leading the subcommittee to "recommend strongly that no consent be given for the erection of overhead wires in any part of the city."[4]

Not that the question was lacking in comic elements, as critics searched for rhetorical flourishes to drive home their antipathy. At Danzig, for example, the opponents of the overhead system of electrification argued that "the overhead wires conveyed the idea of a hopfield, the contact rollers made the noise of a swarm of bees, and the movement of the cars was like the rolling of a ship at sea."[5] This was mild, however, compared to the fury of the Paris city council in 1902. After a decade of successfully defending the center of Paris from the trolley, the central government had decided to overrule the city council and to relax somewhat the total prohibition against all overhead wires within the vast area enclosed by the interior boulevards—that is, within historic Paris before the annexations of the Second Empire. Cries of pain and anti-trolley outrage surged up, as they had for a dozen years, and one member shouted that "if ever they install trolley wires in my quarter of the city, I will cut them down with my own hands."[6]

[4] Report of Birmingham Subcommittee on Tramways, as quoted in *EE* 19 (1897): 569-70.
[5] *EE* 14 (1894): 294.
[6] Meeting of the Conseil Municipal, 1 August 1902, in AN, F 14, 15023. This very full dossier, entitled "Cie Générale Parisienne de Tramways: Substitution de Traction," shows very well the tremendous anti-trolley feeling, on aesthetic grounds, in the French capital. Also

Perhaps this Frenchman was inspired by an 1893 incident in Toronto, Canada. There "the curious spectacle was witnessed of a brigade of axemen merrily chopping down the poles erected by the street railway company of that city." The company had not secured the necessary approval of the city engineer for their "rough, awkward poles that would have disgraced the streets of a backwoods village, more particularly when they were painted a variety of colors, the favorite being a glaring red."[7] In Austria-Hungary, electrification "made for a long time but little progress, as the authorities resolutely opposed the installation of the trolley system."[8] In short, the highly utilitarian and often ugly overhead system did not conform to the ideal of beautiful and harmonious cities, one of the products of Europe's long history and its rich, elitist culture.

There was also an initial distrust of electric traction because critics alleged other serious drawbacks. In addition to "disfiguring the streets with the overhead wire," there was "the danger of the live wire to passengers, the interference of the returning underground current with telephone and telegraph reception and with scientific laboratories, and the electrolysis of gas and water mains."[9] There were also widely expressed fears that the more rapid electric cars on busy streets would lead to more accidents. Critics also charged that falling lines would electrocute pedestrians and horses, and grimly publicized those mishaps that did occur. "The 18th of March, 1897, in Brussels, a telephone wire, suspended above the streetcar, gave way and in falling, made contact with the tram wire. A two-horse van passing by came in contact with the broken wire, the driver received some severe shocks, and both horses were killed on

---

Paul Brousse and Albert Bassède, *Les transports*, 2 vols. (Paris, 1907), 1:139-40.

[7] *EE* 11 (1893): 3.

[8] E. A. Ziffer, "Electric Railway Practice in Austria-Hungary," *SRJ* 15 (1899): 685.

[9] Sternberg, *Das Verkehrsgewerbe Leipzigs*, p. 49.

the spot."[10] Clearly, the new system was extremely dangerous.

These criticisms were basically technical and verifiable; they did not rest upon subjective value judgments, as did the aesthetic critique. Therefore the technicians could respond successfully to them, either through technical modifications when necessary, or through educating or ridiculing the uninformed layman. The telephone companies, which had been using the earth as a ground, were compelled, reluctantly, to insulate their grounds.[11] As for safety, streetcar men argued that current at 500 volts was not dangerous to man, producing, at most, disagreeable shocks. (This voltage could be lethal for horses, probably because the nails of the shoe passed into the hoof and could carry current easily to the nearby nerves.)[12] Furthermore, properly maintained wires broke very rarely. Industry experts also argued convincingly that electric cars were actually less dangerous, because they could be controlled better than horsecars, particularly in the braking.[13]

This still left the strong, even violent criticism of poles and wires. And this criticism could not be answered easily or simply brushed aside by experts and capitalists, however much they might wish to do so. As one American observer of European tramways put it, there "is strict regulation in regard to operation which is exercised over the companies by the municipalities or other governing authorities. . . . It cannot be denied that the city, and often the national government, interferes in the operation of cars in a way unknown in this country." Types of rails, cars, safety devices, and even schedules were set by public authority.[14]

Thus while elected officials reflected general public concern about overhead electric traction, government engi-

[10] Birmingham Report, in *EE* 19 (1897): 569.
[11] *SRJ* 6 (1890): 152, 263-64, 455; *EE* 11 (1893): 401-03.
[12] *SRJ* 5 (1889): 125-26; 6 (1890): 46-47, 151.
[13] Allgemeine Elektricitäts-Gesellschaft, (1899?), pp. 13, 85; *SRJ* 6 (1890): 32; *EE* 8 (1891): 67.
[14] *SRJ* 21 (1903): 18.

neers weighed and evaluated the proposed techniques themselves, just as they had done with steam tram proposals. Little wonder, then, that electrification might be delayed for a considerable period. At Basel, for example, the city's public works department made an "exhaustive investigation" of the various types of mechanical traction before finally recommending the overhead method of the Siemens-Halske variety, which the city fathers then considered and adopted.[15] The city was only following the normal pattern of inquiry and deliberation.

In centralized France there was a special section for "Tramway Regulation" within the Bridges and Roads section of the Ministry of Public Works, staffed by one or more engineers in each of the administrative divisions (*départements*) of the country. Tramway regulation and supervision was thus in the hands of France's engineering elite from its great technical schools. And in the mid-1890s a tramway inspector in Paris received the handsome salary of 5,000 francs per year, all such salaries and related expenses of tramway control being determined by the government and then billed to the companies.[16] Any significant, or even insignificant, deviation from the status quo required the approval of these inspectors.

More important, we must remember that tramway concessions were for fixed and limited periods.[17] At the end of its allotted days the tramway company was normally to turn over all lines and fixed equipment to the city without any

[15] *ZK* 1 (1894): 530.
[16] See, for example, AN, F 14, 15005, "Frais de Contrôle," 5 December 1894.
[17] C. Colson, *Abrege de la législation des chemins de fer et tramways* (2nd ed., Paris, 1905), has a good discussion of the concession system on the continent (pp. 198 ff.), as well as an exhaustive analysis of French practice, a model for much of Europe in tramway as well as in general commercial legislation. (See Rondo Cameron, *France and the Economic Development of Europe* [Princeton, 1961], pp. 21 ff.) Also W. M. Ackworth, "Report on the Law of France Relating to Tramways," Royal Commission on London Traffic, *Report . . . upon . . . Transport in London*, 8 vols. (London, 1905), 4:999-1001.

payment of any kind. Thus the passage of time, the inescapable reality of men and historians, also weighed heavily on these very mortal corporations. This meant that a given company had to recover all its fixed investment through some kind of scheduled repayment (depreciation, sinking fund, bond amortization, etc.) before the concession expired. For at that moment the company's fixed investment would be worthless as far as its shareholders were concerned, independent of what value it might have for the city. And since electrification greatly increased fixed investment, as we have seen, the operating gains had to be great enough for all these expenses to be paid off and amortized before the company's scheduled demise. In concrete terms this meant within the fifteen to twenty years remaining on concessions granted to continental firms.

This was clearly impossible. Therefore, because of both strict regulation and the approaching expiration of its concession, the individual tramway company had to renegotiate *all* the terms of operation with its municipality. And it was precisely such negotiations which gave anti-trolley sentiment a mechanism to push for a public policy that would permit the smallest possible use of what it conceived to be a technology with most undesirable side effects. Thus the carefully regulated companies were totally unable to apportion the indisputable gains of overhead technology as they saw fit, and electrify their operations so as to maximize the private profit. Rather, they had to negotiate the division of those gains with public authority, in what was one of the "most interesting chapters in the history of German [and indeed all continental] municipalities."[18]

Part of the potential gains might thus go to satisfy aesthetic perceptions, through the imposition of less economical methods. Then there were the gains that companies might be required to pass directly to the riding public, principally in the form of lower fares or longer lines than

[18] L. S. Rowe, "Municipal Ownership and Operation of Street Railways in Germany," *AAA* 27 (1906): 40.

a profit-maximizing company would have chosen. Third, there was that part of the gain that might be appropriated by city government through higher taxes, taxes which companies had to accept for permission to electrify. Fourth, a substantial portion might have to go to tramway workers, whose productivity increased substantially with electrification, as did their wages and working conditions.

Finally, lest I be accused of an unseemly sympathy for the problems of capitalists, I should add that the individual operating tramway companies had to share the private profit itself, primarily with the electrical manufacturers who controlled the new techniques. (See chapter IV.) In short, whereas the new technology undoubtedly paid, the individual companies had to bargain for a share of its fruits within the European institutional framework of public control and carefully formulated public policy.

There were, of course, national differences in the institutional framework of tramway regulation in Europe, as the next two chapters illustrate. Yet in the final analysis these differences were variations on the common theme of effective regulation and public policy. The most striking differences at the international level were clearly between the basic European and American patterns. This may be seen in even a brief look at what might be termed the "American model" of tramway institutions.

A distinguishing characteristic of American tramway development from the beginning was the absence of effective public control. In sharp contrast to those in the European states, with their national legislation and regulatory framework, street railway companies in America operated under franchises granted by the different state legislatures and confirmed by the individual cities themselves. Although practice varied widely, the different legal systems shared an inability to control effectively and continuously the various privately owned street railway companies. This did not necessarily mean that relations between companies and local governments were quiet and uneventful. Quite the contrary. Cities often came to resent bitterly the terms under which companies operated, and the litigiously inclined Americans often did their best to enrich the legal profession with suits and countersuits, appeals and counterappeals. Yet until at least the beginning of the twentieth century, when Massachusetts pioneered with a state regulatory agency for street railways,[19] companies and promoters had great freedom of action, for good or for ill as the case might be.

One key to the matter was that early American franchises for street railways were granted for longer periods than were European concessions. As one reformer put it in 1911, "During the years when the neglect of the public interests in franchise negotiations was more the rule than the exception, a great many cities granted perpetual franchises."[20] Until 1884 street railway franchises granted in New York, for example, were unlimited as to time, so that the courts of New York interpreted them as perpetual.[21] (Buffalo and Albany apparently deemed this excessive and limited their franchises to 999 years.) Perpetual franchises were less common in the western than in the eastern states, but in 1898 a special committee in Massachusetts headed by Charles Francis Adams found that almost one-half of the states had no limit regarding the time for which a franchise might be granted. Even when municipalities granted franchises for a fixed term, what was to occur when the franchise expired was "a subject upon which almost all of the limited franchises granted in the United States are silent."[22] In such cir-

[19] See E. S. Mason, *The Street Railway in Massachusetts* (Cambridge, Mass., 1932).

[20] Delos F. Wilson, *Municipal Franchises*, 2 vols. (New York, 1911), 2:44; also Edward Higgins, "Some Differences Between American and British Transportation Methods," *SRJ* 16 (1900): 357; Colson, *Abrégé*, pp. 200-01.

[21] Wilson, *Franchises*, 2:127-28.

[22] Massachusetts, *Report on the Relations between Cities and Towns and Street Railway Companies* (Boston, 1898), p. 74. This excellent report contains considerable material on European as well as American practice.

cumstances the threat of a limited or fixed-term franchise to a company's indefinite operation was more hypothetical than real.

Silence on procedures at the expiration of franchises was matched by vagueness as to the obligations of operating companies toward public and municipalities. In their choice of schedules, fares, routes, extensions, and even mode of traction, companies had great leeway. In 1891, when electrification in the United States was in full swing, an American study of European practice concluded forcefully that "many of the rights the American municipalities have surrendered to the street-railway companies, the municipalities of the Old World have jealously retained."[23] The simple nonspecific clauses of early franchises, particularly perpetual franchises, had forced public authorities into the difficult position of having "to depend for the power of regulation principally upon the police power of the state instead of upon the terms and conditions of the franchises themselves."[24] This lack of specific obligations made effective regulation hard, if not impossible.

A third area of difference was that of financial structure and financial control. Here state and municipal authorities had very little influence on the financial structure of street railway companies. The only limitations on the value a promoter could assign to his properties were his conscience or good sense, and the public's credulity. True, the Massachusetts Street Railway Commission pioneered in this direction in the early twentieth century, when it followed French and German practice and began to verify and regulate subsequent capital increases of companies in that state.[25] But by that time the American industry was mature, and the effect of regulation in and out of Massachusetts in the time of expansion seems to have been minor. The result

[23] Osborne Howes, Jr., *Report on the Transportation of Passengers in and around the Cities of Europe* (Boston, 1891), p. 4.
[24] Wilson, *Franchises*, 2:32.
[25] Mason, *Street Railway*, pp. 21-29.

was a great inflation of stated assets and a "watering" of the capital stock.

This occurred in many ways. Early practice often saw all capital actually expended in construction raised through bonds, which were supplemented by free issuance of capital stock as a bonus to investors.[26] Nor of course was there any legal limit on the ratio of bonded debt to common stock, as in France after 1881, for example, where joint-stock capital had to equal at least half of total capital. Depreciation was inadequate and unsystematic, and old tracks and equipment were often carried on the books as assets long after they had been replaced. Unregulated merging of competing firms into holding companies provided another opportunity to inflate capital, as promoters promised investors huge profits from unrestrained monopoly power. Finally, since franchises obviously represented privileges that might be turned into large profits, the franchise itself—a mere piece of paper in the French view—was capitalized and overcapitalized. No doubt European companies sometimes found ways to overstate their capital, but their freedom in this respect was much less.

We should also note the greater possibilities for the corruption of municipal officials in the United States than in Europe. This malleability of officialdom helps explain the great reliance in the United States on granting competitive franchises: officials were so easily corrupted that the public's best hope for securing good service was competition among rival franchise holders. Some European cities, such as Paris and Leipzig, for example, also resorted to competing franchises, especially in the horsecar era. But they realized sooner and more generally that the need for heavy fixed investment and the possibilities of economies of scale meant that street railways were an inherently monopolistic system of urban public transport, and that there was correspondingly a need for effective public regulation.

We may conclude this discussion with two results of the

[26] Wilson, *Franchises*, 2:26.

American institutional framework of development. First, the lack of careful bureaucratic scrutiny meant that both experimentation and diffusion of innovation were restrained primarily by technical and economic considerations. This helps account for the fact that both experimentation and development could and did proceed much more rapidly in the United States than in Europe. It also helps explain how anti-trolley sentiment could be pushed aside. One American writer summed this up, in passing, when speaking of British conservatism and how it had checked the rate of tramway electrification. "Conservatism . . . has not been unknown when measures of progress have been proposed in the United States, but when the possibility of a new enterprise paying a good dividend has been assured, capital generally has been forthcoming, and the old fogies, if they have not yielded, have simply been ignored."[27]

Second, it seems fair to say that the undisputed primacy of the private entrepreneur resulted not only in rapid development, but also in eventual hostility and a feeling that the division of gains from enterprise and technology needed redressing. Thus we come to one of the paradoxes of American development, which no doubt extends beyond tramways and transport. The free-wheeling entrepreneurial activity, which operated so successfully beyond effective public control, also built up strong antipathies, antipathies which then often had the power to cripple but lacked the means to create.

2. *The Development of Technological Alternatives*

The great initial hostility toward trolleys in Europe because of aesthetic considerations strongly stimulated efforts to find an acceptable alternative. Indeed, the incontestable successes of the American innovation whetted the appetite of engineers and public alike: a giant step had been taken

[27] Hawthorne Hill, "Electric Tramways and British Industry," *Iron Age* 64:7 (23 November 1899).

and the "definitive" solution should follow quickly. Two alternatives to overhead electric traction were already operational and it was only a question of perfecting them. Thus there began a period of experimentation and controversy, a period characterized by the battle of competing systems.

The first of the alternatives was the storage-battery car, mentioned briefly in chapter II, which had many supporters. As one German engineer put it in connection with battery-car experiments in Hamburg in 1890, "every practical engineer, knowing the conditions which exist in large towns," will want a vehicle with its own "independent and self-contained motor-power."[28] Such a vehicle would be safer, since there would be no live conductors, and it would be relatively immune to unexpected accidents in transmission and generation of electricity. And less investment would be required, since even horsecars could be equipped with batteries placed under the seats and no conductors would be necessary.

In addition to the widely noted trial of London's North Metropolitan Company, which is discussed in chapter V, the efforts of the Brussels Tramways Company with Julien battery cars were closely followed, as were similar attempts of various lengths at Hanover, Cologne, Ghent, and Paris.[29] In Brussels they were used on several lines for a number of years. Generally speaking, storage-battery cars worked, but they did not work very well. So engineers and inventors kept trying, anticipating, as one well-known German electrical engineer put it in 1895, "the numerous improvements" in battery (and conduit) systems which "will probably result in many cases in the discontinuance of the use of overhead conductors, while the possibility of doing away

[28] *EE* 1 (1890): 487. Much of the following discussion relies on the *Electrical Engineer* and the *Street Railway Journal*, which followed these experiments with great interest.

[29] Among others, see *EE* 5 (1890): 245; 8 (1891): 229-30; 19 (1897): 413, 733; 20 (1897): 555-56; 21 (1898): 549; Jean Robert, *Les tramways parisiens* (Paris, 1959), pp. 138-44.

with them altogether is not very remote."[30] So hope lingered, and the ultimate triumph was always just around the corner.

There were three principal reasons for this failure. First, battery cars were costly to operate because the expensive batteries were both easily damaged and quickly worn out. Thus the higher cost of power nullified the saving on capital and made most streetcar managers fierce opponents. Second, the great weight of the batteries, which on average added an extra two and one-half tons to the weight of the car, meant that considerably more energy was required to move the car and that the rails and roadbed also wore out more quickly.[31]

Third, and most important for many, accumulator cars "could not be depended upon to give the regularity in service which the public had a right to expect."[32] Part of the problem was that battery cars lacked reserves to meet fluctuating needs for power: either monstrously large batteries had to be built for the largest possible demands, or normally adequate batteries would fail occasionally, just when they were needed most. This lack of reliability led one manager from Ghent to tell his colleagues at the 1900 International Tramway Meetings that he was "absolutely opposed" to battery cars after ten years of trial and "absolute failure." The independence of the car was completely illusory and "horse traction was preferable in every way to that of accumulators."[33] There was the related problem of flexibility. "Every manager recognizes that on certain days and at certain hours it is necessary to double or quadruple the number of cars." And that was impossible with accumulator cars, which could pull no trailers.[34]

Another alternative was the surface-conduit system. The

[30] Oskar von Miller, *Elektrotechnischer Anzeiger*, 8 August 1895, quoted in *EE* 16 (1895): 226.

[31] *EE* 8 (1891): 237, 485; 9 (1892): 187.

[32] Janssen, International Congress of Tramways, 1900 Meeting, as quoted in *SRJ* 16 (1900): 1157.

[33] *Ibid*. [34] *Ibid*.

conduit with its enclosed electric wire—generally placed under one of the specially constructed slotted running rails because European officials felt that a separate conduit in the middle of the tracks would put "too much iron in the streets"[35]—had two great disadvantages, however. Its capital cost was two to three times that of the overhead system. And operating costs were higher, since maintenance and repairs were frequent and more difficult.[36] (Damage from seeping water and mud, and difficulties in cleaning the conduit, were the greatest problems.) Nor were companies slow to stress the fact that the conduit, and especially the long, drawn-out laying of the conduit, interfered with normal traffic in the streets. The method could be justified only in terms of the aesthetic concern, and at Lyons, as elsewhere, "this aesthetic concern cost the company a great deal."[37] No wonder companies tried hard not to use the conduit conductor at all, or demanded compensating advantages in return for its installation.

An interesting variation was the so-called surface-contact system. Here small contact plates were laid in the street between the tracks about every five meters, with each plate connected by a switch to the underground feeders carrying current from the generating station. The switch was designed to pass the current only when the car was over it, each car always being in contact with one of the plates at any moment. There were several varieties of switches, most of which were based upon the action of an electro-magnet. Thus when the plate was not covered by the car, the connection was supposed to be broken and the plate dead and harmless.[38] It was hoped that this system would be cheaper and more easily maintained than the conduit method in those cases where overhead wires were not permitted.

[35] See *SRJ* 20 (1902): 328-32 for a good technical description.
[36] *EE* 14 (1894): 502, 572-75, 602; also, for an inside view, see CL, Cie Gle Parisienne de Tramways, Etude, July 1901.
[37] Arrivetz, *Histoire*, p. 22.
[38] See Robert, *Les tramways parisiens*, pp. 145-49; *EE* 15 (1895): 669; 19 (1902): 662.

Used on the historic Charles Bridge in Prague, experimented with extensively by Schukert of Nuremberg, and most widely installed in Paris, the surface-contact method was an interesting failure. Considerable leakage of current was part of the problem. And the fact that the plates or studs had to be set above the road surface meant that they always obstructed traffic somewhat. But the Achilles' heel was the automatic switch, which did not always break the connection and thereby left a live electric plate in the street. While only quite disagreeable for the pedestrian, the resulting strong shock could be lethal for horses, like the pair of horses which chanced to touch such a plate on Place de la République in Paris in 1897. These horses were "suddenly seen to jump up in the air and then fall to the ground, killed instantaneously."[39] And it was said in Paris that heartless drivers purposely rode their horses over the plates in the hope of finding a lethal one and collecting a goodly indemnity.

Since none of these attempts to develop "pure" alternative technologies ever seriously challenged the overhead system, we might be tempted to suppose that aesthetic concerns were of only passing significance in Europe, in the final analysis. True, there was more hue and cry, but in the end opposition was overpowered by the same powerful economic interests that prevailed in the United States. Such an argument would, however, overlook basic modifications of the original innovation. These modifications, which were clearly responses to aesthetic concerns, added up to two more technological alternatives for Europeans to consider.

The first of these was in the area of "mixed" systems, systems which "mixed" the overhead conductor and some alternative on the same car and the same line. Once again Siemens and Halske led in this experiment, particularly with a widely noted attempt in Berlin to combine the overhead conductor with storage-battery traction.[40] As opposed to the typical "pure" battery, the batteries were not re-

[39] *EE* 19 (1897): 546. [40] See below.

moved from the car for charging at the central power station. Rather, they were charged while the car was on that section of the line equipped with the overhead wire, which at the same time provided current to drive the car on that section. Then, when the car came to zones where no overhead wires were permitted, the bow trolley would be laid on the roof and the car would proceed by battery power alone.

More frequently, the conduit was crossed with the overhead conductor to produce another hybrid. Among the more important examples were Berlin, Prague, Budapest, and Vienna, where the Siemens and Halske variant was usually installed.[41] This mixed method was also used by the French Thomson-Houston Company at Bordeaux, Marseilles, and especially Paris. Equipped with both trolley and conduit contact mechanisms, the car could pass through central areas, historic squares, and in front of great monuments without benefit of the despised wires. Then the cheaper, surer wire could be used on those portions of the same line where aesthetic objections could be overcome. As the Allgemeine Elektricitäts-Gesellschaft explained, "the mixed system is employed in those towns that object to the overhead system in certain squares or streets in the inner part. . . . This system is more or less a compromise to obtain a concession for electric traction."[42] Thus municipalities were presented with another option, another technological alternative. (See figure 9.)

It is important to realize that even where the overhead system was adopted in toto, there were modifications and improvements. These modifications, which responded to aesthetic concerns without sacrificing technical efficiency, added up to another technological alternative to the early American overhead system.

[41] *ZK* 2 (1895): 138; *TH* 2 (1969): 218; Heinrich Vellguth, "Electric Railway Practice on the Continent of Europe," *SRJ* 21 (1903): 354-59; *EE* 7 (1891): 527-29.

[42] Allgemeine Elektricitäts-Gesellschaft publication in John Crerar Library (1899?), pp. 11-12.

In the first place, there was widespread interest in the problem of visual effects. Quite typically, an English engineer studied American practice in its early days and reported his findings in 1891. "Much of the overhead work in America has been done in a hurried manner, and could be made much neater and safer with more care and time being spent upon it. This point should be insisted upon if the system be allowed here."[43] And generally Europeans did insist. Thus an American streetcar expert in Europe noted in 1900 that "overhead pole lines are much neater looking in France than in America. This comes from the fact that all work is treated from an aesthetic as well as from a utilitarian point of view, while in America the former is usually so subordinate to the latter that in actual results it is not visible."[44] This writer was even somewhat puzzled by this undeniable fact, since much of the electrical equipment was practically the same. "The difference in appearance must come then from the greater care in installing the lines not to shock the eye"—the broad interest in visual effects.[45] Figure 10 provides one such example.

This being said, the American expert concluded that the chief substantive difference in French and American practice was in the poles. In contrast to stark wooden American poles, which struck all but the most dedicated philistines as aggressively ugly eyesores, French and European poles were made of steel and handsomely decorated. Indeed, it seems clear that pole decoration and design became a minor art, with crossbars, crowns, lighting fixtures, sections, and bases elaborated in a variety of styles. The products of the Mannesmann Pipe Works of Düsseldorf, which probably supplied more tramway poles throughout Europe than any single firm, could be particularly ornate and stylish, as

[43] *EE* 8 (1891): 67.
[44] A. N. Connett, "Electric Railway Practice in France," *SRJ* 16 (1900): 929.
[45] *Ibid.*, p. 930. See also the good description of this same care at Frankfurt, where the overhead system prevailed, in *60 Jahre Städtische elektrische Strassenbahn*, p. 20.

figure 11 illustrates.[46] Hence poles attained a certain elegance and blended gracefully into the urban scene. Poles also served admirably for electric street lighting, which tramway companies were often required to provide, and when placed in the center of a busy boulevard on an elevated base, they divided traffic and gave crossing pedestrians welcome islands of refuge.

Overhead systems in Europe were neater also because overhead feeders were not allowed. This alone "robs the overhead line of its most hideous feature, and makes the designing of an attractive pole a much simpler problem."[47] The feeders, those heavy insulated cables carrying electricity from the central station and connected with the trolley wire at spaced intervals along the line, were originally strung in the air in America and were "very noticeable."[48] In Europe they were placed underground and completely concealed. The elimination of heavy feeder cables overhead also facilitated construction of central poles on broad boulevards, which allowed one set of poles to serve two tracks. And it made the wire network simpler and much less conspicuous on curves and through squares, which had originally required extra support wires—precisely where they were most objectionable. Now the overhead wires spun only a light and delicate web at such points.

Europeans also modified the overhead system to serve well in narrow streets, where poles would be traffic hazards as well as eyesores. The common practice was to suspend the overhead conductor by means of crosswires attached to brackets embedded in the walls of the abutting buildings, as in figure 12. A spring-and-rubber-cushion arrangement let the bracket absorb the shock and noise, without disturbing the embedded base and damaging the building.

[46] This and other illustrations are taken from Mannesmann's 1898 catalogue for France: Deutsch-Oesterreichische Mannesmann-röhren-Werke, *Poteaux tubulaires Mannesmann pour traction et éclairage électriques* (1898).
[47] Connett, "France," *SRJ* 16 (1900): 930.
[48] E. J. Silcock, "Tramway Haulage," *EE* 20 (1897): 117.

9. Berlin. Conduit traction in front of the Brandenburg *Gate*.

10. Breslau. Wires and poles skillfully arranged.

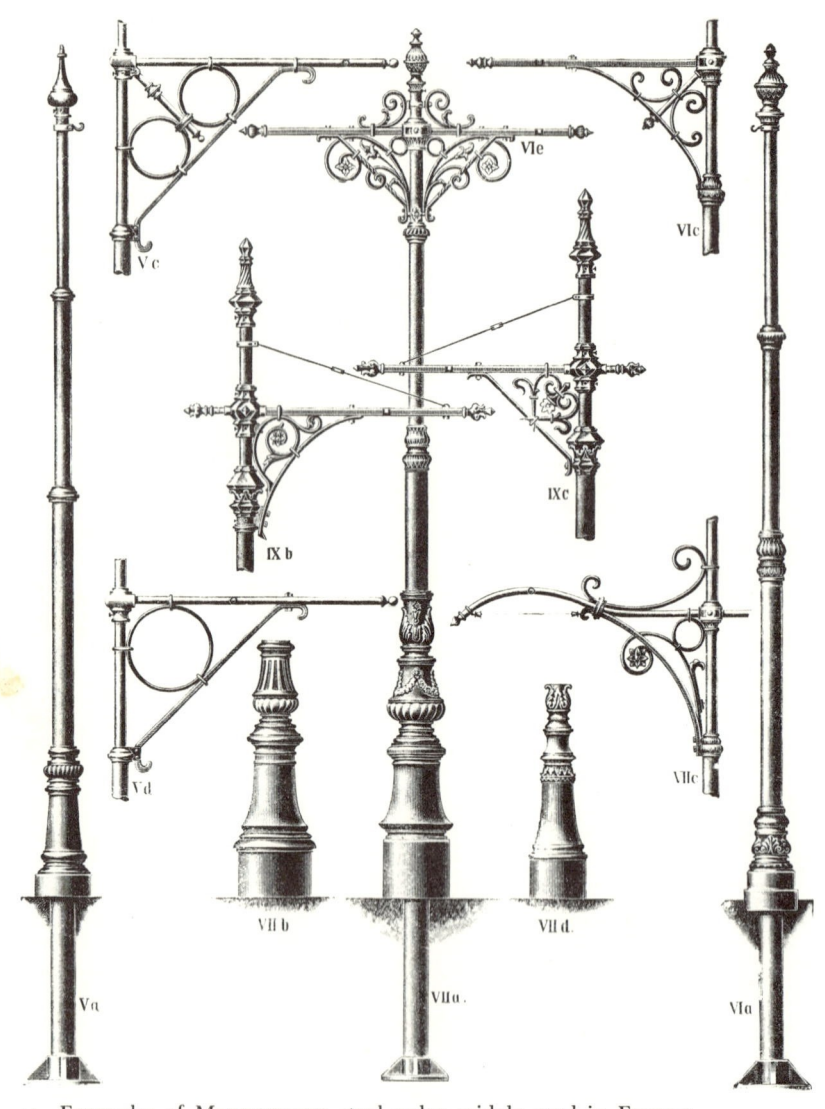

11. Examples of Mannesmann steel poles, widely used in Europe.

12. Heilbronn. A typically festive inauguration of electric traction.

Since most property owners were opposed to poles in front of their buildings, the threat of such an installation or a token rent usually enabled the company to secure permission for its brackets as a decidedly lesser evil. Here again the result was to design a more attractive packaging for the basic overhead technology, which could then be diffused into a different environment.

To sum up, the very negative European reaction to overhead electric traction led engineers and inventors to search for technological alternatives in three different directions. These were: a systemic change through the perfection of a completely different method of traction (primarily battery or conduit); an incorporation of methods of unequal quality into a hybrid mixed system; and a more attractive and sensitive packaging of the basic breakthrough. Each of these had advantages and disadvantages, as we have seen, and it was not always easy to establish the subtleties of the truth in the midst of the claims and counterclaims that marked the battle of the systems.

The basic results of the search for alternatives were increasingly clear, however. First, all three systems—non-overhead, mixed, and overhead—"worked," and could be put into operation. Second, each system surpassed horse traction by a substantial margin. Third, from strictly technical and economic viewpoints, the overhead method was best and the mixed was next best. The conduit was clearly inferior to the overhead conductor because of capital and maintenance costs, but it was nonetheless preferable to the expensive and unreliable batteries. Finally, the ugliness of many early overhead installations in the United States could be greatly reduced. But they could not be eliminated entirely. As one pro-trolley engineer dryly put it, "Trolley wire suspended in any way in the public street cannot from the nature of things be ornamental."[49] Having established the facts, the technical people could present their material, as well as their recommendations, for public discussion and

---

[49] Connett, "France," *SRJ* 16 (1900): 929.

policy formulation. The public and its representatives could then weigh and debate the alternatives intelligently in light of their preferences and aspirations. They could choose their alternative as they sought to design a transport future they could live with and even be proud of. It is to that debate and design that we must now turn.

3. *Negotiations and Agreements*

While opponents were bemoaning the harmful effects of the trolley and while technicians were seeking alternatives, interested and disinterested supporters of the American innovation launched a vigorous counterattack. As might be expected, the stress was on the potential benefits to the riding public in speed, length, frequency, comfort, and price. Proponents of overhead electric traction were also quick to invoke the weighty argument that these advantages had a "great social significance, especially for the poor population."[50] However, we should not overlook the fact that there was also an attempt to meet trolley critics head on, an attempt to show that the overhead system had neutral or even *positive* features from an *aesthetic* point of view.

Again and again writers stressed that in a properly modified trolley installation the wires were hardly visible, or, rather, that they were visible but the people quickly became accustomed to them. "Overhead wires . . . no doubt at first do offend the eye; but this is one of the many things met with in large towns, which, although ugly, are soon unnoticeable by reason of their great utility."[51] As for poles, the decorative character of the mast and crossbar made them no more objectionable than ordinary lampposts already used for arc lighting.

Another tactic was to stress all the unpleasant aesthetic aspects of horse traction which could be reduced with overhead electric traction. Horse manure, that bane of the city,

[50] Sternberg, *Das Verkehrsgewerbe Leipzigs*, p. 49.
[51] Silcock, "Tramway Haulage," *EE* 20 (1897): 117.

was singled out often. The chief engineer of the city of Frankfurt on the Main, Reise, quite typically stressed that "the presence and cleaning up of the dung of 650 tramway horses is an aesthetic and hygenic inconvenience," an inconvenience electric traction would dispose of.[52] As for the ugliness of overhead wires, Reise noted that the experience of all cities showed the public became accustomed to overhead wires very quickly and did not see damage. People did not look at the wires alone but rather at the whole thing, which appeared as a welcome and useful installation for both the city and the public. Another advantage of electric traction for many was that the number of horses using the streets might be reduced by as much as 50 percent. That would "save the wear and tear due to the tramping of these [tramway] horses, and it is no stretch of the imagination to say that the life of the streets is doubled, while the cost of cleansing the streets is reduced."[53] And lower expenses would lead to lower taxes, a consequence hardly in need of debate.

Nor was it necessary to take offense at a horse simply behaving like a horse, to see the positive side. As one writer puts it, "the later nineteenth century generally considered hauling tramcars the most gruelling and deleterious work which could be given a horse," and complaints of their mistreatment was a constant theme of humane societies and animal lovers.[54] Now it was possible to do something about this suffering, and high time.

Finally, these positive aesthetic considerations were very often tied to what might be called the general "price of progress" argument, which, familiar to all, admitted that the overhead system had unfortunate side effects. But it quickly went on to stress that it was nevertheless a most de-

[52] Reise, Denkschrift, Sept. 1896, quoted in *60 Jahre Städtische elektrische Strassenbahn*, pp. 8-9; also Dr. Rasch, "Elektrischen Bahnen mit oberirdischer Stromzufuhrung," *ZVDI* 38 (1894): 485 ff.
[53] *EE* 2 (1888): 99.
[54] Lee, "Tramways of Hull," pp. 43 ff.; Sternberg, *Das Verkehrsgewerbe Leipzigs*, p. 49.

sirable step forward, all things considered. Universally employed, this argument seemed to have struck a particularly responsive chord in Germany. Thus in 1894 a German engineering professor ended a long evaluation of overhead electric traction by calling upon the city of Munich to remember a popular proverb, "The better is the enemy of the good." He then advised the city to permit installation of the overhead system as a "usefully recognized kind of construction and thereby take the certainly still existing inadequacies in the bargain, in order not to remain too far behind as compared to foreign countries."[55] This advice also suggests how Germany's preeminent European position in the electrical industry facilitated overhead electrification. Producers understood what was involved technically, were aware of the competitive implications, and had real influence. In France and Great Britain this indigenous element was lacking, and the new method was more foreign and suspect.

These aesthetic and psychological arguments helped soften up the opposition and convince officials that overhead electric traction could not simply be dismissed out of hand. Rather, it required the same kind of serious consideration which earlier and eventually unsuccessful attempts had received. Street railway companies began to request and receive permission to electrify a certain line, very often a suburban line, on an experimental basis. If the line was strategically situated, like the Thomson-Houston line serving the industrial exhibition in Bremen in 1890, so much the better. In any event, the trial would demonstrate most of the merits of the new system, and allow the public and the municipality to weigh the gravity of the inconveniences.

Some examples show how this was an important step in the process of adoption. In 1890 the French General Tramway Company received permission to substitute overhead electric traction for Rowan fireless steam engines on two

[55] D. E. Voit, *Bayerisches Industrie und Gewerbeblatt*, 1894, pp. 129 ff., as quoted in *ZK* 1 (1894): 322.

lines it was building at Marseilles. The lines, which were clearly suburban in character, posed none of the aesthetic problems of major lines in the city center. This substitution in the form of mechanical traction was then permitted on other new lines, which had already been scheduled to use compressed air power. The electric experiment was predictably successful, and the company won allies for the trolley, which it then proposed for all of Marseilles.[56]

Similarly, the success of a line equipped with Thomson-Houston equipment in Lyons in 1894 led the tramway companies to request electrification throughout the city and bargain for the greatest possible utilization of overhead conductors.[57] In Rome, the municipality first agreed to the trolley on the line from San Silvestro Square to the Termini railroad station in early 1895, and at about the same time the city of Milan agreed to this mode on a single new line from the center to the suburb of Simpton. The clear success of both trials then led to eventual agreement on the general electrification of tramways in both cities.[58] In both Dresden in 1893 and Munich in 1895 the installation of the overhead system on a trial line was a necessary step leading to electrification of the entire streetcar network.[59]

In these, as in many other cases which might be mentioned, demonstration lines showed the effectiveness of electric traction. Henceforth the aesthetic question tended to become *to what extent* the trolley should be permitted, not whether it should be permitted at all. At this point serious negotiation between the municipality and the company (or companies) on the whole range of questions involved in the general adoption of electric traction became possible.

There was certainly considerable variation in the negotia-

[56] AN, 65 AQ, Q 1381, Cie Générale Française de Tramways, Annual Reports, 1888, 1891-93; F 14, 13507, notes, 3 November 1890 and 26 November 1896.
[57] Arrivetz, *Histoire*, pp. 20-23.
[58] CL, Cie Française Thomson-Houston, Italian inquiry, 1896.
[59] Grossmann, *Die kommunale Bedeutung*, pp. 93 ff; Klein-Bader, *75 Jahre Münchner Strassenbahn*, pp. 11-12.

tions between private companies and municipal authorities. And indeed, the British never did reach the kind of renegotiated general agreement with private industry that prevailed on the continent, preferring instead the idiosyncratic pattern examined in chapter v. Yet in spite of the great variation it is possible to establish the general pattern for the continent.

It is clear that private enterprise was almost always the source of initiative, submitting its proposals for electric transformation to the local authorities. Such proposals came not only from the existing tramway companies but also from banks, entrepreneurs, contractors, and especially electrical producers, who had no previous ties to a city's tramways. A major city, like St. Petersburg or Vienna, might be confronted with "a perfect epidemic of electric traction proposals."[60] And indeed by the end of 1895 Vienna had received eight major offers, including ones from Schukert, Allgemeine Elektricitäts-Gesellschaft, the Wiener Bankverein, and the New Vienna Tramway Company working in conjunction with the Anglobank and Siemens-Halske.[61] Thus there were generally many possible suitors competing for the hand of a single gracious lady, and most municipalities were fully occupied in trying to make the best choice. And if the existing tramway company usually had the advantage because of its unexpired concession, the city almost invariably had the possibility of buying up the concession if it chose. This option, which would lead to running the tramways as a municipal enterprise or the granting of a new concession to another entrepreneur who offered better terms, normally forced even existing companies to bargain aggressively.

In presenting their proposals and battling against one another, private entrepreneurs had only two absolutely minimal demands. First, in return for electrification, there had to be a substantial prolongation of the concession. The only other path to electrification, apart from outright mu-

[60] *EE* 14 (1894): 678.   [61] *EE* 16 (1895): 637.

nicipal purchase, was that employed by the city of Munich in 1892—and, rarely, in other cases. There the company agreed to build and operate electric lines for the city's account, thereby relieving the company of the need to amortize completely this new investment before the concession expired in 1907.[62] Second, the authorities had to permit the overhead system on at least a large portion of the tramways. If such conditions were met, then private entrepreneurs could and did offer a whole array of enticing transportation improvements for public consideration.

Just how favorable the terms might be was in turn partly dependent upon the extent to which the most economical system—the overhead system—was permitted. Thus the development of technological alternatives not only meant that aesthetic demands could be met. It also placed those aesthetic values and goals in competition with other values and goals, which were closely linked with social problems and considerations—lower fares, increased suburban service, increased income for the city, and better conditions for tramway workers. Therefore the different publics and their policy makers had to evaluate and reevaluate their preferences and establish the desired trade-offs between two sets of values, one aesthetic and cultural, the other social and utilitarian.

If it has been possible to follow the actual course of negotiations in only a few instances, the terms of the agreements reached are known in many cases. Therefore I shall now try to summarize the general pattern of final agreement, giving particular attention to the choice between aesthetic and social values. These conclusions will then be illustrated through a brief examination of certain leading cities (as well as by some of the material in the next three chapters).

It is obvious from the agreements that municipalities succeeded in winning substantial improvements in all areas, which went well beyond those inherent in the innovation,

---

[62] Klein-Bader, *75 Jahre Münchner Strassenbahn*, p. 11.

such as speedier, more comfortable, and more hygenic service. But there was more to it than that. Most significantly, European cities won specific improvements directed toward ameliorating specific social problems, which weighed heavily on the growing urban civilization. And the search for these specific improvements was clearly a manifestation of one of the powerful organizing concepts of nineteenth-century and particularly late nineteenth-century Europe, the subject of countless studies—the ideal of the amelioration of harmful social conditions through intelligent, compassionate public policy and governmental action. Here, indeed, was a generous ideal that could compete effectively with aesthetic goals, and perhaps make them look petty and retrograde.

We see this social concern in the way in which cities negotiated lower fares. Of course cities sought a general reduction in the level of fares, and they unquestionably achieved this goal. In France, for example, where the carefully renegotiated contract with private industry reigned supreme, the average fare per tramway rider fell from 15.4 centimes in 1896 to 8.8 centimes in 1910.[63]

Part of the mechanism of fare reduction on the continent was often a partial or total abandonment of the long-standing zone system. In that system the second class passenger normally paid 10 or 15 pfennigs in Germany, or 10 or 15 centimes in France, for the first two sections on the line, and another 5 for each additional section, with perhaps a maximum fare of 25 to 30 pfennigs or centimes whatever the distance. Instead, there was widespread adoption of the American fixed fare entitling one to a ride of any distance, and almost invariably for 10 pfennigs in Germany and 10 centimes in France. Such distances might also approach truly American-scale lengths, as in the case of Paris, where one could ride up to 14 kilometers on one line for only 10 cen-

[63] France. Ministère des Travaux Publics. Direction des Chemins de fer. *Statistique des chemins de fer français*, 1906, II, 655, 667; 1912, II, 895, 909.

times in 1900. Fares were also reduced where the zone system was retained. Here, then, was the first manifestation of social preoccupation. Municipalities hoped that lower fares, and particularly a fixed fare for any distance on a given line, would encourage people to commute greater distances and thereby increase suburban expansion. Such expansion would alleviate the severe overcrowding in the central districts, which the early railroad had only increased.

The same high priority on suburban expansion, which is considered in greater detail in chapter VI, was seen in the way in which municipal authorities almost universally linked electrification negotiations with the extension of lines and suburban service. The importance of this concern was also seen in many contracts, especially after 1900, which tied the company's profits to the construction of more lines and extensions. The Paris and Department of the Seine Tramways Company characteristically agreed in 1910 to build another whole series of extensions, which had little likelihood of real profit, once the company had paid 6 percent on its capital two years straight.[64] With such clauses municipalities could rest assured that good profits for the private monopolist, which were by no means certain, would also result in the construction of more lines and the further encouragement of population diffusion.

The city of Leipzig was an excellent example of the way in which electrification was used to achieve the spatial expansion of the tramway network the city had long desired, and it warrants a somewhat closer look.[65] In 1890 the city studied and granted a new omnibus concession to link the city with two outlying districts. When the entrepreneur in question proved unable to finance his concession, the town council decided in late 1892 to substitute electric tramways, if it could. Because of poor relations with the existing Greater Leipzig Tramways Company, an English firm orig-

[64] CL, Cie des Tramways de Paris et du Département de la Seine, Etude, 1910.
[65] Sternberg, *Das Verkehrsgewerbe Leipzigs*, pp. 49-52.

inally formed in 1871, the council rather atypically opted for a new company, which would not only build the proposed electric lines but also force the English horse tramway company to come to heel. After ironing out the juridical problems, whereby the state of Saxony would grant the concession to the city, which would then retrocede it to the new company, the city negotiated with A.E.G. over the terms of the new concession. The agreement was signed in early 1895.

The principal articles of this typical concession are worth noting.[66] The operating company (the Leipzig Electrical Tramway Company) was to be incorporated in Leipzig, was forbidden to sell the electricity it produced, and was to operate for a period of forty years. At that time everything would revert to the city free of charge, except for the company's land holdings, electric power station, and motorcars bought in the last five years. The city had the right to buy the company after twenty years and at five-year intervals thereafter, in a carefully specified manner based on net profits in the five preceding years. The company was to pay initially 2 percent and eventually 5 percent of its gross receipts to the city, or an average of $3\frac{7}{8}$ percent over forty years—ten times what the English company had averaged paying. Routes, speed, type of equipment, etc., were to be approved by the city. The overhead method was accepted, but the city could require new techniques once they were proven cheaper. And of course fares were lower on the new lines: one could ride up to 5 kilometers with unlimited free transfers for a flat 10-pfennig fare.

The instant success of the new company with its better and cheaper transit forced the English company to sell out and retire when the city would not agree on electrification terms, exactly as the city had hoped. The old company was purchased by the local banking house of Becker and Company and the Gesellschaft für elektrischen Unternehm-

[66] *Ibid.*, pp. 52-57.

ungen, U.E.G.'s financial subsidiary. These financial interests then proposed a new Saxon corporation to electrify and extend the old horsecar lines with Thomson-Houston overhead equipment. Agreement was soon reached with the city on terms very similar to those granted the A.E.G.-sponsored firm. The major exception was the requiring of battery cars in the inner city.[67] Thus Leipzig succeeded brilliantly in its principal objective of extending its transport network: the forty kilometers of line in 1895 jumped to 108 kilometers in 1900. It also achieved its secondary goal of sharply reducing fares, which averaged 10.8 pfennigs per passenger carried in 1895 and 6.6 pfennigs in 1900. No wonder the numbers of passengers jumped threefold in the same five years, from 21 million to 64 million.[68]

Perhaps the very best indication of the impact of the social ideal upon tramway policy was the way in which almost every municipality used negotiations over electrification to introduce special trams at reduced fares to benefit the working class. Although not unheard-of in the horsecar era, especially in Great Britain, the workman's ticket was nonetheless a rare phenomenon. The tramway company in Leeds, England, which was supposed to run special workmen's cars "each weekday before 7 A.M. and after 6 P.M. at fares of a half penny per mile, with a minimum fare of a penny, specifically for the benefit of artisans, mechanics and daily labourers . . . appears to have been flatly ignored for many years."[69]

In Paris, and indeed throughout France, there was "no question of workmen's trams in any of the concessions before 1890."[70] This meant that a Parisian worker paid the normal second class fare of 15 centimes within the city, as opposed to 30 centimes in first class. Then in 1891 the government required exclusively second-class service on cer-

[67] *Ibid.*, pp. 57-62.   [68] *Ibid.*, pp. 89-91.
[69] Dickinson, "Leeds," *JTH* 4 (1960): 220-21.
[70] CL, Cie des Tramways de Paris et du Département de la Seine, Etude, 1909.

tain lines in the morning, and the pattern of preferential treatment formed an entering wedge. Subsequently, all the electric concessions required special workmen's trams with fares one-half that of the second-class fare, which normally became 10 centimes. This meant that the French worker—or any passenger—who hopped aboard before 7 or perhaps even 8 A.M. and returned between perhaps 6 and 8 P.M., came to ride for 5 centimes, or only *one-third* the price he would have paid previously.[71] Here, as elsewhere, the goal was extremely cheap fares which would allow the worker to save his energy at the least, and facilitate his quest for better, more distant housing at best.

These most important social objectives relating to tramways were often coupled with the additional goals of better working conditions for tramway men and increased payments by the tramway company to help support the growth of municipal services, many of which were themselves oriented toward the poor and the modest. Altogether, they constituted a set of appeals that put the proponents of the aesthetic ideal on the defense and forced them to retreat to the most sacred monuments and the most exquisite quarters. These they managed to defend from the trolley in many cities, at least for a time, even as the overhead method was accepted outside such special zones.

This result was also achieved because the tramway companies offered a final, rather daring concession. In many instances, such as Rouen, Leipzig, Munich, Berlin, Hamburg, and no doubt many other cities, they agreed to a clause by which public officials could compel them to substitute (either immediately or only some years after the original installation) any other method of traction which the public officials might determine was as cheap and as satisfactory as the overhead method.[72] When we realize that

[71] *Ibid.*; also CL reports on the companies at Bordeaux and Rouen, and Cie Générale Française de Tramways.
[72] Klein-Bader, *75 Jahre Münchner Strassenbahn*, pp. 12-13; CL, Tramways de Rouen, Etude, September 1901; *EE* 16 (1895): 226.

technical men were all too well aware of the difficulties of alternative systems—the Crédit Lyonnais engineer considered the danger of having to abandon the trolley at Rouen "fairly slight"—this final compromise seems worthy of Machiavelli himself. But people could tell themselves that the overhead system really was only temporary. They could wait for a better system, like the citizens of Munich "who are still waiting to this day."[73]

This general pattern of adoption and agreement might be illustrated with many examples, but three should suffice. Let us begin with Marseilles.

After opening the first overhead electric lines in that city in 1892, the General French Tramways Company and the city spent five years in long negotiations before reaching an agreement concerning electric traction. The extent to which overhead wires would be permitted was the single greatest stumbling-block. And although this question was finally resolved in favor of the overhead system for all tramways, the company was still required to adopt yet another not unknown type of mixed system—and continue with only horse omnibuses in the heart of the city.[74] In return for this privilege and a prolongation of the concession to 1940, the company agreed to more than double the tramway network from 54 to 127 kilometers. In addition, the company consented to one-class service with a flat fare of 10 centimes for all lines, which government experts considered a "very low" fare indeed.[75] In view of these terms, the rather low payment to the city of approximately 1 percent of gross receipts below 15,000,000 francs and 2 percent above was quite understandable.

The German city of Hamburg provides another opportunity to see the adoption process in some detail. This example is particularly apt since the terms of the renegotiated

[73] Klein-Bader, *75 Jahre Münchner Strassenbahn*, pp. 12-13.
[74] CL, Cie Gle Française de Tramways, Etude, November 1919; Convention, 21 October 1897.
[75] AN, F 14, 13507, Rapport, 1901.

concession in Hamburg were quite typical and even "served as a model for other cities, on account of the early introduction of electricity."[76] Beginning with horse traction in 1866, Wintertur steam locomotives of the Brown type were used on the main line of one of the four companies in Hamburg from 1879 on. These engines were unpopular—people nicknamed them "the smoking flatirons"—and so the city ordered experiments with Hüber battery cars in 1886 as a possible alternative.[77] Service continued for several months, but the cars were a complete failure. They often stalled on the grades, and it was not uncommon to see passengers compelled to get off in order to lighten the load and relieve the motors.[78]

By 1891 the Hamburg Street Railway Company had succeeded in consolidating three of the four companies and, impressed by the Thomson-Houston line in Bremen in 1890, it proposed to electrify its entire network with the Thomson-Houston overhead method. And although some critics denounced it as dangerous and ugly, the earlier failures with accumulators were fresh in the minds of the authorities. In addition, the company was willing to agree that if another method of electric traction were improved to the point where it would enable successful and profitable working of the lines without overhead wires, then the company would install such a system.[79] Both these factors helped speed negotiations to a conclusion.

The city agreed to extend the concession to 1922, at which time all tracks and buildings within the city limits were to revert to the city, free of charge. In return, the company agreed to pay the city a tax of 1 pfennig per passenger, or about 9 percent of its gross since the average zone-system fare was about 11.5 pfennigs by 1900. In addi-

[76] Heinrich Vellguth, "The Street Railway Company of Hamburg, Germany," *SRJ* 19 (1902): 2.
[77] Erich Staisch, *Die elektrische S-Bahn in Hamburg* (Hamburg, 1964), pp. 58-59.
[78] Vellguth, "Hamburg," *SRJ* 19 (1902): 1.
[79] *EE* 19 (1897): 335.

tion, the city was to share in the profits, beginning with one-fourth of any profits in excess of 6 percent on the company's capital stock and rising by steps to one-half of profits above 10 percent. These large payments to the city coffers were not particularly pleasing to the riding public. Passengers did obtain lower fares, of course, but because of payments to the city the company did not introduce the flat 10-pfennig fare for any trip within the city limits, which had been widely introduced into German cities in the 1890s.[80] As for the company, it was amortizing its capital adequately and paying an 8½ percent dividend by 1898.[81] Thus city, riding public, and private company all benefitted.

Although the city permitted the trolley system throughout the city, steps were required and taken to reduce its unsightly aspects. The company exercised great ingenuity to avoid using poles in open squares. In narrow streets the trolley wire was suspended from wall rosettes, fastened to the buildings, so there was no obstruction. Elsewhere and in the suburbs only Mannesmann steel tube poles were used, and they were capped on top by an ornamental hood to improve their appearance further. On one of the most elegant streets in the city along the harbor, "special and very attractive double bracket poles were used." These handsome poles (see figure 13) were embellished with copper so that "the ornamentation and scrolls are beautiful specimens of coppersmith work."[82] The installed poles with their arc lights on top cost 10,000 marks ($2,500) each, an enormous sum when we consider that in the United States wood poles cost roughly $70 installed and steel poles around $300.[83]

[80] Vellguth, "Hamburg," *SRJ* 19 (1902): 1-12.
[81] *SRJ* 23 (1904): 544-45. Even though electrification occurred at an early date, the company's installation did not suffer from early mistakes. Particularly, "in spite of advice to the contrary and considerable ridicule," the company originally built a very heavy track and substructure. The low, broad rails weighed as much as 53 kg. per meter.
[82] Vellguth, "Hamburg," *SRJ* 19 (1902): 6.
[83] Crosby and Bell, *Electric Railway*, pp. 310-11.

But such effort mollified or even pleased aesthetic sensibilities: a visiting committee from Sheffield, England, could report that "some of the wrought iron work is so artistic that it is an ornament to the streets rather than otherwise."[84] The same sort of concern was also seen in the waiting pavilions the company was required to build wherever the city demanded. In the better quarters of the city in particular (and in other Central European cities as well), these wooden pavilions with stone foundations were elaborately decorated in a half-baroque, half late-Victorian style, harmonizing with the sensibilities of the population. (See figure 14.)

If Hamburg's rapid and relatively easy renegotiation stood at one end of the spectrum, in large part because the city was willing to bargain on the basis of the overhead system as modified to pacify European sensibilities, then Berlin, with its struggle and delay, stood at the other. The well-entrenched, extremely profitable Great Berlin Horse Railway Company began to experiment with battery cars as early as 1884, and continued to do so from time to time through 1895.[85] Little real progress toward electrification was made, however, and for two basic reasons. First, there was hostility toward conduit and especially overhead conductors, on safety and aesthetic grounds.[86] Second, the company's concession expired in 1911 and it refused to consider any general electrification without receiving a substantial extension, an extension the city was reluctant to grant because of considerable sentiment for municipal ownership.[87]

The fact that the Berlin Industrial Exhibition of 1896 would place extraordinary demands upon the city's transit facilities, as well as pressure from the riding public for

[84] *EE* 19 (1897): 332; also U. S., *Consular Reports*, "Electric Streetcar System of Hamburg," vol. 61, no. 229 (October, 1899), pp. 218-21.
[85] *Die Grosse Berliner Strassenbahn, 1871-1902* (Berlin, 1902), pp. 31-32; *SRJ* 16 (1900): 620; *EE* 5 (1889): 339, 399; 11 (1893): 249, 294.
[86] Sheffield Report, in *EE* 19 (1897): 363-66.
[87] Buchmann, *Die Entwickelung*, pp. 15, 39; Edmund James, "Street Railway Policy in Berlin," *AAA* 15 (1900): 125-28.

13. Hamburg. View on Jungferstieg, showing row of handsome double bracket poles.

14. Various types of waiting stations used in Hamburg.

some improvement in service, finally led to a tentative and partial agreement in 1895. The city accepted the electrification of three lines, partly with overhead and partly with conduit conductors, on a two-year trial basis.[88] Opened on the first of May, 1896, the overhead portion of these Thomson-Houston-equipped lines served well and won converts for the trolley, especially as the Thomson-Houston conduit system functioned rather poorly. Thus the experimental phase was an important step toward the general agreement reached in 1897.

The terms of the renegotiated concession, redrawn to expire in 1919, clearly reflected the combination of aesthetic and social goals which has been stressed in this chapter. The company agreed to install a large mixed system combining battery and trolley traction. The overhead conductor serviced most of the lines, but "as in most German installations special care was taken to design and use poles which would thoroughly harmonize with their surroundings."[89] The city required all cars to run on batteries over fully twenty kilometers of line in the inner city, and reserved the right to so order elsewhere.[90] The city also had the right to order construction of 150 kilometers of new lines wherever it desired, which would increase the total network by about 50 percent. A 10-pfennig fare over any distance within the city limits was to be introduced within three years, and this did result in the fall of the average fare from about 11 pfennig in 1896 to 9.2 in 1902. The municipal tax on gross receipts was increased to 8 percent, and one half of all profits of more than 6 percent on the additional capital (and one half of all profits above 12 percent on the old) were to go to the city.[91]

The final resolution of the technical-aesthetic question is extremely revealing. The battery portion of the mixed ser-

[88] *EE* 14 (1894): 85, 347; *Die Grosse Berliner*, pp. 32-33.
[89] *SRJ* 16 (1900): 621.
[90] Buchmann, *Die Entwickelung*, pp. 17-20.
[91] *Ibid.*, pp. 39-43, Appendix Table; *Die Grosse Berliner*, pp. 32-38; James, "Berlin," *AAA* 15 (1900): 126-27.

vice, which the city had required in place of the conduit conductor used on the lines opened in 1896, functioned poorly. The "noisy, odorous, acid-spilling cars" were not popular with the public whose aesthetic sensibilities they were intended to safeguard.[92] They became even less so when heavy snow and cold weather placed exceptional demands on the batteries and produced breakdowns and delays—"a calamity for all the traffic in the congested streets of Berlin."[93] The company, continuously castigated for the failures of a system it had warned against, petitioned first the city and then the Prussian Ministry of Public Works for permission to substitute a continuous conductor, be it the dependable overhead method or the less satisfactory conduit, as the officials might decide.

This request eventually resulted in the reduction of the non-overhead area to five short sections around the grandest and most historic squares, streets, and bridges. The total distance was now only about three kilometers, as opposed to twenty initially. Installed by Siemens and Halske, the mixed system still gave problems. Thus the company continued to petition for changes and chip away at the aesthetic defenses. By 1910 only the stretch in front of the great Brandenburg Gate was free of wires. (See figure 9.) Even there temporary trolley wires were erected each winter, and only in the summer months did conduit service leave an unobstructed view.[94] The passage of time had left only a symbolic vestige to mark what had once been a passionate issue.

[92] *SRJ* 17 (1901): 132.
[93] *Die Grosse Berliner*, pp. 38-41; Buchmann, *Die Entwickelung*, p. 18.
[94] Buchmann, *Die Entwickelung*, p. 18.

IV. Private Enterprise in France

One of the conclusions of chapter III was that the initiative and pressure for electrification in continental Europe almost always came from private firms, and that this pressure developed very shortly after Sprague's breakthrough. More specifically, it seems clear that much of the initiative came from a small group of leading electrical manufacturers, as opposed to the individual tramway companies. These electrical producers sought to sell the equipment needed for street railway electrification to potential buyers, be they independent companies or municipalities. In order to do so they modified the equipment, found financing, gave cost and performance guarantees, and generally did what was necessary to make a sale. Finally, the small number of electrical producers, often allied with general contractors and financial institutions, seem to have competed vigorously along oligopolistic lines for contracts. This meant that the producers were unable to dictate unreasonable, one-sided terms to purchasers, a state of affairs that helped municipalities in their efforts to reap a major portion of the gains from innovation.

Evidence from the relatively well-studied German electrical industry might be expanded and recapitulated to buttress these assertions. After all, the three leading firms accounted for roughly 90 percent of all electric tramway installations in Germany. These same producers set up finance and holding companies for tramway operations, built systems throughout Europe, and developed the technical modifications municipalities demanded.[1] However, such a discussion would repeat a good deal of the material in

[1] See Hermes, *Finanzierung*, 7-14; F. Fasolt, *Die sieben gröszten deutschen Elektricitätsgesellschaften, ihre Entwicklung und Unternehmertätigkeit* (Dresden, 1904); J. Loewe, "Die elektrotechnische Industrie," *Schriften des Vereins für Sozialpolitik* 107 (1903): 110-30.

chapter 11 and would be based almost exclusively upon printed sources. It would not shed light on other continental countries or problems of comparative European economic history, which could confirm or modify German-based findings. Nor would it be possible to show effectively, except through inference, that there was vigorous if oligopolistic competition in the industry—an important point, in my view. Therefore it seems advisable to go in a different direction and, primarily on the basis of unpublished archival materials, to examine a neglected case of entrepreneurship in European electric tramways, the case of France.

1. *The French Thomson-Houston Company*

The electrification of surface transit in France is inextricably bound up with the development of La Compagnie Française pour l'Exploitation des procédés Thomson-Houston. By way of introduction, perhaps three things should be said about this firm, generally known in France simply as Thomson-Houston. First, it was in part an American creation: one of the first examples of important direct American investment in European manufacturing. Second, Thomson-Houston became the dominant firm in the industry, installing and equipping roughly 40 percent of all electric tramways of all types in France by the end of 1898.[2] Finally, Thomson-Houston found and elicited sharp competition from other firms; never by any stretch of the imagination did it "monopolize" the field. With these thoughts in mind we can return briefly to the United States and the origins of this extremely successful firm. For as one well-placed insider put it in 1914, "The Thomson-Houston Group is the most important of the French groups in the electrical industry. . . . It controls, either by itself or in collaboration with

---

[2] *IE* 8 (1899): Supplement, 10 March, 10-15. The origins of United States direct investment in France have been examined by Charles P. Kindleberger, *Business History Review* 48 (1974): 382-413.

its associates, companies with a capital of more than 800 million francs."³

When American electrical manufacturers turned toward Europe to capitalize upon their leadership in urban transport technology, they presented a strong and unified front. Sprague had sold his company to the Edison General Electric Company in 1889, shortly after his initial success. About the same time the Edison Company's Henry Villard began negotiations with the other leading electrical producer, the Thomson-Houston Company, which was equally strong in street railways. These negotiations led to a merger in April 1892 of the two companies into the newly formed General Electric Company. J. P. Morgan and his associates wielded a dominant influence in matters of financial policy, but the top managerial and technical positions went mainly to men from Thomson-Houston.⁴ The strengths of the new firm were so great in electric street railways that it was certain to dominate the field in America.⁵ And it was in a good position to try to capitalize fully upon its advantage in the most advanced, and therefore most promising, foreign market, Europe.

While a German subsidiary was founded at Berlin—the Union Elektricitäts-Gesellschaft—and an English subsidiary planned, so was a French firm projected by the end of 1892. This French company, which took its name from the Thomson-Houston International Company, now a General Electric subsidiary, was by no means merely a branch of the American parent. Rather, as seems very often to be the case with successful foreign investment, it was a joint undertaking enlisting foreign technological superiority, on the one hand, and native management and capital on the other.⁶

³ CL, Etude du Groupe Thomson-Houston, May 1914.
⁴ Passer, *Electrical Manufacturers*, pp. 248-49, 321-29.
⁵ *Ibid.*, pp. 325-26.
⁶ See the striking similarities with foreign behavior in Russia at this time, as analyzed in my *Pioneers for Profit: Foreign Entrepreneur-*

This may be seen by examining the basic agreement upon which the French company was based.

From the American company the new French company received the exclusive right to produce and sell in France and its colonies, as well as in Spain and Portugal, all Thomson-Houston equipment, as well as the exclusive right to all present and future patents, plans, blueprints, information, and experience developed in the United States. In addition, the American firm promised to lend to the French company any engineers and technicians it might need. In payment for this technology the American company was to receive 50 percent of all profits in excess of 5 percent.[7] The French partners consisted mainly of the men from an existing French manufacturer (La Compagnie pour la fabrication des compteurs et matériel d'usines à gaz), which was already licensed by the American Thomson-Houston to produce its electric meters in France. The two sides had therefore already cooperated. The French founders from the Cie des compteurs, including G. Chamon, A. Foiret, and E. Siry, became the guiding force in the French Thomson-Houston Company, where General Electric was represented by Coffin and Rice. In non-technical areas of policy the French founders were apparently ready to exercise effective leadership from the beginning.

This may be seen in the financial arrangements, which resulted in a rapid dilution of American influence. The initial

---

ship and Russian Industrialization, 1885-1913 (Chicago, 1970), particularly, pp. 72-112, 158-241, 379-89, and "Foreign Enterprise in Russian and Soviet Industry: A Long Term Perspective," *Business History Review* 48 (1974): 336-56.

[7] The terms of the agreement are reproduced in *Bulletin financière*, 30 October 1898, found in AN, 65, AQ, G 602¹; also see CL, Etude du Groupe Thomson-Houston, May 1914. Exactly why all contracts were with the wholly owned Thomson-Houston International Company, whereas subsequently contracts were made directly with General Electric, is not clear. The probable reason is that Sprague or the Edison Company had already given some licensing agreements that included France or at least Spain, as for example to A.E.G. Thus General Electric could not give exclusive French rights for all its patents.

agreement between the two groups called for a company with 1,000,000 francs of capital stock, one-tenth of which went to the American firm without any cash payment for its technical contribution. The contract further stated that after a dividend of 5 percent was paid on the capital stock, 90 percent of which was presumably paid in cash by the French founders and investors, then 40 percent of all the remaining profits that might be paid out were to go to the American partner. In short, General Electric might receive large profits without making any cash investment, exactly as if it had received the founders' shares so commonly used in late nineteenth-century Europe.[8] Yet the French had a valuable option. If the French Thomson-Houston's capital stock was raised to 5,000,000 francs, then the new French firm could give General Electric capital shares with a nominal value of 2,000,000 francs and thereby relieve itself of any further payments.

This was done in early 1894. The result was that General Electric received 42 percent of the French Thomson-Houston's capital of 5,000,000 francs in payment for its patents and technology, but it had no claim on future profits. Capital was subsequently increased very rapidly: to 15,000,000 francs in 1896, 25,000,000 francs in 1897, and 40,000,000 francs in 1898. All these issues were at prices well above par, so that the capital raised by the French Thomson-Houston Company from joint-stock flotations was about 75,000,000 francs, plus another 10,000,000 from the sale of bonds.[9] It seems fairly certain that General Electric did not subscribe to these rapid increases and that its portion of the total capitalization declined correspondingly. Indeed, General Electric was near bankruptcy in 1893 and was forced to sell off some of its investment portfolio, and profits remained low until 1898.[10] Thus General Electric's discomfiture and the enormous need for capital for European ex-

[8] See McKay, *Pioneers for Profit*, pp. 201-07.
[9] *Bulletin financière*, 20 November 1898, AN, 65 AQ, G 602¹.
[10] Passer, *Electrical Manufacturers*, pp. 327-29.

pansion facilitated the assimilation of Thomson-Houston as a truly French firm, although with a very valuable American technical assistance contract, and its emergence as a bellwether speculative issue on the Paris Exchange, from its listing in May 1896.[11]

But this is to anticipate events. When founded in early 1893 Thomson-Houston was very much American, its whole *raison d'être* the diffusion of the American system of urban transit. The first year, following the objectives laid down in the articles of incorporation, Thomson-Houston confined itself primarily to selling and installing equipment imported from the United States, very much like an overseas sales office of the parent firm. It had some modest success, selling equipment for a trial line at Milan and a new suburban tramway in the Bordeaux area.[12] Then in late 1893 or early 1894 the firm decided it had to expand its activities if it were to take advantage of its opportunity. Rather than simply sell the foreign equipment, it would engage in "every type of activity related to the electrical industry."[13] In early 1894 Thomson-Houston purchased controlling interest of an existing electrical manufacturer (les Etablissements Postel-Vinay), raised its capital from one to five million francs, paid off General Electric, and set about manufacturing, installing, and financing tramways all over France.

The decision to manufacture and finance large-scale operations through investments in individual tramway companies, as opposed to simply importing and installing foreign equipment, was of crucial importance in the firm's subsequent success. Clearly this decision involved considerable risks. At the very least, the company would need large amounts of capital, which would then be immobilized for considerable periods. At worst, the investments in operating companies might be unprofitable, and such assets could

[11] *Economiste Européen* 9 (1896): 428.
[12] Annual Report, 1893, in *IE* 3 (1894): 287.
[13] Revised articles of incorporation, Special Shareholders' Meeting, 11 July 1894, in *IE* 5 (1896): 285-88.

easily become frozen in any financial crisis, precisely when they would be most needed. Thus the well-informed, conservative analysts at the Crédit Lyonnais only stated with particular authority a common perception when they stressed the dangers of such a policy.[14] Yet if Thomson-Houston were not merely "to vegetate," its French directors apparently had little choice but to accept the risks of a more aggressive policy.

There were various reasons. As one careful study of the firm in the French financial press put it, "People are creatures of habit [très routinier] in France, and if management had waited until it suited the tramway companies to decide to adopt the Thomson-Houston system on their lines, it would have waited a very long time and the patents of the company would no doubt have lapsed before anything happened."[15] As it was, the French company and its subsidiaries had to defend themselves against patent infringement on "innumerable occasions" by 1900.[16]

Thomson-Houston would also have waited for a long time, in many cases, because horse tramways in France were in a very mediocre financial position. One study calculated that a group of twenty-one provincial tramways were paying dividends of only 3½ to 4 percent on their capital stock in the early 1890s.[17] The General French Tramways Company, the largest company in France, with tramways in four major French cities, had to reduce its capital by 50 percent in 1893 after averaging dividends of about 2 percent for many years.[18] Hard-pressed to make such modest payments, few companies could easily find the credit necessary for a total transformation, and Thomson-Houston was

[14] CL, Etude du Groupe Thomson-Houston, May 1914.
[15] Bulletin financière, 11 November 1898, AN, 65 AQ, G 602¹.
[16] Cie d'Electricité Thomson-Houston de la Méditérranée, Special Shareholders' Meeting, 28 April 1900, AN, 65 AQ, G 602².
[17] Fuster, *Annuaire Général des Tramways*, 1901, pp. 38-39.
[18] AN, 65 AQ, Q 1381, Cie Générale Française de Tramways, Annual Reports.

being asked to finance—or find financing for—any large purchases.

There was also the problem of competition with other producers if the company only sold equipment, competition which operating companies could use to beat down the price of equipment. The public works contractor J. Claret and Company had already, in 1890, opened the first electric street railway in France at Clermont-Ferrand. Initially intending to use fireless steam engines on his largely suburban network, Claret decided to substitute the Thury system of overhead traction. This was apparently a variation of Siemens and Halske's old wire-within-a-pipe method, with the contact apparatus attached to the car by means of a loose cable.[19] Claret had constructed all aspects of the new line very profitably, purchasing only the electrical apparatus from an independent supplier.[20] And the Oerlikon Works of Zurich, Switzerland, had been able to provide its own type of overhead equipment for the first electric line at Marseilles, which was opened by the General French Tramways Company in May 1892.[21] The financing of its sales would give Thomson-Houston an additional advantage in its competition with other producers.

Finally, investment in operating tramways seemed to hold the key to really large profits. There would be the substantial manufacturer's profit on the electrical equipment, the profit for engineering and planning the entire installation, and the general contractor's profit. In each case, control of the operating company would enable Thomson-Houston to set high, noncompetitive prices for its goods and services not only for the initial installation, but in the future as well. In addition, there might be large speculative profits as moribund horse tramways were bought cheaply, trans-

[19] Fuster, *Annuaire Général des Tramways*, 1901, pp. 131-35; *IE* 8 (1899): Supplement, 10 March, 10-11.
[20] See AN, F 14, 13520, Clermont-Ferrand.
[21] *EE* 7 (1891): 329, 387; AN, 65 AQ, Q 138¹, Annual Reports, 1891-92.

formed, and converted into good investments, which could eventually be sold in part to the public.[22]

These factors were all present at Rouen, where Thomson-Houston purchased and equipped its first major subsidiary. And because the statistical data are fairly complete for Rouen, and because electrification was quick and decisive there, Rouen is an excellent example of the way in which the electric transit innovation was inherently profitable, even if municipal demands, private competition, and speculative excesses might sometimes obscure that reality. Therefore Rouen deserves rather detailed analysis.

The horse tramways of Rouen were due to the initiative of an English contractor, Palmer Harding, who received a concession for twenty-three kilometers of line in 1877. The Rouen Tramways Company was incorporated the following year with a joint-stock capital of 3,750,000 francs, of which all but 10 percent went to Harding for the tramways he agreed to construct. Since Harding's costs of construction should not have exceeded 2,000,000 francs, he had difficulty securing the administrative approval necessary for a sale of his shares to French investors. He therefore had to cede all his shares to an English holding company formed for that purpose.[23] With inflated capital, poor equipment, and inadequate maintenance—the kind of experience leading to the tough French tramway law of 1881—as well as some expensive and disastrous experiments with steam tramways, the company failed to develop beyond its initial position. All indicators of traffic and finances stagnated. Receipts and passengers carried tended to decline, a decline operating expenses failed to match. The operating margin correspondingly rose from about 85 percent in 1882-83 to a ruinous 92 percent by 1894. Intermittent dividends averaging

[22] See the Annual Reports for 1895, 1896, and 1897, in *IE* 5 (1896): 285-88; 6 (1897): 265-68; 7 (1898): 241-42; also CL, Etude du Groupe Thomson-Houston, May 1914, and discussion below.

[23] CL, Tramways de Rouen, Etude, September 1901; AN, F 14, 13528, Tramways de Rouen, note, 30 April 1881.

less than 1 percent from 1881 to 1889 ceased completely in 1890.[24] Here indeed was a wreck of a "before" which Thomson-Houston might profitably transform into a rejuvenated "after."

Thomson-Houston proceeded on two fronts. First, it worked out an agreement with the English holding company to electrify and then purchase its shares in the French operating company at Rouen. Thomson-Houston's offer was very attractive: it paid the English company 352 francs per share, or about 70 percent of the original inflated par value of 500 francs.[25] After six years of no dividends and prospects of only more of the same, Harding's English successors must have been very pleased by the power of electric traction.

At the same time Thomson-Houston submitted a project for the substitution of electric traction and the extension of the Rouen concession for almost fifty years to the city council and the Ministry of Public Works in 1894. This project was eventually approved after extensive studies, particularly of the results at Le Havre, where Thomson-Houston had installed electric traction for the General French Tramways Company in early 1894. Work on the entire network was then actively pushed, and on May 22, 1896, the first line was inaugurated in a large public ceremony graced by the attendance of many local and national dignitaries.[26] And no wonder: Rouen was far and away the largest electric tramway network in France; only Hamburg's was larger in the whole of Europe.

The total length of track was increased only moderately, although three new lines were opened. All lines received heavy new girder rails of the Broca type, weighing either 56 or 88 pounds per meter, depending on the traffic. Feeders were run from the newly built powerhouse on the left

[24] CL, Tramways de Rouen, Financial Abstracts, reproduced in part in table 7.
[25] CL, Tramways de Rouen, Etude, September 1901.
[26] *EE* 17 (1896); 314-18.

bank of the Seine, in a covered trench along the roadway, to five separate terminals on the lines. The overhead work was patterned on the American kind, although more brackets and steel poles were used. The power station was also similar, though hand stoking as opposed to automatic stoking of the boilers was used because of the lower French wages. The rolling stock consisted of 50 motorcars, each designed to seat 20 passengers with room for another 20 standing on the platforms. The well-lighted cars and the overhead work met with the approval of the population, at least as judged by the local press.[27] In short, the historic capital of the ancient Norman conquerors, now a city of 113,000 inhabitants with perhaps 40,000 more in the surrounding suburbs, a city well along in the process of industrial transformation with its cotton industry, its port, and its expanding administrative and commercial activities, provided an excellent opportunity for contemporaries to judge the possibilities of urban electric traction in France. And, as table 8 shows, the possibilities were very great.

If we examine this statistical picture of tramway development in Rouen, several points stand out. Horse tramways were clearly bad business for both consumers and investors at Rouen. There was no growth in traffic whatsoever before electrification, and investors did worse and worse as dividends were suspended entirely. Everything changed with electrification. Perhaps most striking was the astonishing two-and-one-half-fold increase in passengers in a single year, from 5,000,000 in 1895 to 13,000,000 in 1896. This meant that the number of rides per inhabitant per year jumped from thirty-three in 1895 to eighty-five in 1896 and then 108 in 1900, a fairly respectable figure in terms of international comparisons.

No doubt part of the public's extremely enthusiastic reception was due to the sharp decline in the price of transport. Whereas the horsecar rider averaged paying more

[27] *Ibid.*; also *EE* 19 (1897): 595.

Table 8

THE ROUEN TRAMWAYS COMPANY, 1882-1913

Year	Length of Line	Results per km. of Line (ooos of frs.) Receipts	Expenses	Net	Kms. Run (ooos)	Riders Carried (millions)	Results per Rider (in frs.) Receipts	Expenses	Net	Total Net Receipts[a] (ooos)	Dividends per Share (%)	Rides per Capita
1882	26	34.5	28.8	5.7	965	5,150	.174	.145	.029	153	1.6	—
1887	27	32.4	27.2	5.2	1,076	4,994	.175	.147	.028	157	2.2	—
1892	27	31.1	28.4	2.7	1,074	4,822	.173	.159	.014	71	0	—
1894	31	28.9	26.6	2.3	1,139	5,216	.172	.158	.014	83	0	35
1895	43	20.6	—	—	—	5,162	.171	—	—	159	0	33
1896	44	37.3	—	—	—	13,021	.126	—	—	714	5	85
1897	45	38.2	—	—	2,958	14,492	.119	—	—	777	5	94
1898	45	39.8	23.6	16.2	3,161	15,096	.118	.070	.048	810	5	98
1899	50	39.1	22.5	16.6	3,291	16,141	.121	.069	.052	825	5.5	104
1900	50	41.3	24.3	17.0	3,527	16,988	.121	.071	.050	874	5.5	108
1905	51	40.8	22.6	18.2	3,627	17,105	.121	.068	.054	937	6	100
1909	51	46.6	25.7	20.9	3,798	19,382	.122	.067	.055	1,068	6.27	110
1910	74	40.4	23.7	16.7	4,970	23,733	.126	.074	.052	1,248	6.50	128
1912	78	41.9	24.3	17.6	5,376	25,801	.127	.074	.053	1,365	6.60	—
1913	81	42.9	24.7	18.2	—	—	—	—	—	1,477	6.67	—

SOURCE: Cie des Tramways de Rouen, Statistical Abstracts, CL.

[a] Before debt charges.

than 17 centimes per ride, the electric tram patron paid a fare of about 12 centimes—a reduction of 35 percent. At the same time expenses per passenger carried declined even more sharply, by more than 50 percent, so that the gross profit per passenger jumped almost *fourfold* between 1894 and 1899. Here was the mechanism which resulted in a 5 and 6 percent return on the firm's greatly expanded capital, which had risen to 12,500,000 francs in 1899. Here also was the steady if unspectacular growth of a healthy industry after 1899 and the once-and-for-all change to electric traction: both per capita usage and dividends per share advanced steadily until the outbreak of war. All in all, Thomson-Houston had created a profitable subsidiary. And it had demonstrated to officials, passengers, and investors the promise of electric traction.

According to an analysis by the Crédit Lyonnais, two factors were the key to the very satisfactory results at Rouen, results which contrasted sharply with some of those to follow.[28] First, in the negotiations over electrification the entrepreneurs had to agree to build only a few kilometers of new lines to serve outlying districts. Such lines required somewhat more investment than the old lines and brought in lower receipts, at least in terms of kilometer of line and probably in terms of car-kilometers run as well. And while the length of lines increased only twelve kilometers, the last omnibus lines, which had been extremely unprofitable, were also consolidated into the new electric tramway network. The company benefited from the transformation on the heavily used existing lines with little or no offsetting burden from less profitable, less frequently traveled suburban extensions.

Second, the reductions in fares were considerable, but they were quite "equitable" from the company's point of view. The zone system was retained: a fare of 15 centimes in first class and 10 centimes in second was charged for the first section, with 10 and 5 centimes being required for ad-

[28] CL, Tramways de Rouen, Etude, September 1901.

ditional sections. There were also special workmen's tickets of 10 centimes for a single ride of any distance begun before 8:00 A.M., or 15 centimes for a round-trip ticket.[29] Yet in spite of the various reductions, the average fare of 12 centimes was more than most French electric tramway companies would be able to charge. Finally, we should note that the entire process of electrification occurred at one time, and was not complicated by piecemeal measures, so expensive in terms of traffic problems and management time.

The results of the Rouen Tramways Company, favorable from every point of view, were instrumental in overcoming hostility and inertia. Tramway electrification became the order of the day in France. This was not an unmitigated blessing for Thomson-Houston, for if concern with safety and aesthetic conditions declined to negotiable levels, public officials did not relax their demands. On the contrary, they saw the advantages of electric traction for the private tramway companies as well as the public, and they became more demanding in their negotiations with the operating companies Thomson-Houston sought to acquire and then supply. Municipalities were able to do this in large part because Thomson-Houston's success attracted competitors, latecomers who hustled for the remaining concessions and who were sometimes willing to gamble recklessly with the terms they would accept.

The electrification of the tramways of Bordeaux demonstrates this process admirably. Founded in 1879 by another English group, The Bordeaux Tramways and Omnibus Company Ltd. operated a concession scheduled to expire in 1911. Following the general trend the English directors presented projects for electrification of their tram and omnibus lines in 1897, and they even signed a contract for this purpose with an English equipment maker, the Dickinson Company. But the company "was blocked by the bad faith of the Bordeaux municipal council, which wanted a French

[29] *Ibid.*

company to take the English company's place."[30] At this point Thomson-Houston and the General Traction Company, which is discussed in detail below, presented competing projects. And the Traction Company, a tough competitor in its own way, "intrigued with" and probably bribed certain council members in its pursuit of the concession. However, Thomson-Houston strengthened its hand through purchase of the majority of the existing company's shares from the English owners, subject to approval of electrification from the city council.[31] Unable to influence the horse tramway company, the Traction Company's only hope was to have the city use its right to purchase the English firm whose shares Thomson-Houston now held, and then have the city cede the horse tramways to it for electrification. This meant serious delays, however, and with the public in favor of better transit and the proposed aesthetic compromise, the municipality accepted Thomson-Houston's final proposals.

Yet greater public awareness of the profits inherent in electric traction, which the competition of rival groups placed in sharp relief, enabled the city to obtain excellent terms. In the first place, the new fares were extremely low. One could ride the length of all lines (in most cases from two to four kilometers with one line of seven kilometers) for only 10 centimes, or a round-trip for 15 centimes. More expensive first-class tickets were not permitted. In addition, workmen's tickets could be purchased for trips in the early morning and evening at the extremely low price of 5 centimes for one way.

The overhead trolley was generally accepted. Nevertheless, the more aesthetically satisfying conduit system was required on certain bridges and squares. Although they added up to only two of fifty-three kilometers in 1902 when electrification was completed, they entailed equipping

[30] CL, Cie Française des Tramways électriques et Omnibus de Bordeaux, Etude, 1902.
[31] *Ibid.*; Thomson-Houston, Annual Report, 1898, in *IE* 8 (1899): 380.

many cars for the troublesome mixed system.[32] The company also agreed to extend existing lines by approximately 50 percent. And the city could order the company to make further extensions in the future, though if receipts fell below 30 centimes per car per kilometer on such new sections the city was to make up the difference. The city was also to receive an increased portion of the gross receipts, ranging from a low of 5 to a high of 20 percent depending on the average receipts per kilometer, and indeed the company paid 15 percent in the first year. The company was to use its poles to light the streets, entirely at its own expense. Finally, note that all workers, who were to be of French nationality, were to work a ten-hour day and receive one day off at half pay each week. Conductors were to receive a minimum of 4 francs per day and motormen 5 francs.

Perhaps the best way to appraise the impact of these terms is to compare results in the last year of horsecar service, 1900, with those at the end of that decade, when the population was totally familiar with electric streetcars. Again a threefold increase in passengers carried is striking —from 21,700,000 in 1900 to 63,000,000 in 1909. Only a small portion of this surge in traffic was due to population growth. Rather, usage per capita was the basic factor, jumping from roughly eighty in 1900 to more than twice that in 1909—a very respectable increase. (See chapter VII.) Length of line also increased from forty-one to seventy-one kilometers. All of this went with a 50 percent reduction in the cost of transportation: passengers paid an average of 16.7 centimes per ride in 1900; they paid only 8.8 centimes in 1909. To put it another way, the company carried three times as many passengers but increased its gross revenues only 57 percent (from 3,540,000 to 5,570,000 francs).[33]

As for the new Bordeaux Tramways and Omnibus Company, it was able to pay a steady 5 percent dividend through 1913, with the exception of 1907 and 1908 when the

[32] *Ibid.*; Fuster, *Annuaire Général des Tramways*, 1901, pp. 62-65.
[33] France, *Statistique des chemins de fer*, 1900, II, 344-45; 1909, II, 786-87, 807.

dividend rose almost imperceptibly to 5.1 percent. This was a very mediocre return; investors were receiving 5.3 percent, yield to maturity, on Bordeaux Tramways thirty-five year, first mortgage bonds in 1901, a higher return for much lower risk.[34] The modest return for electric tramways was certainly no better than that of the old horse company, and perhaps worse. The old horse tramways had been "quite prosperous," earning about 600,000 francs per annum in the last three years of its existence, or about half what the electric company was making for its joint-stock capital of 25,000,000 francs in 1908.[35] Actually, the return of 5 percent on capital stock was exaggerated, as both private and state financial analysts agreed that depreciation was inadequate.[36] Clearly Thomson-Houston was less successful in its investments at Bordeaux than it had been at Rouen.

The reasonable conclusion is that city officials were quite successful in using the competing electrification schemes to appropriate a large portion of the gains from technology from the regulated private monopoly for the public's benefit. This is indeed what the Crédit Lyonnais study on the results of electric traction for a number of French tramways concluded at the end of 1900. "It is above all the public which has benefited from the application of electric traction. The companies have not lost by it, but the benefits have rarely been as high as could have been expected."[37] The average investor in French tramway shares gained very modestly from electric traction. Thomson-Houston itself earned a "very small return" of 3.3 percent on its large portfolio of shares in subsidiary companies between 1905 and 1913.[38]

Dividends from operating companies were only part of

[34] AN, F 14, 13512, Tramways de Bordeaux, 1901.
[35] Ibid., 1908; CL, Tramways de Bordeaux, Etude, January 1902; Note, May 1902; Etude, August 1913.
[36] AN, F 14, 13512, 1908; CL, Tramways de Bordeaux, Etude, December 1919.
[37] CL, Etude sur les résultats de la traction électrique . . . en France, December 1900.
[38] CL, Etude du Groupe Thomson-Houston, May 1914.

the profit picture, however. Thomson-Houston was first and foremost in the business of selling street railway equipment and engineering expertise. As we suggested earlier, its development as an investment banker was tied to efforts to secure and control such sales. And if state supervision restrained scandalous overcapitalization, it did not prevent very profitable noncompetitive sales to operating subsidiaries.[39]

The size of such profits from the manufacture and sale of electrical equipment was of course a closely guarded secret. Not surprisingly, contemporary estimates on profits are both rare and vague. Fortunately, however, the impartial and highly confidential studies of engineers at the Crédit Lyonnais cut through this fog to some extent. After buying the almost bankrupt horse tramways at Amiens in 1897, Thomson-Houston spent 3,400,000 francs to electrify that thirteen-and-one-half-kilometer system, or approximately a million more than a substantial but still "reasonable" profit would have left.[40] At Algiers, Thomson-Houston equipped a short, seven-kilometer network for 660,000 francs per kilometer, "a very high figure" equal to that on the so-called penetration lines at Paris. (The Algerian Tramways Company was nonetheless one of the Thomson-Houston's more successful subsidiaries, paying dividends of 10 percent by 1906.)[41] Padding of costs and the accompanying substantial profits apparently continued when Thomson-Houston began to supply affiliated electric power companies in addition of tramways after 1900.[42]

[39] For example, when Claret electrified the first commercial tramway with overhead conductor in France in 1890, the local government inspector tried to show in detail that Claret had paid himself too much for what he had done and had thereby inflated the capital. The inspector general overruled this as a "narrow view," pointing out that the method was new and involved special risks and costs, and was therefore entitled to substantial profits. See AN, F 14, 13520, Clermont-Ferrand.
[40] CL, Tramways d'Amiens, Etude, March 1903.
[41] CL, Sté des Tramways Algériens, July 1902.
[42] CL, Thomson-Houston, 1914. A March 1926 study of the com-

The "largest part of profits" always came from manufacturing and contracting for subsidiaries; dividends were the smallest part. This was because throughout its pre-war existence Thomson-Houston "directed all its efforts toward constructing things for its subsidiaries, and devoted much less attention to the dividends the subsidiaries might pay."[43] The fact that Thomson-Houston came to exercise a powerful influence on the policies of the General French Tramways Company meant, for example, that the interests of the other General Tramways shareholders, which lay in a large return on existing capital, tended to be sacrificed for Thomson-Houston's construction profits on ever less remunerative suburban lines.[44] No wonder Thomson-Houston systematically sold a certain number of shares in subsidiary companies each year on the stock exchange, particularly after 1900, "whenever a favorable moment appears and whenever it can sell for a small profit."[45]

Three further points should be made concerning these construction profits, which allowed Thomson-Houston to pay dividends of 10 and even 11 percent on its very large capital prior to 1900. First, construction profits provided a powerful mechanism for rapid diffusion and maximum extension of electric tramways throughout France. They reintroduced at the producer's level the substantial entrepreneurial profits which public authority denied at the operating level. Second, there was a large element of risk in these construction profits because Thomson-Houston had to finance them through long-term investment. As noted earlier, capital grew very rapidly, so that by 1900 investors had placed about 107 million francs in Thomson-Houston's shares and bonds. This enabled Thomson-Houston to be-

---

pany concluded that the exaggeration of fixed investment (*immobilisations*) of most of its subsidiaries seems to indicate that Thomson-Houston charges a high price for the work and equipment it provides for the companies it controls."
[43] CL, Thomson-Houston, May 1914.
[44] CL, Cie Générale Française de Tramways, September 1902.
[45] CL, Thomson-Houston, May 1914.

come a vast investment bank for the electrical industry, accepting payment for its work and equipment in the shares and occasionally the bonds of its operating subsidiaries. Yet if some of these subsidiaries proved somewhat unsuccessful, then the value of their shares would decline and reduce the value of the original payment Thomson-Houston had received. Thus profits might subsequently need to be restated as losses. This risk puts a different light on the construction profits which very conservative financial analysis might deem excessive: such "profits" necessarily included a premium for the risks involved in long-term financing and uncertain total receipts. Third, whatever the *real* risks were, Thomson-Houston's profits *as reported* soared until 1900. This stimulated the appetite and initiative of individual investors and competing firms, who rushed toward the supposedly wonderful profits in the electric traction industry.

2. *Followers and Competitors*

Thomson-Houston had several major competitors in France. The most important of these was the General Traction Company, a Franco-Belgian concern founded in Paris in January 1896 with a capital of 5,000,000 francs. The French founders included the small Banque Henrotte of Paris and the Parisian engineer Renard, who had been a Thomson-Houston founder. The Belgian founders were more noteworthy, including both Georges Chaudoir, an important industrialist from Liège, and Jules Nagelmackers and his bank from that same city.[46] Indeed, it seems clear that the Belgian partners provided the driving force initially. Such Belgian leadership and foreign investment reflected the large role that Belgian entrepreneurs and engineers played in spreading first horse and then electric

[46] CL, Cie Générale de Traction, Etude, March 1901. Renard had to resign from Thomson-Houston after the General Traction Company was founded. On the enterprising Jules Nagelmackers and the Banque Internationale de Paris, see McKay, *Pioneers for Profit*.

tramways throughout Europe and the world. One well-informed observer summed up the situation in 1902:

> At the present time there are ten or fifteen large tramway investment companies owning tramways throughout Europe, whose headquarters are in Brussels and whose stock is actively quoted on the Brussels stock exchange. The city, in fact, occupies a commanding position in the tramway industry second to no other city in Europe. . . . Tramway syndicates . . . and their operations are not confined to one country, but they are ready to take up enterprises of this character in practically every country of the globe.[47]

In January 1897 the General Traction Company boosted its capital to 15,000,000 francs and a number of major banking firms jumped on board with major subscriptions. The most important of these was the Banque Internationale de Paris and its financial group, which was active in Russia, South Africa and elsewhere, and which deserved its reputation as a fast-stepping speculative entrepreneur. There were also Baron Gunzburg of the Banque de l'Afrique du Sud and a number of English capitalists grouped around the Exploration Company of London, apparently linked to the American streetcar magnate Charles Yerkes, who was active in London underground railway construction at this time.[48] In short, the Traction Company was the product of aggressive major financial interests.

[47] *SRJ* 20 (1902): 328. One such country was tsarist Russia. At the end of 1909 Belgian companies accounted for three-quarters of the capital invested in the electric tramways operating in the Russian Empire. (V. S. Diakin, *Germanskie kapitaly v Rossii: elektroindustriia i elektricheskii transport* [Leningrad, 1971], p. 117; also see McKay, *Pioneers for Profit*, pp. 100-02.) It is my intention to examine Belgian foreign investment in tramways, particularly as it related to Russia in a subsequent publication.

[48] In addition to the Crédit Lyonnais studies, see the debate in the French Chamber of Deputies on the Traction Company, which began 20 November 1902 (1902, pp. 2680 ff.) and is conveniently grouped together in AN, F 14, 15012.

This firm competed for and won a number of concessions, especially for secondary suburban lines at Rouen, Bordeaux, and, above all, Paris. There, after playing a leading role in the successful creation of the Paris subway in 1898 with the Metropolitan Company, it founded or assumed control of a series of new suburban tramway concessions in 1899: the Left Bank Tramways Company, the Mechanical Tramways for the Suburbs of Paris Company, the East Paris Tramways Company, the West Paris Tramways Company, and the Tramways of Paris and the Department of the Seine—to name only the most important. In most instances the General Traction Company competed with Thomson-Houston for these new concessions. Indeed, Thomson-Houston succeeded in electrifying only the existing General Paris Tramways Company.[49] Thus the Traction Company swept everything before it at Paris between 1897 and 1900, and gave rise to predictable cries of monopoly and trustification.[50] In fact, just the opposite was true: Thomson-Houston, the dominant firm, was being effectively challenged at a number of points.

The Traction Company's opportunity must be understood within the context of the extremely complex evolution of Parisian public transportation before 1914. The slow extension of service to outlying areas by the General Omnibus Company after its creation in 1854 led to various attempts to limit that company's power and provide better transport.

[49] This firm was the successor to the South Paris Tramways Company, which had been founded in the mid-1870s, in part by Palmer Harding. The original company had gone backrupt in 1884 following a very complicated legal history, and it was eventually reorganized as the General Paris Tramways Company. Thomson-Houston was successful in this instance primarily because it was able to buy controlling interest in 1896 from the English firm holding most of the shares (The Continental Metropolitan Tramways Company), precisely as Thomson-Houston bought out English interests at Rouen and Bordeaux. CL, Cie Générale Parisienne de Tramways, July 1901; Klapper, *Golden Age*, p. 43.

[50] See the statements by Jules Coutant in the debate in the Chamber of Deputies, cited above.

While the first of innumerable discussions and projects concerning an underground "metro" began in the early 1870s, and finally reached fruition in 1898, new tramway concessions to new companies were granted in the mid 1870s and again at the end of the 1890s, when twenty-two new concessions were approved in 1899 alone. Thus Paris, suffering rather atypically among continental cities from an inability to control effectively the Omnibus Company, which had been founded before regulation procedures were well established, was led to granting concessions to competing companies in an attempt to improve service and lower fares. This meant that there was a great lack of unity in Parisian public transport before 1914, as several companies operated with many different contractual obligations. This problem also opened the opportunity of the late 1890s, when concessions for a whole series of suburban lines for the more outlying and less densely settled areas of greater Paris were granted.[51]

Very much like Thomson-Houston, the Traction Company sought to profit primarily from the sale of equipment and construction services to subsidiary operating companies. It made arrangements to supply completely the individual concessionaires, who were often Traction Company straw men, and the tramway companies they founded. The Traction Company then constructed the tracks, purchased and installed cars and equipment, agreed to sell the needed electricity, and entered into long-term service contracts. In return, the Traction Company agreed to accept full or partial payment in the shares and bonds of the operating companies, companies which had a total stock and bond capital of roughly 140,000,000 francs in 1901.[52]

There were, however, several crucial differences. In the

[51] Materials at the Archives Nationales and the Crédit Lyonnais on Paris urban transport are voluminous and would permit a detailed investigation of developments in this period.
[52] CL, Cie Générale de Traction, Etude, March 1901. On financial operations, AN, F 14, 15024.

first place, the Traction Company was "particularly greedy" and imposed upon the operating companies truly "Draconian conditions," as one top official aptly put it.[53] The lines of the East Paris Company eventually cost 53,000,000 francs, for example, or about twice what they should have. The small Eu to Tréport Tramway Company, for which 1,000,000 francs should have been ample, was capitalized at 1,500,000 francs: "this inflation of 50 percent represented the paper profit the General Traction Company arbitrarily attributed to itself."[54] Indeed, the company said that it added a 30 percent mark-up to all the equipment it sold to its subsidiaries, and to all the work done for them. This meant that the Traction Company stood to gain—on paper —roughly 30,000,000 francs of profit on the more than 100,000,000 francs' worth of tramways it equipped in 1899 and 1900. It begins to be understandable how rumors of a dividend of 15 to 20 percent for 1899, as opposed to 6 percent in 1898, might whip up the Traction Company's shares to three times their par value in late 1899.[55]

The Traction Company and its subsidiaries were correspondingly completely dependent upon the hopes and fantasies of the investing public, and specifically upon the boom in tramway shares. Thus the Traction Company was often paid in the shares of its subsidiaries in advance, long before the firm was operational. This enabled it to try to sell such shares on the exchange quickly, and gain funds for ever more projects. This tactic also made it possible to report as earned the profits that might never materialize. Then the Traction Company could push its own capital to 30,000,000 francs and insiders could sell their Traction shares for large gains.[56] This entire strategy of profit through stock-market speculation was clear to one keen observer at the Crédit Lyonnais in late 1899. "In short, the Traction Company serves as the pretext and the means for

[53] E. Rousseau, Note, 22 January 1907, AN, F 14, 15023.
[54] CL, Cie Générale de Traction, Etude, March 1901.
[55] *Ibid.*, Etude, n.d. [late 1899]. [56] *Ibid.*, Etude, March 1901.

speculation by the Banque Internationale and its group, whose goal is to profit from the present favor of the public for all traction companies. The reason for that favor was the legitimate expansion of all those companies, and particularly the very real accomplishments of the Thomson-Houston Company. Today that favor appears to be primarily manipulated by the tricks of speculators."[57]

For a while these tricks appeared eminently successful. The shares of the subsidiary firms rose well above their already inflated par values. The 500-franc shares of the Tramways of Paris and the Department of the Seine went as high as 1,160 francs; the 250-franc shares of the "Metro" (control of which quickly passed to the Belgian Empain group) hit 470; the East Paris Tramways Company's 500-franc shares started at 710, the price at which they were first offered to the public; and West Paris reached 674.

Most startling by far, however, was the Traction Company itself: its 100-franc-par-value shares leaped more than 200 percent to 315 francs in late 1899. At that price, concluded the highly confidential Crédit Lyonnais report, Traction Company shares "were very inflated and extremely dangerous in case of a [financial] crisis." Yet, most significantly, this sharp critic was infected to some extent and was moderately optimistic: if the subsidiaries paid little or no dividends yet, and if their capital was often inflated, and if their fares were unquestionably low, "nevertheless it seems that their worth as a whole is quite real and that their success seems assured." The subsidiaries had "undeniable intrinsic value," and Traction shares were probably worth about 175 francs each.[58]

Another difference from Thomson-Houston was that the Traction Company was willing to accept almost any conditions to outbid its rivals and win concessions. Thus it universally accepted what one state engineer later called the "exaggeratedly low fares" of 15 centimes in first class and 10 centimes in second class for a ride of any distance within

[57] *Ibid.*, Etude, n.d. [late 1899].   [58] *Ibid.*

the Paris city limits.[59] The fare for going beyond the city limits varied, from nothing at all for Left Bank Tramways to an additional 15 and 10 centimes for the West Paris Tramways, with other companies somewhere in between.[60]

Of many examples let us consider only the Left Bank Tramways. On one of the company's lines an unusual passenger could ride twenty-two kilometers from Boulogne on the southwest of Paris to Vincennes on the east of Paris, through modest, predominantly working-class southern suburbs such as Vanves, Montrouge, and Charenton—all for the incredibly low fare of 10 centimes. On another line he could ride twenty kilometers from Montreuil to Boulogne (fourteen kilometers of which were within the city limits of Paris) for the same low fare.[61] Indeed, the Minister of Public Works, Maruéjouls, could state in the Chamber of Deputies in 1902 that "according to my information Paris is the only city in the world where there is such a cheap fare for a ride of more than fourteen kilometers."[62]

As if this were not enough, the subsidiaries of the Traction Company accepted the total prohibition on electric overhead wires *anywhere* within the city limits of Paris. Then they set off to electrify many kilometers with the Diatto surface contact system of electric traction, a supposed simplification of the Claret-Vuilleumier contact method discussed earlier. At best the still experimental Diatto system would be quite expensive; at worst, an expensive failure. The latter proved to be the case.

This result was related to the fact that the men behind the Traction had neither technical experience nor proprietary technology. Nor could the Traction Company expect to earn a profit on its manufacturing operations, since it had

[59] Rousseau, Note, 22 January 1907, AN, F 14, 15023.
[60] CL, Tramways de la Rive Gauche de Paris, notes, 1907, 1911; Tramways de l'Ouest Parisien, Etude, February 1911.
[61] *Ibid.*
[62] Chamber of Deputies, Coutant interpellation, 1902, pp. 2680 ff., in AN, F 14, 15012.

to buy every bit of its equipment and material from unrelated firms. "Owning neither special patents nor its own manufacturing plants, the Traction Company could [in the long run] expect only one basic kind of profit: the profit from advantageously selling shares of profitable operating companies, which it had either founded or equipped in return for the shares it accepted."[63]

All these factors culminated in the ultimate deficiency which punctured the Traction Company's balloon: the disastrous financial results of its operating tramways, in conjunction with a Europe-wide stock-market break in 1900. In that year the three most important of its Paris tramways had operating costs in excess of operating revenues. The Left Bank Company, for example, was spending almost two francs for each one it took in.[64] Nor was the improvement very substantial in 1901 and 1902. Now the Traction Company's speculative directors found themselves with rapidly declining, unsalable shares and a number of half-finished lines. The company could continue construction only by means of large bank loans, totaling 40,000,000 francs, from a syndicate headed by the Société Générale of Paris. This in turn required placing all the Traction's portfolio as security, so that by March 1901—little more than a year after its heady triumphs—the Traction Company existed "only nominally." Its liquidation was considered—quite correctly —"inevitable."[65]

Perhaps it will be reassuring to the moralist that, by every available indication, the speculators grouped around the Banque Internationale de Paris and the English Exploration Company lost heavily in their manipulations with the Traction Company. First and foremost, they were able to sell to the public only a small portion of all the shares of the street railway companies they had founded. For example, the Traction Company, the Banque Internationale de Paris,

[63] CL, Cie Générale de Traction, March 1901.
[64] France. *Statistique des chemins de fer*, 1900, II, 340-43.
[65] CL, Cie Générale de Traction, Etude, March 1901.

the Exploration Company, and their affiliates and directors subscribed at least three-fourths of the 24,000,000 francs raised by the Mechanical Tramways for the Suburbs of Paris Company by September 1899. "There really was no public participation" in the company initially, and this situation had not changed significantly by 1902, according to government investigators.[66]

Similarly, the 12,000,000 francs of the Left Bank Company were subscribed in 1899 by these groups as a "sort of syndicate and the public did not participate. . . . No doubt the syndicate hoped to sell these shares well above par after the company proved profitable in 1900, but circumstances declared otherwise."[67] As the Minister of Public Works, Maruéjouls, put it in answer to Coutant's charge that the Traction Company had defrauded the investing public, it was not the little investor but rather the founders themselves who had been taken as far as the Left Bank Company was concerned.[68] And if the shares of the Traction's largest enterprises, those serving Paris and its suburbs, were "not widely diffused" to the investing public in 1903,[69] the smaller tramways built by the company—at Caen, Châlons-sur-Marne, Eu-Tréport, Mézières, Montpellier, and for the suburbs of Bordeaux—were 90 to 99 percent owned by the Traction Company as late as 1911. Unlike the shares of the Parisian tramways, which to a considerable extent had been sold off at great loss by 1911, the shares of such small companies could not be sold at all.[70]

The founder-speculators were no doubt more successful in selling off some of their own shares in the Traction Company itself, and this counterbalanced to an unknown extent the losses they took directly and indirectly through the

[66] AN, F 14, 15024. Blondel, 25 October 1902.
[67] *Ibid.*, Blondel, 7 November 1902.
[68] Chamber of Deputies, Coutant interpellation, 1902, pp. 2680 ff., in AN, F 14, 15012.
[69] AN, F 14, 15024, Réorganisation des entreprises de tramways de Paris, n.d. [1903].
[70] CL, Cie Générale de Traction, note, February 1911.

Traction Company on the various operating companies. Yet they certainly had little to cheer about. A special shareholders meeting in late 1902, which saw the Traction Company reduce the value of its joint-stock capital by 70 percent, only very reluctantly certified that the founding directors had properly performed their duties and agreed not to bring legal actions against them for any cause. In return, however, the retiring directors agreed to subscribe 1,600,000 francs of new Traction shares, to cancel loans of 4,500,000 francs which they had advanced to the Traction Company for its projects, and to reduce the rate of interest on a large loan (apparently about 20,000,000 francs) from 7 to 3 percent. The founders who had led the firm admitted that they had been incompetent and had exercised bad judgment, at the very least, and paid heavy fines for their behavior.

Yet we must realize that even if the founders of the Traction Company had been models of probity and technical acumen they would have still done rather poorly, unless, of course, they had simply refused to accept the stringent terms the competition for French concessions demanded after Thomson-Houston's early success. This may be seen in the history of the Lyons Tramways Omnium Company, which also sought to emulate Thomson-Houston's successes, as did the Fives-Lille Company, a well-established French producer of heavy equipment.[71]

Founded in early 1896 by substantial and successful capitalists from Lyons, including Edouard de Billy and Louis Neyrand, the Lyons Omnium sought concessions to equip and to operate electric tramways. The firm had solid technical competence, which was considerably strengthened in 1898 when it acquired for stock the tramway construction

[71] In 1896 Fives-Lille was moving into the electric field and had finally reached an agreement for an important electric tramway concession. By the beginning of 1899 it had equipped lines in nine cities: Angers, Avignon, Douai, Le Mans, Lyons, Oran, Rennes, Roubaix-Tourcoing, and Vals-les-Bains. *Economiste Européen* 9 (1896): 11; *IE* 8 (1899): 10 March, Supplement, 10-15.

division of the large Sté Alsacienne de Constructions Mécaniques. That firm was licensed to manufacture and install Siemens equipment in France and had worked closely with the Lyons Omnium from its inception.[72] With such financial and technical assets the Lyons Omnium succeeded in establishing electric tramways in at least nine small cities across France—Fontainebleau, Bourges, Cannes, Saint-Quentin, Poitiers, Cette, Avignon, and Pau.

Unlike the Traction Company, the Lyons Omnium neither inflated the capital of its subsidiaries nor tried to sell the shares of its operating companies to the public. Rather, it directed all its efforts toward creating conservatively capitalized operating companies, which the Omnium planned to own indefinitely. The fact that the results of those operating subsidiaries, concentrated in the smaller cities of France, were quite poor, and that their dividends averaged less than 2 percent, shows how competitive the search for tramway electrification had become. Subsequently, in 1903, the Lyons Omnium reduced its joint-stock capital by 50 percent to 10,000,000 francs, a figure closer to the actual value of its portfolio of tramway shares. From that time on, the company concentrated on electrical contracting and engineering, most notably in connection with the North-South subway line in Paris. These engineering projects were profitable, as were continuing service contracts with the tramway companies. By 1910 the company was paying 8 percent on its reduced capital—or 4 percent on the original capital investment.

3. *The Mature Industry After 1900*

By the end of 1900 only five of the sixty-nine cities of France with a population of more than 30,000 inhabitants did not have their own tramway networks (Montluçon, Rochefort, Saint-Nazaire, Le Creusot, and Montauban). Al-

[72] CL, Sté Omnium Lyonnais de chemins de fer et tramways, Etude, January 1903; Special Shareholders' Meeting, 18 August 1898.

most every conceivable opportunity for electric tramways had been exploited and "the grand period of construction is pretty well closed, at least as far as urban tramways are concerned."[73] Both private entrepreneurs and public officials were now faced primarily with the operation of a mature industry rather than with the creation of a new one.

Another major difference was that the electric tramway industry found itself in a very altered economic climate after 1900. The upright directors of the Lyons Omnium summed up the situation very well for their shareholders in late 1901. "The industrial crisis throughout all Europe, the result of overproduction and speculative excesses, has hit traction companies particularly hard. To the extent that the investing public was seduced by the brilliant profits which the electric tramway industry seemed to promise, so to that same extent has it condemned it on the basis of incomplete results."[74] As tramway shares fell precipitously and turned paper profits into losses, each constructor was hard-pressed to find cash to complete existing contracts. The most recent agreements were often canceled or postponed, as each of the leading firms entered a period of retrenchment.

As mentioned above, the Traction Company was saved from bankruptcy in 1900 only by an emergency construction loan of 40,000,000 francs from the Société Générale. This allowed the Traction Company to fulfill its commitments to its Parisian subsidiaries, but there was never any effort to gain further concessions. Noting investor disfavor, the stringent terms for concessions, and higher-than-expected operating expenses, the Lyons Omnium stated that in the course of 1901 it canceled every possible contract and project, even at the cost of penalties and forfeiture payments. These projects, including suburban lines for Paris, electric tram and light companies for Toulouse, Bucharest, and Tsaritsyn (Russia), would have "given im-

[73] Fuster, *Annuaire Général des Tramways*, 1901, p. 18.
[74] CL, Omnium Lyonnais, Annual Report, 7 December 1901.

portant construction profits, but these engagements would have been able to place our company in a critical situation due to the obligation to make substantial investments at the very moment the public was turning away."[75]

The dominant firm, Thomson-Houston, was subject to the same factors, though its stronger position allowed it to put them in a less damaging light. A new president, F. Guillain, presented shareholders with the need to take an extraordinary loss of 25,000,000 francs in December 1902, in order to reflect more realistically the value of its portfolio of tramway shares. Guillain also acknowledged the fears of his shareholders in the face of the collapse in tramway shares, due mainly to "the difficulties of other companies, which would seem to place even their existence in danger." And he acknowledged that these fears were compounded by the erroneous belief that Thomson-Houston was basically a financial holding company, almost exclusively interested in electric traction. Then—no doubt to the amazement of many shareholders who had responded to management's loudly-trumpeted calls to electrify the tramways of France with more than a hundred million francs—Guillain stated emphatically that there was nothing to this mistaken idea. Thomson-Houston was rather an electrical manufacturer, a manufacturer which had begun with electric tramways but would not stop there. Electric power and lighting were now growing rapidly, for example, and "in reality we are only at the beginning of our development." The financing of subsidiaries was only a temporary expedient, and such subsidiaries would be sold off to the public as they yielded the normal profits of normal operations.[76]

This statement reflects less what Thomson-Houston had been than what it wanted to be, and what it would become. Thus the only important new tramway operations after 1902 were those undertaken in connection with the 1910

[75] *Ibid.*
[76] AN, 65 AQ, G 602², Special Shareholders' Meeting, 3 December 1902.

reorganization of Paris's urban transit. Working together with the Empain interests—indicative of the tendency of major constructors in the industry to cooperate more and compete less after 1900—Thomson-Houston unified the diverse systems of the Tramways of Paris and the Department of the Seine. It also purchased control of the General Omnibus Company in order to transform Paris's most antiquated transit company, as part of the city's general transit reorganization. This was far less than was being invested in electric power companies in the same period.

Even such power company investments were of secondary importance, and increasingly Thomson-Houston was primarily if not exclusively an electrical manufacturer. Until 1908 large electrical equipment, for example, was purchased primarily from America and General Electric. But extensive expansion in all areas before the war meant that by 1914 all the equipment Thomson-Houston sold was made in France, although the technical assistance contracts with General Electric (and A.E.G.) remained a valuable asset.[77] The new orientation was reflected in the profit mix: profits from construction, equipment sales, and patent rights tripled from 2,500,000 francs in 1905 to 6,500,000 francs in 1913; revenue from portfolio investment declined from 2,250,000 to 1,670,000 francs as shares were steadily sold off.[78] Tramways had provided a wonderful launching pad, a launching pad Thomson-Houston was leaving far behind.

The drastically altered conditions of the "tramway crisis" also presented government regulators with a different problem. Now there was no strong tendency toward expansion, particularly between 1901 and about 1904, when the abandonment of a very few lines suggested that a substantial portion of the benefits of greatly increased service achieved in the 1890s were even in danger of being lost. The Vanves to Paris (Champ de Mars) Tramway Company, for example,

[77] CL, Etude du Groupe Thomson-Houston, May 1914.
[78] Ibid.

opened in July 1900 with its costly Diatto system, installed by the general contractor Brancion for a company financed primarily by Belgian bankers and speculators. Even with the extraordinary traffic of the Paris Exposition of 1900, the company ran a large deficit from the beginning. A government expert concluded, after service was stopped in February 1902, that "the line will have to be abandoned and nothing can be done to avoid the company's liquidation."[79]

Yet this remained a very atypical occurrence. Total trackage and passengers carried in France increased substantially. Net receipts from operations almost doubled from 18,700,000 to 33,600,000 francs between 1902 and 1909, while capital invested increased by only 20 percent.[80] On the eve of the war tramways were a well-established but still growing sector (7 percent per annum for receipts), moderately but adequately profitable for the private investors who owned them. That reversals were limited and healthy growth predominated was due in no small part to a continuing strategy of intelligent public regulation.

For the well-managed, solid tramways companies of provincial cities state policy could remain unchanged. All modifications of the capital structure of operating companies, and particularly the sale of first mortgage bonds, were thus scrupulously examined by the state's engineers and required the approval of the Ministry of Public Works. This permitted the state to verify not only that the debt capital did not normally exceed one-half of the capital actually expended, but that interest on such bonds was well covered by net operating profits. This meant that a company like the General French Tramways Company was scrutinized every three or four years on the average, as it needed to raise its stock capital from 4,600,000 in 1894 to 50,000,000 by 1914, when another 66,000,000 francs of its well-secured bonds were also outstanding.[81] The goal, it would seem, was maxi-

[79] AN, F 14, 15024, Blondel, Note, 17 October 1902.
[80] France, *Statistique des chemins de fer*, 1909, II, 796-97.
[81] AN, F 14, 13507, Cie Générale Française des Tramways.

mum expansion of service by the regulated public monopoly consistent with providing a return (5 to 5½ percent on the common stock, 4 to 5 percent on the bonds) capable of attracting private capital. In the smaller cities the capital stock might fare worse, as we have seen, but the bonds were fairly well secured.

The situation at Paris was more complicated. There the machinations of the Traction Company were easily uncovered by state engineers, and in most cases the state compelled the Traction Company to restitute large sums to its operating companies before approving their investment account, a not insignificant factor in the Traction's well-deserved demise.[82] But very low fares, expensive and undependable surface-contact equipment within the city limits, and competition from the very successful underground Metro meant large operating losses for these suburban latecomers in any event. In 1902 a government report lumped them all together as companies "headed toward total ruin."[83] And although the older firms—the General Omnibus Company, the General Paris Tramways Company, and the Tramways of Paris and the Department of the Seine—were much better off, they too were not in a position to attract the capital necessary to complete their transformations. In both cases streetcar service promised to be drastically curtailed, as the private companies would surely go bankrupt if the terms accepted by or imposed on them between 1897 and 1900 were maintained.

Since tramways were an essential public service, however, the city and the department would then be required to take over the bankrupt firms and operate them at a loss, with the taxpayer contributing the difference. Yet the cen-

[82] For example, the State Council refused to accept the substitution of the Traction Company for the original concessionaire on the Montmorency to Enghien line; it also gave up 10 percent of the cost of construction originally agreed upon for the Left Bank Company. See notes by Blondel on these firms in AN, F 14, 15024.

[83] AN, F 14, 15024, Réorganisation des entreprises de tramways de Paris; also, 15023, Note, Rousseau, 22 January 1907.

tral government and the departmental administration were strongly opposed to any such measures.[84] Therefore the only solution to the common problem was to provide "temporary aids," so that the companies could at least meet their daily operating expenses and continue to function until some definitive reorganization of Paris's public transportation was worked out.

This was done in two ways. First, the state permitted the various companies to raise their fares from 15 and 10 centimes in first and second class within the city limits to 20 and 15 centimes on average, with similar increases for the suburban portions. This helped permit the East, West, and Left Bank Companies to move from large operating deficits in 1903 to modest operating surpluses in 1905.[85] Of course the lack of depreciation meant that the companies were only covering their variable costs and that large net losses were still being incurred. But the trams were running and that was the main thing: the shareholder's investment was already irrevocably lost in any event.

The second aid was that the central government belatedly authorized the trolley for much of Paris. The central government had already considered permitting the trolley in the so-called peripheral quarters in 1897, but following the wishes of the municipal council all neighborhoods had been treated equally and the trolley banned throughout the city.[86] After 1901, however, the government overruled the objections of the municipal council and allowed the trolley in large portions of the city.

Thus a governmental investigation in 1902 concluded that tramway operating expenses had to be reduced and that to do so

> it is necessary to authorize the trolley in the peripheral areas of the city. For today it is clear that the only system

[84] AN, F 14, 15024, Conseil Général de la Seine, 7 June 1903, Caplain; also debate on Coutant interpellation, F 14, 15023.
[85] Note 83 above, plus Coutant, letter 16 September 1906, in F 14, 15023, and *Le Temps*, 12 January 1903.
[86] AN, F 14, 15012, Cie des Omnibus, 23 November 1897.

of mechanical traction that works well for intensive service is that with a continuous conductor—either the overhead or the conduit. But the conduit costs 150,000 francs more than the trolley per kilometer. It is admissible only in the center and in those quarters where aesthetic considerations should predominate. In other cases the trolley may be permitted; the overhead conductor, established with elegant poles and without a spider's web of crosswires, is quite acceptable. It should therefore be permitted everywhere beyond the old exterior boulevards, with the exception of the Champs Elysees.[87]

Nor was this concession extended only to the financially weak firms. The Omnibus Company and the Thomson-Houston-backed General Paris Tramways Company were similarly treated, in order that these companies might not simply find themselves unable to raise the capital necessary for their long-discussed electrifications.[88] Not that the central zone was breached: the General Parisian Company, for example, at great expense electrified the entire line from the Etoile to Montparnasse and from Montparnasse to the Bastille with conduit conductors. The point was that the central government balanced reduced aesthetic demands against the goals of maintaining low fares and adequate service. Thus, in spite of the phenomenal success of the Metro, which carried roughly 16,000,000 passengers in 1900 and 312,000,000 in 1909, and in spite of the initial speculative excesses, the tramways of Paris continued to do their job. In 1909 they still carried almost as many passengers (263,000,000) as in 1901 (277,000,000).[89] For that, intelligent public policy deserves much of the credit.

[87] AN, F 14, 15024, Réorganisation des entreprises de tramways de Paris.

[88] For details, see in particular F 14, 15023, on the substitution of electric traction by the Cie Générale Parisienne de Tramways, 1901; and F 14, 15012, the Cie Générale des Omnibus, 1902-1904, and Zone d'établissement du trolley, 1907.

[89] CL, Cie du Chemin de Fer Métropolitan de Paris, Statistical Tables; France, *Statistique des Chemins de fer*, 1901, II, 352-53; 1909, II, 810-11.

To summarize, France offered an outstanding example of the way in which private enterprise, particularly in the form of the leading electrical producers, spread the new transport technology throughout the world. And this was the general pattern: only Great Britain deviated markedly, as we shall see in the next chapter. Seeking large construction profits, the leading electrical producers aggressively competed for old and new concessions, bargained with regulating municipalities over terms, and altered their technologies to reflect noneconomic demands. In all this, public authorities succeeded in winning many marked improvements for their populations.

As for entrepreneurship in France, there was no lack of it in this new industry, in a country where businessmen have often appeared to avoid risk and lack dynamism. There was no lack of entrepreneurship for at least two reasons. First, American entrepreneurs took the lead by founding the French Thomson-Houston Company, which was a joint venture with French businessmen and which was assimilated quite quickly. Thus, to the extent that entrepreneurship might have posed a problem, the foreign component was substituted, at least initially, for domestic deficiencies. Second, the success of the leading firm brought indigenous followers and foreign competitors, who often daringly spread the new transport system. These competitors snapped at the heels of Thomson-Houston and forced the dominant firm to run hard to hold its early position, as late nineteenth-century capitalism functioned effectively.

V. Municipal Enterprise in Great Britain

1. Early Efforts

The numerous, largely unsuccessful attempts with steam tramways, coupled with the fact that British horse tramways had not done as well for their shareholders as "could reasonably be desired,"[1] meant that there was great interest in the American breakthrough in urban transit. From its inception in 1888 *The Electrical Engineer* of London, for example, was fascinated with the possibilities of electric traction and conscientiously reported all proposed or attempted electrification schemes. At the same time this leading trade and professional journal accepted as axiomatic that the technically feasible overhead system was unacceptable for aesthetic reasons.

There was correspondingly a great interest in battery traction, which in September 1888 was judged "likely to prove most useful on English tramways for two reasons: first, because in this country it will be impossible to line the city streets with poles strung with electric wires, and second because it requires no great immediate outlay, nor extensive change of plant. For ordinary city and suburban tramways . . . the accumulator system . . . will be most preferable in every respect."[2] Six months later *The Electrical Engineer* discussed in great detail the first "series" conduit tramway in Europe, at Northfleet: whatever practice in America might be, it was certain that for English towns "accumulator cars carrying their own battery and lines with

[1] A. Dickenson, "Electric Traction," *EE* 6 (1890): 26. If all net operating income had been paid as dividends, tramway shareholders as a group would have received 5¼ percent on their investment. The true rate of return was in fact less, as Dickenson pointed out, because in many instances depreciation rates were unrealistically low.
[2] *EE* 2 (1888): 261.

underground conductors in conduits . . . are alone allowable."[3]

We might wonder if aesthetic conditions were so central and if the multi-faceted experimentation with alternative technologies did not suggest that English technicians were generally unwilling to acknowledge the superiority of overhead conductors on purely technical and economic grounds. This was hardly the case, however. A long paper by Edward Hopkinson, of the firm of Mather and Platt, delivered before the Institute of Civil Engineers, for example, showed how he had successfully perfected his own overhead system to haul freight and passengers on the curious Bessbrook and Newry Tramway in Ireland. Work had begun in July 1884, when Mr. Henry Bercroft of the Bessbrook Spinning Company (whose extensive flax mills and stone quarries were situated at Bessbrook, about three miles from Newry on Carlingford Lough) suggested to Dr. Hopkinson that a line between Newry and Bessbrook for the carriage of coal and flax from the wharves to the mills and the down traffic of manufactured goods might be worked electrically. Employing both third-rail and overhead conductor—the latter for a long crossing of a public highway—the line was successfully opened in October 1885. Hopkinson convincingly showed that operating costs and capital costs were much less for his continuous conductor than would have been the case with battery traction.[4]

In a more general vein another technical man, discussing the different systems of traction in 1891, began by saying that although each had advantages and disadvantages, "most will agree with me that the overhead is most seductive, and if the prejudices of various local authorities could be overcome in districts where the streets are suitable, no

[3] *EE* 3 (1889): 215.
[4] In *EE* 1 (1888): 353-55, 376-78, 400-02, 423-25. Klapper, *Golden Age*, pp. 59-60, considers that "the historical importance of the Bessbrook and Newry is immense," because it led directly to Hopkinson's equipping the world's first underground electric railway in London in 1890.

doubt it would be as suitable in this country as in America."⁵ Nonetheless, it was the different aesthetic perception that led yet another technician to conclude that "In England the storage system in most situations has immense advantages over the overhead systems, in as much as the exterior construction necessary for the latter often would not be tolerated in our towns."⁶

Of the various attempts to find an acceptable alternative technology in battery traction, that of the North Metropolitan was most important, so much so that beside it "other trials pale to insignificance."⁷ Formed in 1869 and experimenting with battery cars as early as 1882 and again in 1887, this large company serving greater London decided to introduce accumulator traction on its Barking Road Line from Canning Town to Plaistow. The system was installed by the General Electric Power and Traction Company. This firm had been occupied with various experimental accumulator lines for some years, as at Southwick and on the West Brighton and Shoreham Tramway in 1887, and was prepared for what it no doubt hoped would be the decisive success. The risks of the General Electric Power and Traction Company were substantial, for it agreed to equip and run six cars for a fixed fee of 4½d. per car-mile for six months, a full 1½d. less than the North Metropolitan's operating costs with horse traction. With moderate inclines and a none-too-smooth track, the one-and-a-quarter-mile section offered battery traction a fair trial.⁸

Many companies were watching this trial in late 1888 "and the favorable certificate would result, without doubt,

⁵ *EE* 6 (1891): 26-27.   ⁶ *EE* 4 (1889): 484.
⁷ Klapper, *Golden Age*, p. 72.
⁸ *EE* 2 (1888): 261-62. The batteries were mounted on sliding trays, lodged under the seats, and could easily be pulled through the detachable side panels at the depot and replaced by recharged batteries. The operation took no more time than changing horses and was easily performed by the same unskilled laborers. Charging of the batteries took eight or nine hours and could run a car for thirty-six miles, or somewhat more than one-half a day's run of fifty to sixty miles.

in a very general adoption of electric traction in English tramways."[9] The results were not unpromising, and the tramway company labeled them "satisfactory" after six months, while requesting Parliamentary sanction to extend the experiment to other lines.[10] The leading trade journal was much more positive.

> The status of the electric car in England may now be considered secure. Other companies will follow suit, and, as with electric lighting, the eventual state of the mother country will not be found behind that of the States, with the double advantage of having a practically thorough and perfect system, not requiring to be altered after a year's use, and without the constant unsightliness of long lines of electric wire posts.[11]

Others were less certain. After a visit to the Canning Town line the chairman of the Wigam Tramway Company concluded that low mechanical efficiency, rapid deterioration of batteries through jolting and variable loads, and the "bad small of unhealthy gases" added up to a system to be avoided.[12] A Glasgow delegation thought fifteen months of operation left "little doubt of the successful issue of the experiment," although there was still the big question of the life of the batteries and therefore the proper rate of depreciation in determining total expense.[13] When the contract with the General Electric Power and Traction Company was renewed in April 1891, however, the North Metropolitan Company agreed to pay 5½d. per car-mile, or 1d. more than previously.[14]

Disappointing costs were matched by regulatory setbacks. Although the North Metropolitan secured a license from Parliament and the London County Council to use electric traction for seven years, the West Ham Corpora-

[9] *EE* 2 (1888): 376; also 3 (1889): 44; 4 (1889): 463.
[10] *EE* 5 (1890): 83.   [11] *EE* 5 (1890): 104.
[12] Report by the Chairman, in *EE* 6 (1890): 185.
[13] Report . . . on Tramways, in *EE* 6 (1890): 361.
[14] *EE* 7 (1891): 402.

tion refused to grant similar terms for lines running through its territory. That corporation stubbornly refused to grant anything more than a temporary license which could be canceled upon twenty-four hours' notice. The Company presented a special bill to Parliament to secure the seven-year license in West Ham but the application was "curtly refused . . . as an attempt, on the part of the tramway authority, to override the local authorities."[15] In the face of these combined difficulties the North Metropolitan precipitately canceled its contract with General Electric Traction in late 1892 and reinstituted horse-drawn service on the Canning Town line. The high hopes of four years earlier had come to naught.[16]

This result contrasted sharply with another widely studied, slightly later experiment with Thomson-Houston overhead equipment on the Roundhay Park line at Leeds. In an excellent example of the demonstration-line technique, the American producer offered in September 1890 to build and equip this new line for the city at its own expense and then remove it if requested, whereas the city would purchase the installation only if fully satisfied. "The Committee [on Tramways] seems not unwilling, but the question of unsightliness or otherwise of the poles and conductors is, as would be expected, the crucial point of the scheme."[17] Yet because the line was fairly long (five and a half miles) and rather suburban in character, running out to the park that "is to become the playground of Leeds," the city accepted the offer.[18] Working up to the very last moment because of bad weather, and without proper shakedown runs, the new line operated perfectly and quickly drew a very large holiday traffic. Proposals for more overhead traction followed, as did great debate over its extent in combination with some conduit traction in the city center.[19]

[15] *EE* 7 (1891): 252.   [16] *EE* 10 (1892): 154.
[17] *EE* 6 (1890): 256.   [18] *EE* 8 (1891): 421.
[19] *EE* 8 (1891): 421, 446-50, 461; 9 (1892): 217, 290, 340; Leeds Tramways Committee Report, in *EE* 15 (1895): 746-50.

These and other experiments, as well as developments elsewhere, resulted in English technical men having made up their minds by 1894 or 1895 at the latest on what had initially been an open and hotly debated question. Thus when the prestigious Institution of Electrical Engineers met in late 1894 and devoted a long session to electric tramways and traction there was "the almost unanimous feeling among the members of the Institution in favor of the overhead trolley system as being by far the best and cheapest in every way."[20] Interestingly enough, this resolution of the technical question actually increased the engineers' frustration (judging by *The Electrical Engineer*), because "it is just this particular method or system which has the hardest battle to fight—the battle against foolish and ignorant prejudice.... There seems a by no means remote possibility that the building and equipment of electric lines will only begin to afford profitable occupation for our children's children after the generation of today has vanished into dust or senility."[21]

There was more to Britain's immobility in tramway electrification in the first half of the 1890s than the conflict between technical and economic expediency on the one hand, and cultural and aesthetic perceptions on the other. The entire institutional structure of British tramway enterprise was uncertain and inadequate. Indeed, as far as tramway development was concerned, any decisive action was stalled in a sort of "institutional blockage." And within that institutional blockage public hostility to the overhead system was increasingly used as a pretext to reject every serious electrification project which private enterprise might advance.

The Tramway Act of 1870 had established that cities could finance and own their tramways but that actual operation had to be vested with private companies. The private tramway company, whether owner-operator or only operator, was limited to a lease of twenty-one years, however. At the end of that time the city was authorized to pur-

[20] *EE* 14 (1894): 715. [21] *Ibid.*

chase the tramways at their physical or "then" value.[22] Obviously companies would not electrify without renegotiated leases. It was also most questionable whether extensions of twenty-one years would be long enough for the full amortization of investment in electric traction. Private interests were urging, therefore, that the law be rewritten to allow the maximum of forty-two years which English electric lighting companies were permitted to negotiate, a period much more in harmony with continental tramway concessions.

An obvious solution lay in renegotiating and extending the basic contract, within the institutional framework of strictly regulated private monopoly. Yet relations between private operating companies and municipal administrations had been deteriorating steadily, and there was widespread public hostility toward the companies in Great Britain. The companies had been increasingly unwilling to make investments and improve service—with battery cars, for example —because their leases were expiring soon; and cities "were then unwilling to grant new leases to companies which they felt had misused their powers, even though the failure of the companies to properly equip their systems was due to their inability to meet the financial burdens incident to the reequipment."[23] Unlike their continental counterparts, British operating companies were also in a weak bargaining position: they could not hold out the alternative of years more of their horse tram service if no agreement were reached.

There was another important difference. British electrical producers were not as concentrated and monopolistically organized as those on the continent or in the United States. This meant that they were relatively weaker and less effective in coaxing and bulldozing city officials into new agreements. In the years between 1890 and the end of 1894 five

[22] Frederic C. Howe, "Municipal Ownership in Great Britain," *Bulletin of the Bureau of Labor*, No. 62 (January 1906), pp. 42-45; Klapper, *Golden Age*, pp. 32-33; Lee, "Tramways of Hull," pp. 14-17.
[23] Howe, "Municipal Ownership," p. 3.

British tramways obtained overhead electric traction from five competing firms with five different systems. Three of these were British firms: Anderson and Munro; the Electric Construction Corporation; and Mather and Platt. Mather and Platt's electric engineering section continued under the direction of Edward Hopkinson, who had electrified the Bessbrook and Newry in 1885 and who made the City and South London Railway the world's first underground electric railway when he completed a third-rail system in 1890. The Electric Construction Corporation had its origins in accumulator traction and was also active with third-rail systems.[24] No doubt both firms were outstanding, but electric traction for street railways was the primary concern of neither. The same thing might be said of the well-established British branch of Siemens and Halske. In 1892 this firm electrified a small line at St. Peter Port, Guernsey, but that was almost ten years after its first third-rail electrification in Ireland and Great Britain in 1883.

This leaves the fifth early supplier, the British Thomson-Houston Company, which opened the Roundhay Park line at Leeds as early as October 1891, as we have seen. Yet although it played an important role in British electric traction, this creation of America's General Electric Company never achieved the commanding position that might have been expected on the basis of the French experience. It was not until 1895 that British Thomson-Houston electrified a second major tramway line at Bristol and began to transform Dublin's system for the Dublin United Tramways Company. Of the forty-one electric railways of all types operating in the United Kingdom at the beginning of 1900 twelve had been equipped by British Thomson-Houston, often working together with other companies. And in only six cases did the company install both the line and the pow-

[24] *EE* 14 (1894): 19; *Electrician* (London), supplement to January 26, 1900; I.C.R. Byatt, "Electrical Products," in Derek Aldcroft, ed., *The Development of British Industry and Foreign Competition, 1875-1914* (London, 1968), pp. 249-50.

er station.[25] Thus, instead of handling all aspects of installation and car building in a standardized way as in France, the British Thomson-Houston tended to be an important subcontractor for motors and electric gear toward which a variety of manufacturing and construction firms often turned.

This lesser role reflected the fact that throughout the 1890s British Thomson-Houston seems to have functioned primarily as a sales agency for imported American equipment from General Electric. It was not until 1902 that it established major manufacturing facilities in Great Britain.[26] Limiting itself in this way, it was hardly likely to exert decisive influence as in France, where the French Thomson-Houston Company represented an ideal marriage of foreign technology with domestic management and capital resources.

The blockage of the early 1890s in British street railway development encouraged some of the most uncompromising critics of the horsecar companies to call for municipalization as the way out of the impasse they had helped create. Municipal ownership and operation of gas and water works had of course become well established in England after Chamberlain's famous initiative at Birmingham in 1873, and England was widely acknowledged as the "classic example" of municipal ownership and initiative.[27] Thus the advocates of municipal tramway operation were well-versed in the basic arguments of the municipal movement.

Three basic arguments seem to have been of particular importance. First, there was the desire to reverse the deterioration of private operation and provide better service for the riding public in all its manifold aspects: lower fares, more frequent and more extended service, more comfort-

[25] *Electrician* (London), supplement to January 26, 1900.
[26] Byatt, "Electrical Products," pp. 250-56.
[27] André Bussy, *La municipalisation des tramways: Ses résultats financiers à l'étranger* (Paris, 1908), p. 3. Also see Sidney Webb's famous *Socialism in England* (London, 1893).

able cars, some kind of mechanical traction, etc.[28] Related to this was the idea of better planning and coordination of all activities related to the streets. No more, for example, would municipalities laboriously tear up and repave their streets in connection with gas or water services, only to see the tramway company repeat in its turn the costly and disruptive process. City engineers and street departments were particularly inclined to make this argument, and their influence was of course considerable.[29]

Second was the economic argument. Tramways were the monopoly of a public necessity, "and, as such, should not be used to put large dividends into the pockets of shareholders."[30] Such profits should instead flow into the public purse. Advocates of municipalization also claimed that better management and maintenance would give profit "in some cases even greater than the company was making for itself."[31] The superior credit rating of cities would permit, for example, lower interest rates on borrowed money, a major factor given the importance of capital requirements in improved transport. This idea—that tramways could make handsome profits and thereby contribute to lower city taxes—was particularly important to business leaders who were by no means doctrinaire socialists.[32]

Third, municipal operation could result in much better wages and working conditions for tramway employees. Rather than simply follow the wage and hours norms for unskilled labor set by the market, as private companies did, municipal tramways could become enlightened pace-set-

[28] Howe, "Municipal Ownership," p. 4, and following interviews with municipal tramway managers.
[29] *Ibid.*, p. 117; Municipal Electrical Association Meetings, 1898, Stewart paper, quoted in *EE* 22 (1898): 18.
[30] Manchester, Special Committee, 1896, in *EE* 17 (1896): 628.
[31] *Fabian Tracts*, No. 33: "The Fabian Municipal Program" (1900), p. 1.
[32] Howe, "Municipal Ownership," pp. 17-18; Bussy, *La municipalisation*, pp. 1-3, 171, 194-97.

ters, exerting real upward pressure on unskilled wage rates that would go far beyond their own workers.[33]

All such arguments were quite hypothetical in late 1893. Only the tramways of Huddersfield were operated municipally at that time, and they only because no private company had been found to lease them.[34] There was still the long-standing Parliamentary prohibition on municipal operation, as well as threatened legal action by some companies over the real meaning of the 1870 law. And there were clearly risks in tramway investment, despite the talk of large profits. Indeed, so great were the forces of inertia that *The Electrical Engineer* could pessimistically conclude in late 1894 that "it is almost certain no change whatever would be made" if British tramways were taken over by municipalities.

If this prediction proved mistaken, it was in no small part due to the model of institutional innovation which the city of Glasgow developed, a model which other cities could seek to emulate. Indeed, it is fair to say that the development of Glasgow's system "had a vast influence on the history of British tramways."[35] What the French Thomson-Houston Company was to France and private enterprise, Glasgow Corporation Tramways was to Great Britain and the entire municipalization movement. As such, it deserves special attention.

2. *The Glasgow Model*

The Glasgow Tramways and Omnibus Company was formed in 1870 in the first tram boom, the result of a merger between two rival company schemes. Almost immediately

[33] Howe, "Municipal Ownership," pp. 4, 65-72; also below and chapter VI.
[34] Roy Brook, *The Tramways of Huddersfield* (Huddersfield, 1959), pp. 13-14.
[35] Robert Crawford, "Glasgow's Experience with Municipal Ownership and Operation," *AAA*, 27 (1906), 27.

the city of Glasgow (Glasgow Corporation) availed itself of the option to build the lines, leasing them to the company for twenty-three years ending in June 1894.[36] The company was to pay the city 4 percent of the total initial capital cost each year plus interest at 3 percent in order to amortize the city's investment during the course of the lease, plus rent of £150 per mile of line in use. Future extensions sanctioned by Parliament were to be paid for in the same manner, although the company had the right to oppose extensions if it felt that they would be unprofitable.

Relations between city and company appear to have been rather poor from the beginning. The company opposed—to no avail—extensions of its lines in 1875, 1879, 1884, and 1885, and the city successfully thwarted an attempt by the company before Parliament in 1887 to enter into nontransportation businesses. At that time, however, the city did agree to negotiate seriously in 1889 with a view toward extending the company's lease expiring on June 30, 1894. Long, heated, and confusing, these negotiations eventually ended in total failure.

Two questions seem to have been crucial. The city was unwilling to consider a renewal of more than five years and wanted the right to take over the lines two years before expiration if it decided to adopt mechanical traction. The city also wanted a sixty-hour work week for tramway employees, who also were to be properly dressed in uniforms provided at company expense. These provisions regarding workers were the most popular with the public, which felt that "poor working conditions made it difficult to get a good class of men on the trams."[37] Though the company might

[36] See James Bell and James Paton, *Glasgow, Its Municipal Organization and Administration* (Glasgow, 1896), pp. 292-303, for early developments; also Klapper, *Golden Age*, p. 211, and Ian Cormack, *Glasgow Tramways, 1872-1962* (Glasgow, 1962).

[37] Testimony of Walter Paton, Chairman, Tramways Committee, Glasgow, HC, 1893-94, XXXIII, Report of Commissioners on labour in agriculture, railways, shipping, canals, docks, and tramways, pp. 126-29; Bell and Paton, *Glasgow*, p. 298.

grudgingly have accepted the clauses concerning working conditions, it was adamant in its refusal to accept an extension of only five years. The result of these abortive negotiations was that by the end of 1889 the city had set its mind on municipal ownership, more than four years before expiration of the Glasgow Tramway Company's lease. Thereafter the city steadfastly opposed the company's attempt to introduce battery traction, even on an experimental basis, while seeking for itself authority to use electricity.[38]

The company fought back as best it could. Against the city's strong opposition it successfully petitioned the Court of Sessions for powers to widen the scope of its articles of incorporation in order to operate omnibuses, cabs, coaches, freight wagons and so forth, in addition to tramways. Thus even though their trams were to pass to the city at an early date, the directors of the company were putting themselves in a position to compete with the Corporation for the street traffic of Glasgow. "They anticipated that with their large capital, their hands free from all Corporation control, and unhampered by mileage rate, sinking fund and other charges, and with liberty to charge such fares as they considered expedient, they would be able to control the passenger traffic of the city. Naturally, they set themselves to encourage their non-tramway trade, and smart 'buses drawn by four horses were placed as models on certain important routes, and off-the-rails traffic was fostered in the most careful and painstaking manner."[39] These moves and ploys were followed with great interest by the public: indeed, the question of municipal working of the tramways figured prominently in local elections of November 1890 and November 1891.

The victory of the advocates of municipalization was strengthened by an opinion of the Attorney General of England to the effect that under the Act of 1870 the city could work as well as own its tramways. Thus in December 1891

[38] *EE* 6 (1890): 492, 515; 7 (1891): 177; 8 (1891): 289, 484.
[39] Bell and Paton, *Glasgow*, p. 299.

the company offered to sell its tramway equipment to the city in 1892.[40] Agreement seemed close, but when the company told its shareholders it also intended to expand its omnibus service to cover the entire city, the Tramways Committee asked that, as a condition for purchase, the company agree not to compete with the city's tramways. The company refused and the city withdrew its proposal. Nor was the company ever to sell any of its cars or horses to the city. Rather, it simply withdrew all its tramways at midnight on June 30, 1894, placing the city in the difficult position of having to begin a complete service with its own equipment the following day. This total lack of continuity between the two operators, indicative of the intense bad feeling, greatly complicated the Corporation's task of starting up its own service. No doubt it was intended to do so.

Adversity had its uses, however, and Glasgow Corporation responded in a way that was to have important consequences for the development of British electric tramways. In early 1894 the new tramways department took over from the city 14,000 square yards of vacant land at Coplawhill, and proceeded to erect its own car barns, stables, workshops, and offices. From the very begining these installations at Coplawhill included a large factory, for they were fully equipped to build as well as repair all the tramcars the department needed.[41] This unusual situation, whereby manufacturing and transportation were joined under the same management, gave Glasgow Corporation a broad scope for enterprise and an excellent opportunity to provide British tramways with badly needed leadership

The tramways department passed its first test successfully. When the cars it had built rolled out on the first of July, it was able "to offer a service little short of that till then conducted by the tramway company."[42] In the mean-

---

[40] D. M. Stevenson, *Municipal Glasgow, Its Evolution and Enterprises* (Glasgow, 1914), pp. 70-71; Bell and Paton, *Glasgow*, 299-300.
[41] *Ibid.*; A. C. Shaw, "Glasgow's Tramway System," *SRJ* 17 (1901): 623-41, especially 639-40; Klapper, *Golden Age*, pp. 215-16.
[42] Bell and Paton, *Glasgow*, p. 301.

time the company blanketed Glasgow with 175 omnibuses, as opposed to the city's 108 tramcars, and on some streets at first outdrew the tramways.[43] From the beginning, however, Glasgow Corporation Tramways introduced half-penny stages of about half a mile, forcing the company's omnibuses to adopt this 50 percent reduction of the minimum fare shortly thereafter. The half-penny fare must have stimulated short rides from citizens who would otherwise have walked, for in the first year of operation almost 40 percent of all fares taken were for that amount.

The city also greatly extended the distance passengers could cover for the old fares and introduced special workmen's fares for early-morning and evening trips. This reduction was all the more remarkable in that it occurred immediately and preceded electrification. Traffic jumped sharply—the second year of municipal ownership saw 60 percent more tramway passengers than had the last year of company operations—and the company was progressively forced to withdraw its omnibuses in total defeat. Glasgow's tramways were thus municipalized only after a bitter struggle with a tough opponent, and they succeeded only after that opponent was beaten once again in a "war to the knife."[44] No doubt this conquering in response to a challenge contributed to the appeal and mysticism of the Glasgow experiment.

From the beginning Glasgow Corporation Tramways implemented other policies in keeping with the avowed intent of better serving the general public interest. The hours of labor were lowered from roughly twelve hours to ten hours per day, and wages per hour were increased by about 15 percent. Drivers and conductors were provided with neat uniforms at no cost and instructed to be polite and obliging.[45] These great improvements meant that by 1905 "the

[43] Ian Cormack, "1894 and All That" (Glasgow, n.d.), pp. 6-7.
[44] Bell and Paton, *Glasgow*, p. 301.
[45] *Ibid.*; Robert Donald, "Success of Municipal Ownership in Great Britain" *SRJ*, 21 (1903), 34-35; Howe, "Municipal Ownership," pp. 72, 89-90.

wages and general conditions are distinctly better than those paid by private employers for a similar kind of service, and the supply of suitable men seeking corporation employment is always far in excess of the demand."[46] Strikes and the threat of strikes were not a problem. All this meant that advocates of municipalization throughout Great Britain could point to improved social relations and better conditions for the working class, in addition to cheaper transport for the riding public.

They soon had a third powerful argument as well: Glasgow municipal tramways made substantial profits for the city, considering the extent of fare reductions and salary increases. Surely this result goes far to explain why tramway municipalization swept all in its path in Great Britain. With all due respect to municipal managerial acumen, however, we must note the effect of extremely favorable purchase terms for the new owners. The Tramways Committee obtained possession of sixty miles of (single) track when the lease expired for only £143,000—the portion of the £345,000 which had been spent by the city after 1870 for the company's account and was not yet repaid by the company. This was only about one-fourth the payment received by the old English company at Bordeaux, for example, which had only thirteen years left on its smaller network. The company at Glasgow received absolutely nothing for its earning power, which was producing a 15-percent profit and a 9.5-percent dividend at the time of expiration.[47]

The financial charges of the past were thus extremely light, and this helped the city earn a surplus of £43,000 in its first year and £83,000 in its second. This meant that the city could write off its small initial investment very quickly. In its annual report of May 1902 the Tramways Committee could state, for example, that "the success which has at-

[46] Robert Crawford, "Glasgow's Experience with Municipal Ownership and Operation," *AAA* 27 (1906): 17-18.

[47] Walter Paton, HC, 1893-94, XXXIII, p. 127; Bell and Paton, *Glasgow*, 302-03.

tended the [tramway] department during the last eight years has enabled the committee, out of revenue, to renew the whole of the track and to write down the disused horse traction plant to scrap value. The capital account, therefore, contains only expenditure applicable to the electric traction system."[48]

The political and ideological decision to establish municipal operation was the fundamental turning-point in Glasgow tramway development. Yet that once-and-for-all decision was simple compared to the complex challenge of technological choice and management.

In early 1890 the Tramways Committee began investigating electricity, visiting accumulator car lines of the North Metropolitan and the Birmingham Tramways that same year, as well as those of Frankfurt, Germany, in 1891.[49] The committee was favorably impressed and on the point of accepting an offer from the General Electrical Power and Traction Company to work accumulator cars for a fixed charge of 4½d. per mile. Unfortunately, the very poor relations between the city and the Glasgow Tramways Company made it impossible to work out the details of this or any other mechanical traction experiments prior to the expiration of the company's lease in 1894.[50] This meant that the city was limited to the consideration of committee reports, tours of inspection, and public discussion. And it encouraged the city to fall back on the technologically conservative alternative of preparing its own horse-drawn system.[51]

[48] Quoted in Donald, *SRJ*, 21 (1903): 34.
[49] *EE* 6 (1890): 3: 305-06; 8 (1891): 397-80.
[50] *EE* 6 (1890): 492; 8 (1891): 289; 9 (1892): 69.
[51] In this connection a Mr. Murphy, connected with the Dublin United Tramways Company stated in early 1896 that according to his experience "Great Britain was behind the whole world in the matter of electric traction." He felt that this "could not be better illustrated than by saying that the city of Glasgow, having acquired the tramways a little more than a year ago, bought a new horse plant to work them instead of an electric plant." *EE* 17 (1896): 714.

The result of continuous investigation was, as might be expected, to discredit accumulator traction but without proving the acceptability of overhead electric methods. Thus the subcommittee visited Leeds's Roundhay overhead line in March 1892, and "was extremely pleased with what they had seen." The cost estimates were firm, whereas those on battery cars had varied enormously.[52] But others intoned the established shibboleth with undiminished conviction. A writer in the *Glasgow Herald* concluded, in a series of articles on the tramway question in October 1892, that overhead wires were acceptable only in suburban areas, as their "absolute unsuitability for heavy city work has been demonstrated." There he felt cable traction was probably most satisfactory.[53] A subcomittee from Leeds found similar opinion three years later in June 1895 among Glasgow's town councillors. "Their general conclusion appears to be that horse haulage should be discontinued as soon as possible, . . . that as between cable and electricity their town is well-suited for cable, that overhead electricity would not suit them in the heart of the city on account of its unsightliness, though it might do in the outskirts."[54]

This predisposition died very hard and was the major factor in postponing until January 1899 the ultimate decision to electrify all lines on the overhead system. True, some members of the Council were opposed even to considering any mechanical system until the city had time to amortize more of its recent investment in horse haulage, but they were a small minority.[55] The basic factor was the hope that the technicians might yet solve the problem with another technological alternative. As one member of the Council put it in August 1896, they were "on the eve of great developments in electric haulage. Perhaps within six months the conduit system might be demonstrated to be the

[52] Report of Tramways Committee, in *EE* 9 (1892): 243; also 10 (1892): 322.
[53] Quoted in *EE* 10 (1892): 463-64.
[54] Report, June 1895, as quoted in *EE* 15 (1895): 747.
[55] Report and discussion in *EE* 16 (1895): 306-07.

best."⁵⁶ Thus the tentative decision which had just been made to equip a short section from Springburn to Mitchell Street with overhead wires was sent back to the committee. Public hostility was clearly important, as the self-criticism of Walter Paton, an overhead supporter, showed. According to Paton, the English public unfortunately did not know much about electric traction and therefore the committee had possibly made a mistake in going too rapidly when they should have been educating the public.⁵⁷ It was not until October 1898 that the Springburn line was finally opened, with overhead trolley wires, on an experimental basis.

Good initial reception to the line permitted John Young, the famous general manager of the Glasgow Corporation Tramways, to push successfully for the decision of January 5, 1899, to electrify all tramways lines with overhead wires whenever suitable. At the same time a long-studied electric conduit line was held in reserve as a possible experimental line, which the Council might immediately implement if it chose to do so.⁵⁸

Young clearly leaned toward a city-wide trolley system, but he presented fairly both sides of the case for the final decision. The disadvantages of underground conductors—higher capital costs, the difficulties inherent in mixed systems, and the great interference with the streets during construction—were all stressed by Young, as might have been expected. Yet, on the basis of the most favorable assumptions, he concluded that the total price of these deficiencies might not exceed 1d. per car mile, or about 16 percent more than the 6¼d. eventually obtained with trolley conductors by 1901. And no one, said Young, would disagree with the tramway committee report of July 1896, which stated that "All things being equal, a system which provides the power without any overhead wire is preferable." How close then was 1d. more per car mile to equality? And was "the gain, which is almost entirely aesthetic,

⁵⁶ Quoted in *EE* 18 (1896): 195. ⁵⁷ *Ibid.*
⁵⁸ Special Report by John Young, in *SRJ* 15 (1899): 39-40.

worth the difference?"[59] Seldom did public authority have a better chance to weigh technological alternatives in the light of the societal values it reflected and formed. Perhaps this is precisely the key to the responsible management of technology in democratic societies, and perhaps Young's mastery of it goes far to explain his great reputation and influence.

Young also followed the continental practice and showed that the unsightliness of overhead construction was not a constant. Thus, in equipping the Springburn route in 1898 he used three different methods of supporting trolley wires: side poles, with a set on each side of the street; center poles with crossbars to serve both tracks; and brackets for span-wires attached to the buildings on either side. Opinion was strongly in favor of the bracket method, which was then specified wherever possible throughout the city. Exceptionally, where the street was too wide, as on Glasgow Bridge or the Great Western Road, ornamental steel center-pole construction was used, with electric lamps atop the masts. The visual effect was agreed to be much more handsome than side-pole construction, which was almost totally avoided. Feeder lines were all underground, though feeder pillars of cast iron were of necessity placed at the edge of the sidewalk at the feeder points. But after all the debate and delay there was no battery or conduit traction on the entire "magnificent system" of electric tramways.[60]

Glasgow drew heavily upon American technology, but it was not subservient to American enterprise. The primary contractor for the new track and tasteful overhead construction was Macartney, McElroy and Company of New York, which used Westinghouse electrical equipment from the United States. All the equipment for the power station was also manufactured in the United States and installed by British Westinghouse Electric. Westinghouse was now

[59] *Ibid.*
[60] A. C. Shaw, "Glasgow's Tramway System," *SRJ* 17 (1901): 623-41 for details and photographs.

competing effectively with Thomson-Houston in Britain as well as with General Electric in the United States, and Glasgow was using this competition to its advantage. The city also purchased American equipment and technology to the extent necessary in order to manufacture all the electric streetcars it required in its own workshops at Coplawhill. Thus the electrical equipment for the cars came mainly from the world-famous J. G. Brill Company of Philadelphia, while the bulk of the other materials were British. By the middle of 1901 the 400 employees at Coplawhill had built more than 300 electric cars and converted many of the old horsecars to electric traction.[61] Subsequently, the city continued to build and overhaul all its own cars and remained a major manufacturer in the industry. In short, the municipal tramway system of Glasgow purchased advanced foreign technology to fit its specifications at competitive prices when that was expedient, and continued to rely on its own skill and initiative for operations.

No doubt this combination contributed to Glasgow's success as "a great system in the best sense, led by inspired management and giving a service of very high quality."[62] And, indeed, all the indicators were very favorable. Substantial profits flowed into the Common Good Fund each year. Fares were sharply reduced. In 1894 there was no half-penny fare, and the average for 1d. was 1.1 miles. By 1905 a half-penny fare allowed a ride averaging 0.6 miles, and a penny purchased 2.3 miles, on average.[63] The tramway network had increased from sixty miles of line to 196 miles in 1914, with a total of 239 miles planned. This increase had contributed to a third zone of suburbanization extending up to ten miles from the city center.[64] Finally, the citizens of Glasgow averaged riding the tramways fully 271

[61] *Ibid.*   [62] Klapper, *Golden Age*, p. 216.
[63] Crawford, *AAA* 27 (1906): 15; Donald, *SRJ* 21 (1903): 34.
[64] *Municipal Glasgow*, p. 60; Michael Simpson, "Urban Transport and the Development of Glasgow's West End, 1830-1914," *JTH*, new series, 1 (1972): 153.

times per year in 1913, or three and one-half times more often than a generation earlier, in 1887.[65] This meant that Glasgow stood well above all other British cities in per capita usage—a handsome tribute to Scottish enterprise and Glasgow's enduring leadership.

3. *The New Institutional Framework*

The success of Glasgow, first with its own horsecars and then with its trolley cars, encouraged widespread emulation. As one American enthusiast put it, "the signal achievement of Glasgow has never been equalled by any company. . . . There was never such a quick transition or such a splendid object lesson in the superiority of municipal management."[66]

Followers were also strengthened because the ambiguities of the 1870 Tramway Act were resolved in favor of municipalities. First, "then" value was determined to be essentially scrap value, so that in the case of the London Street Tramway Company the court awarded the company only one-sixth of what it had claimed.[67] Second, the standing order against the introduction of bills to provide local authorities with exceptional authority for the working of tramways was eliminated after 1896, and such petitions were favorably received.[68] Thus whereas 32 tramways were owned by local authorities in 1892 and 42 in 1897, 70 were so owned by 1900 and 174 by 1904. Of that 174 roughly two-thirds were also operated by local authorities, whereas only four had been through 1896.[69] This trend continued:

[65] Manchester, Tramways Department, *The Passenger Transportation Problem* (Manchester, 1914), p. 89. See chapter VII for extended discussion on suburbanization and per capita usage.

[66] Donald, *SRJ* 21 (1903): 33.

[67] Howe, "Municipal Ownership," p. 43; Massachusetts, *Report on . . . Street Railways*, pp. 78-80.

[68] *Fabian Tracts*, No. 33, pp. 1-3. See the introduction of a bill to facilitate the working of tramways by local authorities, HC, 1893-94, VIII, p. 381, for an indication of the change in spirit.

[69] HC, Tramway Reports, various years; *Municipal Year Book*, 1906, p. 392.

in 1911 local authorities were operating 90 percent of the trackage they owned, and they were carrying four times as many passengers as private companies.[70] Local authorities also had the large and potentially profitable networks; only marginal urban enterprises and some light railways running through a number of political jurisdictions were in private hands.

The great preponderance of public ownership meant that British electric tramways never became captive markets for electrical producers, which always lacked the ownership and control necessary to assure sales at noncompetitive prices. Rather, municipalities were able to shop around and buy their equipment at the best price from any of several sellers. British industry remained relatively fragmented at the beginning of the twentieth century, and a whole series of companies were active as prime contractors for electric traction. The American-based firms, British Thomson-Houston and British Westinghouse, plus Siemens Brothers, the Brush Electrical Engineering Company, and Dick, Kerr and Company were probably most important; but the British Insulated Wire Company, the Electric Construction Corporation, Macartney, McElroy and Company, Mather and Platt, R. W. Blackwell and Company, and several smaller firms were also active.[71] The existence of several sellers in a highly competitive market—British Thomson-Houston and British Westinghouse averaged net profits of less than 3 percent on invested capital between 1903 and 1913[72]—enabled municipal managements to drive good bargains with suppliers. The principal drawback of this municipal independence or even dominance was probably the lack of standardization and the unnecessarily wide variation in design of tramway equipment, which Byatt has observed in the analogous municipally owned electrical utili-

---

[70] Bussy, *La municipalisation*, p. 191; *Municipal Year Book*, 1913, p. 626-27. See also table 4 above.

[71] *Electrician* (London), supplements to January 26, 1900, and January 24, 1902.

[72] Byatt, "Electrical Products," pp. 262-63.

ties.[73] Yet lack of standardization does not appear to have posed major difficulties.

Indeed, it probably reflected the fact that British municipalities developed competent if somewhat idiosyncratic specialists and procedures to manage their transport enterprises. Let us take, for example, the guidelines given by the borough engineer J. E. Stewart of Derby to the annual meeting of the Municipal Electrical Association in 1898 on the crucial question of how best to take over existing private companies.[74] Stewart advised local authorities to purchase their respective tramway companies about three years before the operating company's lease expired. The disadvantage of paying two or three years of dividends would be more than compensated for by the advantage of eliminating the possibility of the sneaky company maneuvers that advocates of municipalization seemed to expect. For example, the company might lay a whole system of new rails, purposely unsuitable for power traction, in order to make "the purchase as expensive as possible" and thereby "choke off" a city waiting until the last minute. Quick action was much cheaper.

As for the managerial problem, the key lay in preventing confusion and friction between the new city tramway department, which would be the city's largest purchaser of power, and the existing municipal electric power department, the unique seller of electricity. The best arrangement was to have a committee of councilmen charged with setting fair and proper terms for transactions between the two departments, which would be considered as working subcommittees. In the broader context, these concerns, and those of countless similar papers before the Municipal Tramway Association, which began in 1902, show the devel-

---

[73] *Ibid.*, pp. 271-73. For a capsule view of British diversity see the surveys of all functioning electric tramways in *Electrician* (London), supplements to January 26, 1900, and January 24, 1902; also Klapper, *Golden Age*, a wealth of information on local peculiarities.

[74] See *EE* 22 (1898): 17-19.

INSTITUTIONAL FRAMEWORK 187

opment of dedicated managers capable of exploiting the opportunities before them.

This goes with a related point. In spite of all the initial hostility, almost all British towns and their managers adopted the overhead system when they finally faced up to operating their own tramways. Indeed, only in London was the scope of the electric wire successfully limited, as horse trams themselves had previously been excluded from the center of the city. Glasgow's unbroken overhead system was the model. Birmingham, for example, which showed a desire to have all its lines equipped with conduit traction but which would not grant a forty-two-year lease to a private company willing to follow these wishes, finally took over operation of its network in 1904 and proceeded to equip all lines with overhead wires.[75] The period of successful municipal operation after 1900 was in the end a period of the ubiquitous overhead system.

The reason for this, in addition to the modifications to placate aesthetic sensibilities and to assure more trouble-free maintenance, was that "properly installed" overhead systems allowed municipalities not only to improve service but also to earn ardently desired "surpluses." These surpluses—a euphemism for profits—could then be turned over to the city, perhaps to reduce taxes. Indeed, by 1910 British municipal tramways were turning over about £280,000 to town councils after having met all operating and financial expenses on a total investment of roughly £50,000,000. It seems that with municipalization voters and public officials considered the economic costs and benefits of alternative technologies, and learned to act very much like the supposedly rapacious shareholders and directors they had so often castigated.

Some thought far too much so for the good of public transport. In the years before 1914 the meetings of the Municipal Tramways Association saw its members increasingly

[75] Massachusetts, *Report on . . . Street Railways*, pp. 142-43; Klapper, *Golden Age*, p. 150.

concerned with municipal efforts to extract large profits from tramways and the possible consequences of such action. Unfortunately, said one tramway expert, the

> process of milking is applied . . . to all prosperous municipal undertakings. Every authority has someone who is responsible for levying the rates. This individual . . . is designated the "chancellor of the exchequer." It appears to be a general practice of his to swoop down upon any pecuniary balance capable of appropriation, for the purpose of reducing the rates. The more he can "hypothecate," the better "chancellor" he is, and, acting upon this assumption he attacks any surpluses made by an undertaking, more often than not without the consent of, or, for that matter, even consulting the manager or committee concerned. This is a very unsatisfactory state of things, for he may be starving the undertaking and thereby depriving the travelling public of something which is necessary to their security. . . . Necessary renewals or renovations may therefore be neglected or postponed, involving a serious disregard of the trust reposed in the committee.[76]

"Milking," "depriving the public," "financial attack," etc.—here were the echoes of criticisms against private companies.

Various factors contributed to these misgivings, but none was more central than that of overstating surpluses because of inadequate depreciation. Obviously if depreciation—the amount set aside for the eventual rebuilding and replacing of lines and equipment—were less than necessary, then surpluses would be artificially and incorrectly inflated. In such cases committees might "hand their surplus over to the rates" and bring themselves "a great deal of eclat," only to force future committees "to levy a rate so that the system may be again put into proper working order." This would mean that "the ratepayers of one period should have to

[76] S.C.T. Neumann, "Tramway Administration by Municipalities," *MTA*, 1911-12, p. 62.

make good that which had been unwisely given to the ratepayers of the past."⁷⁷ The implication was clear: British municipal tramways might in fact be much less a financial success than they were trumpeted to be.

The question was complex, but a complete investigation on this subject in 1910 by J. H. Rogers, Chairman of the Newcastle Corporation Tramways, reached the conclusion that this was the case for "several of our Tramway Committees." According to Rogers, only thirty of the cities paying surpluses were depreciating adequately. On the basis of the same criterion another fourteen municipal tramways were showing "fairly good" results. Yet in Rogers' opinion the tramway committees of these cities "were not justified in paying the amounts they did toward the rates, taking into full consideration the low state of their Reserve and Renewal Funds." A third group of sixteen municipalities was reporting small gross operating profits, but depreciation was inadequate. They were considered to be in an unsound financial position, though not as bad as that of the fourth and last group of municipal tramways, which had gross operating deficits. In short, in 1910 only about one-third of British municipal tramways were generating fully adequate funds to maintain operations properly in the long run. One can see how systems might run down rapidly, until the moment that they had to be either scrapped or rebuilt completely—with very inadequate or even nonexistent funds for renewal.

Speaking from considerable experience as a practical municipal tramway administrator, Rogers believed that the basic reason for this worrisome financial situation was that municipal tramways were not operating on "purely business lines" as self-sufficient enterprises. Furthermore, "any Chairman or Manager will tell you that at the present time it is almost impossible to do this." Instead the members of Councils voted away profits to the relief of rates, irrespec-

[77] J. H. Rogers, "Tramways Finance and Policy," *MTA*, 1910-11, p. 94.

tive of renewal requirements, or else they argued that such surpluses go toward ever more frequent and ever cheaper transportation. "This may please their constituents for the time being, and perhaps that is all they really care about, but the time will undoubtedly come when many will have good cause to regret it."[78] The future was being sacrificed for the present by politicians who were *too* responsive to the immediate wishes of the people.

In this British municipal tramways as a group failed to follow Glasgow, which by 1903 clearly offered

> the best example of municipally controlled tramways in Great Britain, the tramway committee having adopted rather different tactics in its management from those of other cities. The true reason of Glasgow's success in tramway management is undoubtedly owing to the fact that the municipality, through its tramway committee, has placed the entire management of its system in the hands of one man, John Young, who occupies the position of general manager, and who really runs the tramway department as if it were a private company, and is independent, to a very large extent, from the meddling of committees, the division of authority, and the petty annoyances which thus arise, particularly from political aspirants.[79]

Thus indecisive, bickering, and politically preoccupied management combined with and contributed to the inadequate depreciation and the shortsighted financial planning to create serious problems in the minds of some British experts.

It seems likely that these problems played a significant role in the decline of electric tramways in Great Britain, which began in the 1920s and 1930s. In those sorry years and after, the British, unlike some continental nationalities, foolishly matched the Americans in their devotion to the

[78] *Ibid.*, p. 103.   [79] Shaw, *SRJ* 17 (1901): 636.

cause of rooting up magnificent street railway systems in the name of short-term financial expedience. Like the Americans, they would leave themselves dependent upon noisy, dirty internal combustion engines with their insatiable demand for increasingly expensive petroleum. Before 1914 such problems were only small clouds on a distant horizon, however, and there was plenty of time to take proper precautions.

For most, then, the British innovation of city-owned and operated tramways was a great success, a success that joined genuine concern for the public and profitable operations in happy harmony. The establishment of new institutional arrangements had made British municipal tramways a new model for urban transport.

After 1900 this model was diffused throughout Europe, where every leading country except France municipalized at least some of its street railways, and it was studied with interest and even awe in the United States. Paradoxically, slow-to-electrify Britain became a pioneer in her own right with a new institutional model for urban transportation. For many "progressive" people this put her clearly in the lead in this area in the first decade of this century, and more than compensated for the hesitations and conflicts that made her a laggard in the 1890s. As in other questions of change and development, judgments will vary with the criteria used.

VI. The Impact on Society

A revolution—even a public transit revolution—is hardly worthy of the name unless it goes beyond its own domain and produces important consequences in other areas of human experience. Without such subsequent effects the "revolution" is probably better termed an invention, a noteworthy change, or an evolution, as the case may be. What, then, were some of the consequences of the adoption and development of electric traction, and to what extent were they profound and revolutionary? This chapter is a response to these questions: an attempt to show some of the ways in which electric streetcars had a major impact on European society. At the same time we must remember that the whole question of the social impact of European urban transportation has been neglected. The following findings are no doubt somewhat preliminary, and more nearly the first word than the last.

1. *The Riding Public*

The first and most obvious consequence was that public transport came to occupy a much greater place in the daily life of urban inhabitants. Whereas horsecars were used with any degree of frequency in only a few of the largest European cities in 1890, as we saw in chapter 1, the electric streetcar was used intensively and increasingly as an indispensable service by the broad masses of urban population. As a newspaper in one small English city put it after a typically successful electrification, "trams have ceased to be a luxury and are now a necessity of town life."[1]

Perhaps the best way to see this is to look at per capita use of streetcars—what contemporaries termed "the growth

---

[1] *Keighley News*, early 1904, as quoted by J. S. King, *Keighley Corporation Transport* (Huddersfield, 1964), p. 20.

of the riding habit." Generally speaking, we find that in the years immediately preceding the First World War every urban inhabitant of large and medium-sized European cities was using electric streetcars roughly *four times* as much as he had used horse trams a generation earlier. That is, whereas the European city dweller was averaging between a low of 20 and a high of 80 tramway rides per year when Von Lindheim studied the situation at the end of the 1880s, the city dweller was riding from roughly 80 to 270 times per year in 1913. So great was the growth of the riding habit.

In Great Britain, for example, three leading provincial cities averaged only 50 rides annually per head in 1887: Glasgow, 61; Liverpool, 51; and Birmingham, 37.[2] In 1913 the magnificent municipal tramways of Glasgow, those pace-setters for a nation, were carrying each member of its population 271 times per year, while the figures for Liverpool and Birmingham were 187 and 149 respectively, giving an average for the three of 202.[3] Other major provincial cities were within this range, so that when Manchester (201), Leeds (179), Sheffield (207), Nottingham (146), and Bradford (174) were included, the arithmetical average of the eight British cities was 189 rides per year per head in these cities in 1913.

The same leaps can be noted for the major continental cities, although the data are very incomplete. It seems preferable therefore to concentrate upon the German Empire and to present fairly complete figures on the growth of the riding habit in all large German cities between 1890 and 1910. These figures, processed and grouped together for the first time, are presented in table 9.

As this table shows, use of streetcars not only increased dramatically, but tended to vary directly with the size of the city. Therefore, if the arithmetical average in 1910 for

[2] United States, Census, *Transportation Business, 1890*, I, 684.
[3] Manchester, Tramways Department, *The Passenger Transportation Problem* (Manchester, 1914), pp. 89-90.

Table 9

STREETCAR RIDES PER CAPITA IN LARGE GERMAN CITIES[a]

Cities	1890	1895	1900	1910
Berlin	91[b]	96	135	229
Bremen	34	46	74	126
Breslau	23	49[c]	73	139
Chemnitz	9	30	58	91
Cologne	31	49	73	188
Dortmund	20	28[c]	56	93
Dresden	53	117	187	205
Duisberg	14	16	65	66
Dusseldorf	14	32[c]	89	159
Essen	—	42	109	115
Frankfurt	79	117	122	221
Hamburg	86[b]	83[c]	112	133
Hannover	47	60	88	169
Kiel	14	27[c]	37	71
Konigsberg	19	30	48	61
Leipzig	48	65	143	189
Magdeburg	47	45[c]	96	111
Munich	53	62[c]	92	173
Nuremberg	28	33[c]	57	111
Stettin	—	24[c]	52	81
Stuttgart	36	47	80	136
Average:	39	52	88	137

SOURCE: 1890, 1895, N. Neefe, ed., *Statistisches Jahrbuch Deutscher Städte* 4 (1894): 96; 7 (1898): 144-47. 1900, 1910, *Ibid.*, for total rides; population from *Statistisches Jahrbuch für das Deutsche Reich*; my calculations for rides per capita and the arithmetical average of rides per capita in all these cities.

[a] Cities with population of more than 200,000 in 1910.

[b] Does not include Charlottenburg for Berlin, nor Altona for Hamburg.

[c] Does not include subscription tickets (*Abonnement-Fahrten*).

all urban agglomerations with population over 200,000 was 137 rides, the average for those over 400,000 (Berlin, Breslau, Cologne, Dresden, Frankfurt, Hamburg, Leipzig, and Munich), at the same time, was substantially higher—185 tramway rides per person. Nor had per capita tramway usage reached the limit of its development; in fact, it continued to rise until 1914, and indeed into the early 1920s in most cities.

In short, growth in per capita usage in Great Britain and Germany was quite similar. In both cases there was the same fourfold increase in the average large city, from roughly 50 to about 200 rides per person per year, in the course of the generation that saw electric trams replace horsecars. When we remember that about 300 rides per capita seems to have been an historical, "demographic maximum" for even the largest cities with the most highly developed public transit, then it is clear just how profound a change this growth represented.

This growth in per capita usage becomes even more impressive when it is placed in perspective by means of comparison with that in the United States in the same period. In 1890, streetcar usage in the United States exceeded that in Europe by a very wide margin. This greater usage clearly reflected the long-standing leadership of the United States in the development of urban public transport, for although electric traction was spreading rapidly it still accounted for less than 7 percent of passengers carried in the census year ending June 30, 1890. Yet within the twenty-seven metropolitan areas of the United States with population over 100,000 in 1890, the geometric average of street rides per capita per year in these cities—which included cable and elevated railways as well—was already 172 and the arithmetical average was 143.[4] The range was considerable. There were five cities with over 200 rides per capita: Boston and suburbs (225), Denver (202), Kansas City (286), New York (297), and San Francisco (270). Nine were under 100 rides: Baltimore (94), Buffalo (63), Indianapolis (94), Milwaukee (71), Minneapolis (89), Newark (91), Omaha (85), Rochester (85), and St. Paul (84); 13 were between 100 and 199.

[4] United States, Census, *Transportation Business, 1890*, I, 683-84.

Primarily on the basis of von Lindheim's data on the riding habit in Europe circa 1887, the 1890 American transportation census went on to compare American and European patterns of usage. The census admitted that "comparisons much to our disadvantage are frequently made between street railway systems of our own and foreign cities, the grounds of conclusions favorable to the foreign service being that it is managed with more regard for public convenience and made to contribute more to municipal expense." But with evident pride in the American achievement the writer concluded that in their "most important function"—that of carrying passengers—"our lines have attained a development unapproached in Europe.... In the average number of rides per inhabitant the highest number given for a foreign city [of more than 300,000] is little over one-half the lowest figure among the American cities [of the same size]. The street railway system of Berlin, justly regarded as the most perfect in Europe, carried in proportion to the inhabitants of the city less than one-third as many passengers as the city of New York."[5] Indeed, when the German arithmetical average in table 9 is compared with the American average, it seems clear that the urban inhabitants of Germany were using street railways only about *one-fourth* as often as their American urban counterparts in 1890. Unquestionably, European usage lagged far behind and tramways played a much smaller role in European urban life.

By 1910 the electric tramway revolution in Europe had created a totally different situation and relative standing. Unfortunately, direct comparison is difficult, because beginning in 1902 the published American street railway censuses used either the individual states or the entire urban population, as opposed to cities or metropolitan areas for the relevant geographical unit.[6] Thus I have been able to

[5] *Ibid.*, 685.
[6] United States Bureau of the Census, *Special Reports: Street and Electric Railways*, published at five-year intervals from 1902.

find annual rides on public transit (mainly but not exclusively street railways) for only the four largest American metropolitan areas in 1910, which are compared with similar European metropolitan areas in table 10.

Table 10

ANNUAL RIDES PER CAPITA ON PUBLIC TRANSIT

Year	1890	1910
American Cities		
Greater New York	233[c]	330
Chicago	164	285
Boston and suburbs	225	280
Philadelphia	158	275
Average	195	293
British Cities		
London and suburbs[d]	74[a]	245[b]
Glasgow and suburbs	61[a]	271[b]
Manchester and suburbs	38	201[b]
Liverpool	51[a]	187[b]
Average	56	226
German Cities		
Berlin	91	226
Dresden	53	205
Cologne	31	188
Leipzig	48	189
Average	56	203
Vienna	43[a]	175

SOURCE: American cities: U.S., Census, *Transportation Business, 1890*, I, 684-85; F. W. Doolittle, *Studies in the Cost of Urban Transportation Service* (New York, 1916), p. 254. English cities, von Lindheim, *Strassenbahnen*, p. 6; Manchester, *Passenger Transportation Problem*, pp. 89-90. German cities, table 9. Vienna: von Lindheim, p. 7; Doolittle, p. 254.

[a] 1887.

[b] 1913.

[c] New York City, Brooklyn, Newark and Elizabeth, Jersey City and Hoboken combined.

[d] Includes underground and omnibus traffic.

The comparison is very striking. Whereas American per capita usage in the largest cities increased by about 50 percent between 1890 and 1910, European usage jumped roughly 300 percent in the same period. In short, much more rapid European growth meant that the great quantitative gap of 1890 had largely disappeared on the eve of World War I.

Qualitative data confirm these quantitative data regarding Europe's closing of the urban transport gap. Indeed, there is ample evidence that Americans looked increasingly to Europe for leadership and direction in street railway matters, and that, all things considered, America itself was beginning to fall behind.

Take, for example, the transit views of a typical American progressive like Frederic Howe. Beating the drum for municipal reform, Howe was impressed by British tramways at an early date, and by 1913 he found almost every aspect of European urban transport far in advance of American practice.[7] By socializing the means of transport, some German cities and almost all major British cities had transformed a private business into a social agency. And even when German street railways were in private hands, as in Berlin, Howe graded the service as excellent. Of course municipal ownership was superior, even when the most rigid regulation was possible. For regulation could touch "only the evils of overcapitalization, excess charges, and obviously bad service," without permitting the city to plan and build its transport facilities in a farsighted way.[8] The complaints of an increasingly frustrated, defensive, and less profitable American streetcar industry from about 1900 on showed that this type of criticism was widespread.[9]

[7] "Municipal Ownership in Great Britain," *Bulletin of the Bureau of Labor*, No. 62 (January 1906), 1-123; *European Cities at Work* (New York, 1913), pp. 177-88.

[8] *Ibid.*, p. 179.

[9] The hostile environment as a cause for decline, recently set forward by Albro Martin regarding American railroads (*Enterprise Denied: The Origins of the Decline of American Railroads* [New

Nowhere, perhaps, was the turning of the tide and the new wave of criticism more apparent than in Chicago, a paradigm of American vigor and corruption—and not just in streetcars. There Charles T. Yerkes succeeded in forming one of the very largest consolidated street railway systems in the country in the late 1880s and early 1890s, a buccaneering achievement of heroic proportions which inspired a great trilogy—Theodore Dreiser's fictionalized account of Yerke's career.[10] There also raged "a continual warfare between the companies and the people of the city" from about 1895 to the final settlement in 1907.[11] And, indeed, there was also a war between the people of Chicago and their elected city officials, who were widely suspected of being tools of the streetcar interests and all too eager to extend—for a consideration—the original twenty-year franchises for another ninety-nine years.[12]

So strong did popular feeling become that a reform mayor, Judge Edward Dunne, was elected by a substantial majority in 1905 on the platform of immediate municipal ownership of all street railways. Clearly those Americans like Robert P. Porter, who had been ridiculing for years the results of municipal tramway ownership in Great Britain in general and Glasgow in particular as grossly inferior to the "magnificent systems" of the United States, were in full retreat.[13] The British-launched and perfected municipali-

York, 1971]), was often present in the frustrations and apprehensions of street railway managers. See, for example, *ASRA*, Annual Meetings, 1900, 48-51; 1901, 64-68; 1911, 245-46; and Thomas Conway, Jr., "The Decreasing Financial Returns upon Urban Street Railway Properties," *AAA* 37 (1911): 14-30. On the other side see Wilcox, *Municipal Franchises*, for an encyclopedia of alleged abuse.

[10] *The Financier, The Titan, The Stoic*; also see Miller, *Fares, Please!*, pp. 106-07.

[11] Wilcox, *Municipal Franchises*, 2: 148-49.

[12] Ralph Heilman, "Chicago Traction: A Study of the Effects of the Public to Secure Good Service," *American Economic Association Quarterly*, 3rd ser., 9:2 (July 1908): 1-97.

[13] Robert P. Porter, "Statement in Relation to Municipal Ownership and Operation of Street Railways in England," in Mass., *Report*,

zation movement was finally spreading to the United States, where many saw it as the institutional equivalent of the earlier technological breakthrough to electric traction—and just as needed.

Thus it was fitting that good Mayor Dunne and the people of Chicago turned toward the mecca of municipal ownership and asked the general manager of Glasgow Tramways, James Dalrymple, to visit Chicago and give his advice. The famous Scottish tram man inspected carefully and then did not mince words. "The present tramway system of Chicago is, comparatively speaking, altogether out of date, and it has been rapidly going downhill in recent years from various causes. There is no wonder that the inhabitants are intensely dissatisfied with their transit facilities." One of the principal reasons for the decay, according to Dalrymple, had been "the disputes between the municipality and the tramway companies in regard to franchise and other matters. . . . In the light of the experience of other cities, the citizens not unnaturally look to a municipalized system as providing the best way out of the difficulty." Still, Chicago in 1905 provided "a really magnificent opportunity . . . and it has all the makings of the finest electric tramway system in the world."[14]

But not necessarily with municipal ownership, according to Dalrymple. "I should be very sorry, however, were you forced to take such a step, as, speaking generally, I should say, from my knowledge and experience of what it means to operate a municipal street railway system, that the municipalities of the United States are not quite ready to successfully undertake this work."[15] In short, Dalrymple ended by accepting the industry's argument that in America politicians and cities were too dishonest and too corrupt for

pp. 205-261, as well as a shorter version in *SRJ* 20 (1902): 153-55, 312-14, which is ably answered by Robert Donald, "Success of Municipal Ownership in Great Britain," *SRJ* 21 (1903): 30-34, 74-76, and 376-77.
[14] "Interview with Mr. Dalrymple," *SRJ* 26 (1905): 222.
[15] "The Dalrymple Report," *SRJ* 27 (1906): 423.

efficient and successful municipal enterprise. And if Mayor Dunne publicly objected to this unflattering view of American civic spirit, the 1907 agreement he negotiated nevertheless extended the franchises of the Chicago street railway companies, while establishing greater municipal control along rather classic continental lines.[16] In America, that was the most progressive people could reasonably work for.

The comparative quantitative and qualitative data on the growth of per capita use and public attitudes on the quality of service lead to a new and rather surprising conclusion. They suggest that, in keeping with the much more rapid growth of per capita utilization and the development of more socially oriented operations, the impact of electric tramways in Europe over the course of a generation was not only as great as in the United States but was probably *considerably greater*. Thus, although it seems fair to say that the horse streetcar "exerted a much greater influence upon the growth and upon the social and economic life of American cities" than upon British and continental ones,[17] it appears that in the case of the electric streetcar it was just the reverse. In the United States electric street railways were admittedly a remarkable achievement, particularly in the 1890s, before public hostility began to develop and perhaps sow the seeds of decline. But electric traction clearly built on the no less remarkable American development of the horsecar era, and therefore it seems likely that it strengthened primarily existing social and urban trends. In Europe the early achievements were quite modest, and this meant that electric traction carried society relatively farther and in new directions to a greater extent.

The importance of public transit in the lives of those of modest means and its extension to previously unaffected groups was one such new direction. True, horse tramways

[16] *SRJ* 24 (1906): 478; Wilcox, *Municipal Franchises*, 2: 149 ff.
[17] David Ward, "A Comparative Historical Geography of Streetcar Suburbs in Boston, Massachusetts, and Leeds, England," *Association of American Geographers Annals* 54 (1964): 477.

had moved timidly in the direction of a more democratic and less exclusive means of conveyance. But it seems undeniable that cheap, universal, *mass-oriented* urban transport in Europe was a product of the electric streetcar revolution. In Great Britain, "school children who formerly walked now ride. The same is true of millions of workingmen, as well as thousands of men and women whose only outing is taken on the top of a car."[18] Housewives used cheap, quick transit to run errands, do shopping, amuse and rest the children, and generally lighten their efforts. School children, workmen, excursionists, housewives: here are some of the new groups of passengers.

Indeed, the emerging mass character of European urban transit may be most reasonably inferred from much of the data we have presented throughout this study. The tremendous growth in per capita usage, for example, actually understates the increase in lower-class usage because horse tramways had a fairly strong middle-class bias. Similarly, the cultivation of the lower classes by means of very low workmen's fares and better service for poorer neighborhoods was completely indicative of the social direction of electric tramways.

Such evidence may not be entirely convincing, however. The increase in usage for the middle class might still have been almost as great as for the lower, for example. As for workmen's fares, they were normally available to all who rode at the designated hours, whatever their status or income. What is needed is some additional evidence which relates specifically to the working class or those of modest means.

Changes in usage within working-class districts would be one such indication. And indeed, in our discussion of private enterprise in France we saw how the development of electric tramways for the suburbs of Paris (at least for those to the north, east, and south) were largely directed toward serving those of modest means. The problem with such ex-

[18] Howe, "Municipal Ownership," p. 52.

amples is that they are scattered and incomplete, or else they require a precise delineation of lines, quarters, and social classes which would go beyond our scope. Therefore I propose to look briefly at a very atypical city—Essen, Germany—which nevertheless represented the "ideal type" of the industrial, working-class district, although of mammoth proportions. And I will assume that the transport development of this city will allow us to isolate and therefore assess the importance of electric tramways for the lower classes, and particularly the industrial working class.

From only 3,500 inhabitants in 1805, Essen had mushroomed to 57,000 in 1880, when fully 9,000 people were employed by the world-famous Krupp steel and munitions works, which dominated the town. This population was not less than that of other towns obtaining tramways at the time, and neither the railroad running north and south, nor the omnibuses running basically east and west from one to three times per day, met purely urban needs. Thus, in 1878 the city administration decided to investigate the possibility of an ordinary horse tramway, a step that led to a favorable report in 1880, the search for a concessionaire, and a provisional agreement with the constructor Gülich and Company of Potsdam.[19] However, when the city then decided that the thirty-year concession should substitute steam tramways giving off neither smoke nor steam, negotiations fell through. Another entrepreneur then agreed to build the lines but had to withdraw shortly thereafter in 1883, blaming particularly those people in Essen who said publicly and forcefully that public transportation would never make money in their city.[20]

Here, then, was the crucial problem which would delay all tramways until 1893—the problem of profitability. In perhaps the largest company town in Europe, where the small middle class was uninterested in or even opposed to

[19] My basic source has been *40 Jahre Essener Strassenbahnen, 1893-1933* (Essen, 1933), a book-length account.
[20] *Ibid.*, 13-15.

tramways, Krupp workers and employees—a majority of whom had at least a half hour's walk to the plant in 1884— would be the principal and probably inadequate source of passengers. This being the case, entrepreneurs steadfastly demanded some form of subsidy from the city in return for laying their rails in the streets. And this the "comfortable and influential" people of Essen adamantly opposed, while proclaiming loudly that any private money invested—which they would certainly never provide—would be totally lost. Finally, the great Krupp himself argued that his workers needed tramways, and tipped the scale in favor of those on the city council who were willing to grant a construction subsidy of 300,000 marks, in 1888.[21]

At this point another entrepreneur, who had previously been interested, stepped forward at the very end of 1888 and offered to build steam tramways without any subsidy from the city whatsoever. Yet after this bold move the entrepreneur (Die Eisenbahnkonsortium Bank für Handel und Industrie Hermann Bachstein of Berlin) dallied, even after agreements with Essen and four surrounding communities were reached and the concession was granted in September 1889. Possibly the bank was interested in installing electric traction from the beginning and accepted what it had previously rejected in order to freeze out the competition. In any event, the winning entrepreneur began new discussions in 1890, this time concerning electrification. After another firm established an electric power company in 1891, a new agreement with Bachstein for electric tramways was finally concluded in May 1892. The financial prospects were still considered rather dubious, however, and a clause calling for the city's sharing in any profits over 6 percent was inserted mainly for form, as few if any ex-

[21] Interestingly enough, there had been earlier appeals to Krupp to build trams for his workers, and even some negotiations with the city to this end. Nothing came of them, however—another excellent indication of the poor prospects for tramways in working-class Essen. *Ibid.*, pp. 16-17.

pected such a return from the company's three lines totaling eighteen kilometers.

Instead, the success of the tramways opened in August 1893 exceeded the most optimistic expectations. Within the year the city and the provincial government formulated a master plan calling for ten more lines, which were snapped up by the original banking group. In April 1895 further extension with nine more lines was agreed upon. By 1898 the company had built thirty-seven kilometers of line and this figure doubled again by 1913. In that year the people of Essen, who had done without trams completely until 1892, were on average riding roughly 150 times per year.[22] This traffic permitted the company to pay a 5- to 7-percent return, a return which would decline slightly after a set of new and less productive lines were opened and then built up again in cyclical fashion.

Thus the very heavily working-class population of Essen, which never seemed to justify the construction of horse trams, used the electric cars with great and ever-increasing frequency. The electric tramway stood as the common man's vehicle *par excellence*. Surely this tremendous consumer acceptance indicates just how useful electric tramways really were. In Essen, as elsewhere, they bestowed upon ordinary people great benefits with their cheaper, faster, more frequent, more extensive, and more comfortable service. With this general conclusion in mind, we will now turn to two of the most important areas of specific improvement.

2. *Suburbs and Cities*

No doubt there are those who will question the last statement concerning the tie between increased usage and greater welfare. After all, it is a common complaint that increased output and "growth," which has long been the

[22] *Ibid.*, pp. 27-35.

god of industrial man, may in fact be his Baal or his golden calf. Correspondingly, it might plausibly be argued that the growth of sophisticated urban transit is the growth of an inconvenience, wherein countless hours are wasted in ever more rapid, more crowded, and more dehumanizing conveyances. From this point of view, the arrival of the electric tramway with its "improvements" was in reality a fatal departure in the wrong direction, and particularly in the direction of sprawling suburbs and fragmenting cities.

Of course I have thought of this question, which is only a small part of the whole problem of the relationship of economic progress to general human progress. (And I must confess that it is easier to feel "better off" in this respect in a small city, where a person may walk to his work in half an hour, than in a gigantic metropolitan area where a daily commuting trip of an hour each way is often deemed a bargain.) The basic point, however, is that it is meaningless to compare the realities of the mass-transit metropolis with some idealized walking city of the past. We must remember that the relevant initial conditions for purposes of comparison were those of the increasingly centralized and terribly overcrowded nineteenth-century European city discussed in chapter 1. It it against that reality that the impact of electric trams on urban areas must be judged.

We may begin with three of many possible representative statements reflecting the views of contemporaries on the link between public transit, spatial expansion, and human welfare. In 1904 a special subcommittee on the Housing of the Working Class, set up by the city of Manchester, declared that "cheap and rapid transit is the only cure" for the working-class housing problem. And although this had become a ritualistic formula repeated in England without much success since the advent of the railroads, the committee now foresaw a solution: "The modern electric tramway will come to the rescue."[23] Similarly, speaking of urban cen-

[23] Sanitary Committee, *Housing of the Working Class, History of the Schemes and Description etc.* (Manchester, 1910), p. 10, as quoted by Kellett, *Impact of Railways*, p. 359.

ters, where the worker and his family were crowded together in "hives without air near their place of work," the general secretary of the industry-wide Union of French Tramways concluded that electric tramways "will change everything little by little. . . . Railroads build cities, and they are undeniably a centralizing force. Against this the modern tramway opposes its decentralizing force and corrects what was dangerous in the urban agglomeration."[24] Finally, let us note the German writer in 1909 who believed that "residential decentralization to the fringes and suburbs, where there are cheap and healthy dwellings, ought to be for the urban population, and especially those of modest means, the most important and welcome by-product of the development of modern transit." Thus "in most recent times it is better and better understood that the solution to the whole question of housing shortages and housing reform lies essentially in the design of the transport facilities. The housing question is above all a transport question."[25]

On the basis of such statements and data presented in earlier chapters, it is possible to distinguish three generally held beliefs about the relationship between cities, social welfare, and electric tramways. First, European cities were badly overcrowded, plagued with poor, unhealthy, and relatively expensive housing, especially for the lower classes in the old buildings of the central quarters. Second, the way to deal with this overcrowding was to "spread out the population" into the older and newer suburbs with their "pure air and more wholesome surroundings," by means of "cheap and expeditious transit."[26] Such a diffusion would be extremely beneficial for the lower classes, as it already had been for the upper and middle classes. Here then was the social ideal of good service for outlying areas which played such an important role in the renegotiation of the conces-

[24] Fuster, *Annuaire Général des Tramways*, p. 25.
[25] Alfred Haselmann, *Die Aachener Kleinbahnen* (Jena, 1909), pp. 69, 71; also Blum, "Zur Verkehrspolitik der Grosstadte, mit besonderer Berücksichtigung der Berliner Verhältnisse," *ZVDI* 52 (1908): 1083.
[26] *EE* 14 (1894): 18-19.

sion and in the overcoming of aesthetic opposition to overhead wires. Third, expectations were terribly high. For many the electric tramway was little less than the *deus ex machina*, descending miraculously upon the urban stage to resolve the entire social drama.

About the actual impact of electric tramways upon European cities it is hard to speak with such certainty. The secondary and monographic literature is scattered and underdeveloped. And then there is the problem of the idiosyncratic character of the unit of investigation. Each city was different and, as the manager of Manchester's tramways said,[27] "it may be very misleading to draw general inferences [from traffic statistics] unless the local circumstances in each case are fully recognized and kept fully in mind"—a well-nigh impossible task. With these caveats in mind, it nevertheless seems clear that electric tramways contributed markedly to lower population densities and suburban expansion.

Some other investigators have reached this conclusion. Dickinson distinguished a new phrase in the development of the West European city which began "towards the end of the 19th century" and ended in 1914. It was marked by better housing and the fact that "the electric tramway enabled the city to expand."[28] A detailed scholarly study in 1909 of the large electric tramway network of Aachen, Germany, concluded that it had helped create both special suburbs and a general widening of the city. And since the tramways extended far into the countryside and also served as light railways, they permitted peasants in the area to give up farming for the mine and the factory while continuing to live in their houses and villages. This occurred elsewhere, and particularly in Belgium.[29]

In Great Britain, a major 1905 report concluded that the data on the impact of tramways upon the housing problem

[27] Manchester, *Passenger Transportation Problem*, p. 87.
[28] Dickinson, *West European City*, p. 463.
[29] Haselmann, *Aachener Kleinbahnen*, pp. 70-73; Emile Vandervelde, *L'exode rural et le retour aux champs* (Paris, 1910), pp. 151-55.

were "unanimous to the effect that congested districts have been relieved and that tramways have promoted the development of outlying areas for workmen's and middle-class houses." The report clearly noted how tramway lines caused the population to spread out in strips along the route, as well as back from it for a quarter or even a half a mile.[30] Thus in Europe before 1914, as well as North America, the tramway route "was the spinal column of each suburban extension, the whole city having an attenuated plan, its long fingers stretching out into the countryside."[31]

In the course of this study I have found other evidence to suggest that electric tramways caused and facilitated European suburban expansion. The rash of electric lines for Paris suburbs discussed in chapter iv, Hendlmeier's material on Munich and Buchmann's on Berlin, scattered discussions in the popular and technical journals, traffic statistics for individual lines: all these and other data might be presented to bolster the argument. But I fear that such a shotgun approach would remain vague and convince few skeptics. Therefore it seems better to try to penetrate further into this question with brief case studies of two leading and historic cities—Brussels, Belgium, and Manchester, England.

Until at least 1840 the urban growth of Brussels was almost totally confined to the area originally enclosed by city walls built in the fourteenth century, as was noted in chapter i. True, the walls began to be destroyed by order of Napoleon in 1810, and by 1840 they had been replaced by wide circular boulevards. But the *octroi* separating city and country, with its ditch, taxes, and administrative apparatus, remained at the ancient city limits. This actually encour

---

[30] Stephen Sellon, "Report on the Tramway Systems in the Principal Cities and Towns in the United Kingdom," in *Royal Commission on London Traffic, Report . . . upon . . . Transport in London*, 8 vols. (London, 1905), 4:968. Also C. R. Bellany, "Public Transportation with Special Reference to Liverpool Tramways," *MA* 6 (1902): 709.

[31] Humphrey Carver, *Cities in the Suburbs* (Toronto, 1962), p. 8.

aged development beyond the boulevards, where land and materials were cheaper, and the first suburban expansion began in the 1840s.

Generally speaking, the fashionable new quarters lay to the east and south—the royal side of the city. The aristocratic Leopold quarter grew to the east and was incorporated in 1853, and another new area was developed along the Avenue Louise toward the Cambre Woods and was incorporated into the city in 1864.[32] New industrial and working-class areas formed to the north and south, behind the North and South Railroad Stations, and by 1880 the total population had grown from 282,000 in 1831 to 421,000.[33] Yet the development did not expand the built-up area more than a kilometer beyond the ring boulevards, where the walls had formerly stood. In short, Brussels in 1880 remained a highly concentrated city in the midst of a plain of fields, villages, and forests stretching out in all directions, as may be clearly seen in a very revealing contemporary map, which is reproduced as figure 15. As one good middle-class citizen later remembered, Brussels in the 1880s was a small, almost silent city, a city marked by a great sense of security and slow, unhurried movement.[34]

After 1880 the population of greater Brussels grew rapidly, as may be seen in table 11. Almost all this growth was beyond the city limits of Brussels proper, which grew only about 10 percent between 1880 and 1920. It was in the inner and outer suburbs that population increased rapidly. (The inner suburbs are basically the communes adjacent to the city; the outer suburbs are those communes beyond the inner ring, as may be seen to some extent by an examination of place names in figure 16.)

---

[32] "Le Développement de l'Agglomération bruxelloise" (Brussels, 1935), pp. 10-15. (Extract from *Bulletin de la Banque de Bruxelles*, in Bibliothèque Royale, Brussels); L. Verniers, "Les Transformations de Bruxelles et L'Urbanisation de sa Banlieue depuis 1795," *Annales de la Société Royale d'Archéologie de Bruxelles* 37 (1934): 104-58.

[33] "Le Développement," p. 9; table 10.

[34] C. Vanzype, *Au temps du silence* (Brussels, 1939).

15. Brussels. The built-up and surrounding area in 1880.

Table 11

GROWTH OF POPULATION IN METROPOLITAN BRUSSELS

(in thousands)

	1880	1890	1900	1910	1930
Brussels[a]	162.5	176.1	183.7	177.1	200.4
Inner Suburbs					
Anderlecht	22.8	32.3	47.9	64.1	80.0
Etterbeek	11.8	17.7	20.8	33.2	45.3
Ixelles	36.3	44.5	58.6	73.0	83.9
Laeken[a]	17.9	25.3	30.4	35.0	—
Molenbeek-St.-Jean	41.7	48.7	58.4	72.8	64.8
Saint-Gilles	33.2	40.3	51.8	63.1	64.1
Saint-Josse-ten-Noode	28.1	29.7	32.1	31.9	30.9
Scharbeek	40.8	50.9	63.5	82.5	118.7
Outer Suburbs					
Anderghem	2.4	?	4.7	7.4	14.0
Forest	4.2	5.9	9.5	24.3	39.6
Jette	4.7	6.6	10.1	14.8	22.2
Koekelberg	4.9	6.3	10.7	12.8	13.9
Uccle	10.7	13.4	18.0	27.0	43.3
Watermael-Boisfort	3.6	?	6.5	8.4	16.1
Woluwe-St.-Lambert	1.7	2.3	3.5	8.9	24.7
Woluwe-St.-Pierre	1.6	?	2.9	5.2	13.5
Metropolitan Brussels	421.1	500.0	599.1	720.3	902.9

SOURCE: For 1880-1910, Belgium, Ministre de l'Interieur, Statistique de la Belgique, Population, *Recensement général*, 1910, I (Brussels, 1916), 175; for 1930, *ibid.*, 1930, I (Brussels, 1937), 153 (as quoted by Dickinson, *European City*, p. 159).

[a] Laeken and two small communes became part of Brussels in 1921.

This table and the map of Brussels show that although the inner suburbs were only partly built up in 1880, they had grown greatly by 1910. Indeed, they were (with the exception of the very large commune of Anderlecht) almost fully built up and "saturated" by 1910, as population densities per hectare approached or even exceeded that of Brussels proper.³⁵ It is also clear that the outer communes attracted a greater and greater population, and that they were far from saturated, as their continued growth to 1930 shows. Finally, and perhaps most significantly, suburban expansion ultimately resulted in a sharp decline in the density of population for the entire metropolitan area, but this did not set in until after 1890. It occurred as the number of inhabitants per hectare of land with buildings (streets, parks, boulevards being excluded), which had actually risen from 443 in 1880 (and 463 in 1866) to 457 in 1890, dropped to 434 in 1900 and 391 in 1910. The further decline to 344 in 1920 was also part of the same prewar movement, reflecting building decisions generally made before August 1914.³⁶ Clearly, metropolitan Brussels experienced substantial suburban expansion and reduced urban congestion prior to 1914. We will now try to assess the place of urban transit in that development.

We begin with the fact that "until 1870 the means of transport remained rare and rudimentary."³⁷ The various suburban omnibus lines which were tried between 1835 and 1867 failed for a want of passengers. The first successful "American railroad" appeared in 1868, and in the next six years a number of similar tram lines were opened by different companies. These companies were then merged in 1874 and, almost incredibly, not a single new line was opened through the year 1890. Here, then, was the pattern of growth followed by stagnation: the 10,000,000 passengers carried in 1874 had jumped to about 20,000,000 in 1881 as the area served filled in, but only about 25,000,000 rode the trams in 1894, on the eve of electrification.³⁸ In terms of usage per capita there was no increase between 1881 and

³⁵ *Recensement général*, 1910, II, 186.
³⁶ "Développement," p. 15.
³⁷ Guillaume Jacquemyns, *Histoire contemporaine de Grand-Bruxelles* (Brussels, 1936), p. 177.
³⁸ *Ibid.*, pp. 177-94; AN, 65, AQ, Q 508, Tramways Bruxellois, Annual Report, 1895.

1894, as each inhabitant of metropolitan Brussels rode the tramways roughly forty-five times per year at both dates. Here is another confirmation of our position that horse tramways had generally reached the limits of their development by the early 1880s and had ceased to foster further spatial expansion.

A rapid transformation began in 1892, when the Brussels Tramways Company received a concession (expiring in 1942) for the construction of fifteen kilometers of new electric lines, which would be added to the existing network of thirty-nine kilometers all built before 1875. The response of the public was enthusiastic, leading to the conclusion of "difficult negotiations" over more new lines to serve Uccle to the south in 1896.[39] At the same time the company successfully bargained over the old network, which the company refused to electrify until it was unified with the new network and the original concession was extended from 1909 to 1942.[40] The predictable aesthetic problem was solved first by the acceptance of the underground conduit system for certain new lines passing through showpiece areas, such as the Rue de la Loi and along the Leopold Park and the Cambre Woods.[41] Following the agreement of 1899, the tramway network of Brussels expanded very rapidly to 128 kilometers of line in 1911 (or 156 kilometers when the lines of a smaller company were included). Tramway passengers carried in metropolitan Brussels jumped four-fold from about 40,000,000 in 1899 to 165,000,000 in 1913, or from roughly 65 to 220 rides per capita. This meant a fivefold increase in per capita usage in two decades.[42]

Clearly the growth of population in the second zone of suburban communes and tramway development went hand in hand. But which of these mutually reinforcing move-

[39] AN, 65 AQ, Q 508, Annual Reports, 1895-97.
[40] Various newspaper extracts in Jacquemyns, *Histoire contemporaine*, pp. 200-06.
[41] *Ibid.*; SRJ 20 (1902): 328-32; 21 (1903): 658-59.
[42] Jacquemyns, *Histoire contemporaine*, p. 213.

ments was more nearly the cause of the other? To this hard question detailed but by no means exhaustive analysis of specific lines and communes suggests that electric tramway construction tended to lead population increases in the outer communes, and therefore caused and accounted for suburban expansion and less overcrowding, along with other factors to be sure.

An hour's walk from the center of Brussels, the old southern communes of Forest and Uccle, for example, "remained essentially agricultural villages until just toward the end of the century . . . and it was really only from 1890 that the censuses registered a substantial growth in the number of houses."[43] Although a single "American railroad" to Uccle dated from the early 1870s, transit remained poor until new electric tramways were begun about 1892 and finished in 1894 and 1896.[44] Then the population of Forest almost doubled in the 1890s, and more than doubled again by 1910. The number of houses in the larger village of Uccle, which was already a sizable agricultural community in 1846, doubled between 1890 and 1910. Rapid population growth followed adequate transit facilities.

Similarly, the entire area to the southeast and east between the Cambre Woods and the Soignes Forest was provided with good tramway service and a vast, scarcely developed area was opened for reasonable commuting. (See map of Brussels.) The principal lines left from the Namur Gate on the ring boulevards and passed along the Cambre Woods to Boendall and Boisfort, and then swung north along the Soignes Forest to the east of Auderghem and then all the way to the new race track at Stockel.[45] Another set of lines served Auderghem and Watermael directly. And,

[43] Verniers, "Les Transformations," *Annales de la Société Royale d'Archéologie de Bruxelles* 37 (1934): 178.
[44] Jacquemyns, *Histoire contemporaine*, p. 182; AN, 65 AQ, Q 508, Tramways Bruxellois, Annual Reports, 1895-98.
[45] *Ibid.*, Annual Report, 1901; *Horaire des Tramways, Omnibus et Chemins de fer desservant Bruxelles et la banlieue avec plan des lignes*, Brussels, 1914. (In Bibliothèque Royale.)

as anyone who takes the very agreeable thirty-minute tram ride from the Bourse to Boisfort today, and who then explores on foot the surrounding neighborhoods, can testify, here is surely one of the most attractive areas of solid homes and spacious yards in all Europe—a handsome tribute to the electric tram.

There were other even more purely suburban lines, like that of thirteen kilometers to Tervueren, a well-served village to the east in today's third zone of suburbs. The longest line of all—nineteen kilometers—was opened in 1908 and tied Vilvorde, an industrial town far to the north, with Forest, to the south, by means of the grand transversal connecting the North and South Stations through the center of town. Not that the tramway company always wanted to push out to ever more distant points in the sea of towns and hamlets. As the company reported in connection with negotiations over further extensions in 1910, "these lines will be unprofitable for various lengths of time. We are building them only in order to respond to the desires of the various communal governments, and to encourage the development of new housing areas for the benefit of the whole metropolis."[46] But the result was that once again the company built to outlying communities and villages, opening up new land for suburban expansion. And if such lines were not always immediately profitable, this was no doubt an intelligent policy of enlightened self-interest for a company that had paid no dividends in 1893, 6 francs per share in 1896 and 1899, 11 francs in 1903, 24 francs in 1906, and 29 francs in 1913.[47]

A more rapid look at the evidence on Manchester and its surrounding districts shows striking parallels with Brussels. As might be expected, this cradle of the industrial revolution lagged badly in urban transport usage until about 1902, when Manchester and the surrounding towns took over the

[46] AN, 65 AQ, Q 508, Annual Report, 1910.
[47] *La Belgique financier*, 25 March 1909; Annual Report, 1913; both in AN, 65 AQ, Q 508.

tramway network of the Manchester Carriage and Tramway Company. Then usage accelerated dramatically in the first years of the twentieth century.[48]

Table 12

TRAMWAY DEVELOPMENT IN GREATER MANCHESTER[a]

Year of Census	Passengers Carried	Population Served	Journeys Per Head of Population
1881	16,371,000	930,000	18
1891	41,808,000	1,105,000	38
1901	71,991,000	1,287,000	56
1911	264,039,000	1,683,000	157

SOURCE: Manchester, Tramways Department, *The Passenger Transportation Problem* (Manchester, 1914), p. 89.

[a] Including Salford, Oldham, Ashton-under-Lyne, Stockport, etc.

In the same period there was substantial suburban expansion. Whereas the built-up area in 1900 included an area with a radius averaging two to two-and-one-half miles, the area of intensive development in 1914 spread out like a starfish in all directions for up to four miles along the principal roads the tramways served.[49] And the less densely settled area of more spacious living spread out toward the built-up areas of more distant independent towns, such as Stockport to the southeast or Oldham to the northeast.

This distribution of population may be compared with the distribution of tramway service. This has been done in figure 16, where a time-zone map for tramway travel to the center of the city has been superimposed upon a map showing the distribution of population and the tramway net-

[48] For pictures, reminiscences, and technical details on Manchester trams, see the publications of Manchester Transport Museum Society: *Manchester Tramway Album* (1960); Edward Gray, *The Tramways of Salford* (1967); A. K. Kirby, *Manchester's Little Tram* (1964); as well as Ian Yearsley, *The Manchester Tram* (Huddersfield, 1962).

[49] Kellett, *Impact of Railways*, p. xxiii; Manchester, *Passenger Transportation Problem*, Map 2.

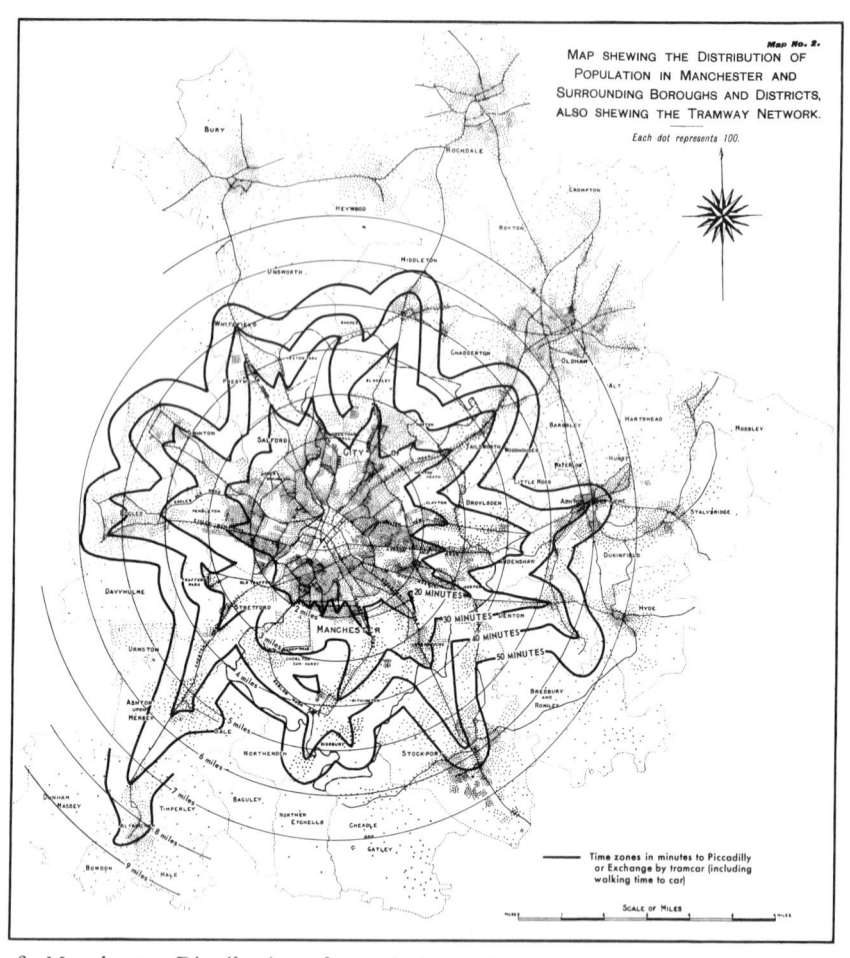

16. Manchester. Distribution of population and transport, circa 1913.

work. The first thing to note is that almost all the intensively built-up area within three miles of the center (Piccadilly or the Exchange) could be reached by tram in a total of twenty to thirty minutes, which included the time spent walking from home to stop and waiting for the car. And the one-way fare in this area would be only a penny, since Manchester's trams give the longest (2.9 miles on average) one-penny ride in England.[50] The time zones also show that much of the star-shaped, intensively built-up area of up to five miles from the center could be reached in the same twenty to thirty minutes. Indeed, the borough of Altrincham eight miles to the southwest was provided with nearly non-stop service so that it was the same twenty- to thirty-minute commuting trip—a true trolley-car suburb. The time zones further show that lines to old and intensively built-up towns like Stockport or Ashton-under-Lyne, which were forty to fifty minutes from the center of Manchester, passed through a large area thirty to forty minutes away that was settled very lightly, or built up only along the roads. Thus the undeveloped area suitable for comfortable commuting was enormous.

This leads to an important point. Certainly the expanding star-shaped periphery of Manchester was well served by urban tramways in 1914. And because the trams were running through to more distant, well-established towns and villages, as they had been for over a decade, they were constantly serving a large area *beyond* the newest and most distant Manchester suburbs. Thus in Manchester, as in Brussels, tramways were not simply following suburban development, but they were leading that development by extending their service in advance of existing demand. If this was the general pattern in most European cities, and I believe that further detailed investigation will confirm that it was, then electric tramways did indeed open up large areas for new residential construction and thereby greatly facilitate socially desirable decentralization.

[50] *Ibid.*, p. 135.

Two more related consequences for the European urban habitat should be noted, if only very briefly. First, just as tramways fostered a decentralization and spreading out of residential areas, so did they also tend to concentrate commercial and administrative activity in a small and quite compact, centrally located business district. This concentration of work and services was most pronounced in North America, where the creation of the sharply defined "down town" went hand in hand with suburban expansion.[51] British cities also experienced this "city-building" to a considerable extent. In Manchester, for example, great and unmistakable concentration was evidenced by both the absence of residential population in the central business district and by very pronounced rush-hour surges of traffic inward and outward on lines serving the center.[52] Continental cities, like Paris or Berlin, continued to weave residential areas and a multiplicity of commercial and business centers together to a greater extent. Nevertheless, the absolute decline in the population within the city limits of Brussels between 1900 and 1910, or the greater concentration of offices and commerce in Dresden, were indicative of the same general trend.[53]

Second, electric tramways had a strong effect on land values, increasing the price of land located on the fringes and in the emerging central business district. Speaking of the United Kingdom, one report concluded that the only exceptions were large residences with large grounds, which might temporarily fall in value as a new tramway line promised to lower the tone of previously exclusive and secluded areas. However, such estates would then appreciate and be sold for smaller house construction, so that "always

[51] Carver, *Cities*, pp. 8-10; Richard Hurd, "The Structure of Cities," *MA* 6 (1902): 40-41.
[52] See figure 17 and Manchester, *Passenger Transportation Problem*, pp. 108-13.
[53] Belgium, *Recensement général*, 1910, I, 175; Grossmann, *Die kommunale Bedeutung*, pp. 233-35.

the ultimate effect is to increase the value of the land."[54] Thus what was always noted about America, where the link between land speculation and street railway construction was very close, was also true of Europe.[55] Tramway extensions made more distant land more accessible and hence desirable, and therefore increased its price.

This result no doubt brought joy to the speculator's heart and was indeed a major achievement. But it also had a negative side, because higher land values tended to frustrate efforts to enable the poor to leap dramatically from old congested tenements to cheap, healthful housing on the fringes, by means of electric tramways. "In Great Britain . . . lines are built into the suburbs for the purpose of increasing the building area and thus relieving the population. The results of this policy, however, are not very apparent, because of the immediate increase in the value of suburban land, coincident with the coming of the cars. The workingmen, for whom homes are desired, find the land held at a much higher price because of the very act of the city aimed at their betterment."[56] A German investigator could similarly conclude that a solution to the housing problem, "which today is essentially a land problem," was beyond the power of better transport alone, especially if there were a close tie between line construction and land speculation.[57] Allowing for the unmistakable socialistic bias of many such statements, it seems clear that municipal officials and transport experts did increasingly realize that tramways by themselves would not automatically provide the greatest possible benefits in

[54] Sellon, "Report," . . . *Transport in London*, 4:968. The point is amply illustrated, 976-81.
[55] John Dickson-Poynder, "Notes on a Visit to the United States of America," . . . *Transport in London*, 4:616. Henri Ruhlmann, *Les chemins de fer urbains; Etude économique et sociale* (Paris, 1936), pp. 169-170; Marcel Chassaigne, *Etude économique sur les moyens de transport en commun dans Paris* (Paris, 1912), pp. 164-67, and sources cited below.
[56] Howe, "Municipal Ownership," p. 56.
[57] Sternberg, *Das Verkehrsgewerbe Leipzigs*, pp. 82-83.

decentralization and better housing. Thus the years before the war were marked by attempts to utilize tramways still more effectively as a decentralizing force, and thereby offset the constraint of the higher land values they created.

Part of the answer was to establish much closer collaboration and planning between tramway managers and municipal officials, as Mr. Hartmann, the director of the municipal tramways of Cologne, emphatically urged his colleagues at the sixteenth meeting of the International Congress of Tramways in Brussels in 1910.[58] Building development, and most specifically the construction of new streets and the widening of old ones, had to be dovetailed with tramway construction and the traffic pattern, according to Hartmann. And for good reason. As one American put it with pardonable exaggeration, "the location and street construction of most European cities do not lend themselves readily to tramway building." Narrow, crooked streets meant that "in many places it is absolutely impossible to enter or cross the center of a city in a tramway . . . and this tends to cut the tramway system into a number of unconnected disjointed lines."[59]

No wonder, then, that more effective utilization of trams often required the cutting of new streets through historic centers, or the widening of narrow streets. This in turn was tremendously complicated by the desire to maintain the traditional beauty and charm of the historic center—the aesthetic dimension once again. Similarly, the layout of new thoroughfares—their width, the number of stops, the size of the cross-streets, etc.—very largely determined how fast tramways might run and how useful they might be.[60] Such careful planning could then be closely coordinated with

[58] As reported in *Verkehrstechnische Woche* 8 (1911): 668-69.
[59] Richard McCulloch, "European Tramways," *Journal of the Western Society of Engineers* 8 (1903): 282-84.
[60] Hartmann, *Verkehrstechnische Woche* 8 (1911): 669-71; also C. T. Bartley, "Visit to European Cities," . . . *Transport in London*, 4:633-40.

municipal efforts to build cheap housing in the suburbs, as was very effectively done by the municipal tramways of Frankfurt on the Main.[61]

In short, there is much evidence to suggest that the director of Nuremberg's tramways was right and also representative in believing that improvement in the layout of the tram network was one of the keys to continued increases in usage and to further expansion on the periphery.[62] Let two examples, one from Germany and one from France, suffice. In 1912 Nuremberg-Furth, an agglomeration of 400,000 inhabitants, lagged badly in tramway development with only ninety-two rides per capita, or about one-half that registered in the leading German cities of roughly the same size. The key to the problem was that although Nuremberg had good east-west lines through the center, and consequently was tending to grow in those directions, it was totally lacking in any direct north-south lines through the city. This meant that a passenger going north-south through the center had to go by way of the circular boulevard and would arrive no sooner than he would had he walked directly through the historic core. The proposed answer was for the city and its municipal tramways to raze certain "uninteresting" buildings in the inner city for new street construction, and couple that construction with a tunnel under the old fortress area in the center to provide through north-south tramway service. According to the city planners, this scheme would result in the triumph of both efficiency and aesthetic sensibilities, a theme we have seen before. This crosstown linkage, combined with relatively short extensions to the north and south, would greatly increase the network's usefulness. In particular, it would allow workers to flow into the largely undeveloped area north of the city and still easily reach their industrial plants, located mainly to

[61] *Verkehrstechnische Woche* 8 (1911): 703.

[62] P. Scholtes, "Ein kritischer Vergleich über Benutzung und Ausbreitung von Strassenbahnen," *Elektrische Kraftbetriebe und Bahnen* 10 (1912): 31, 38-39, 44-47.

the south of the city.⁶³ The goal of adequate housing for all would be closer to realization.

In France the Lille-Roubaix-Tourcoing "Electric" Company, approved in 1904 and in operation well before the war, was combined with new boulevard construction toward which the new company contributed 1,000,000 francs. This made possible twenty-two kilometers of essentially interurban electric railway, complete with a special right of way to the side of the new boulevard. And this meant high speeds and intensive service—a train every five minutes, as opposed to every hour on the local railroad. In addition to this interurban service, the company built thirty-eight kilometers of ordinary tramway lines to dovetail with its interurban and to serve the three cities and the surrounding area.⁶⁴ Here were two examples of the coordination of street and tramway construction that were essential to more effective tram networks.

Another part of the answer was to realize the limitations of electric tramways in the mass-transit urban world which they had done so much to call into existence. Such limitations were most apparent in the largest cities. There the great increase in tramway traffic could end in a congestion that threatened to choke the "arterial lines near the central parts of the city." And when that happened, "when the traffic on these lines approaches the 'saturation' point, then additional main arteries must be opened out or other transit facilities provided."⁶⁵ Since new streets were expensive and often brought devastating destruction upon the cultural and artistic past—witness the battle over the possible introduction of electric tramways into the center of Vienna⁶⁶— often the only alternative was to go underground. Of course such underground (and elevated) urban railways already existed before 1900, principally in New York, Boston, and

⁶³ *Ibid.*
⁶⁴ For details, see AN, 65 AQ, Q 270, and CL, L'Electrique Lille-Roubaix-Tourcoing, Etude, May 1913.
⁶⁵ Manchester, *Passenger Transportation Problem*, p. 100.
⁶⁶ *ZOIAV* 60 (1908): 775-76; 61 (1909): 413-17, 432-36.

London. But with the opening of the Paris Metropolitan in 1900, after years of acrimonious debate, subway construction stood poised on the threshold of a new era.

For the new Paris Metro was extremely successful, both for the public who patronized it and for the private capitalists who built it. This may be seen in the ambitious plans of a single company, the Lyons Tramways Omnium Company, which was moderately successful in 1905 with the North-South Company, Paris's second metro company. By 1912 the Lyons Omnium had completed the planning and arranged much of the financing for another subway, this time for Naples, Italy. As the Lyons Omnium told the financiers who were to underwrite the new company, "in the central portion of Naples it is almost impossible to get on the tramways in the rush hours." Thus even though tram traffic had grown three-fold in little more than fifteen years since electrification, many citizens of Naples used it only rarely. The tramways could not satisfy the demand, a demand which the metro would meet and stimulate further.[67] And with a dividend of 6.5 percent on the private company's capital anticipated, it is easy to see why the Lyons Omnium in 1914 looked forward to building similar underground systems in Vienna, Madrid, Genoa, and Moscow. And this was only one of many engineering firms with the capacity to plan and build such transit systems. Had Archduke Francis Ferdinand never gone to Sarajevo, and had the great civil war of 1914-1918 been averted, it seems fairly certain that metros would have been built in perhaps a dozen major cities in the next decade to complement overworked tram systems.

3. Leisure and Recreation

In addition to fostering suburbanization, which from the vantage point of today's exploding city assumes particular significance, the electric tramway had another major effect

[67] BUP, Métropolitan de Naples, no. 105, Etude de l'Omnium Lyonnais, March 1911.

we would be less likely to expect. This was the impact upon leisure and recreation, an impact which was particularly strong among the lower classes. For if low incomes were a crucial factor limiting permanent migration of these classes toward "pure air and better surroundings," cheap electric trams nevertheless provided the means for a regular if temporary exodus from the most modest domicile in the most congested quarters. It opened up new possibilities of excursions and outings on those increasingly frequent days of leisure and relaxation. The trolley car helped democratize recreation as well as the journey to work.

The importance of recreational travel was readily apparent to contemporaries, even if social historians have hardly noticed it. As one somewhat surprised American streetcar engineer put it after two years of work in Europe in 1903, "the banner days are the pleasant Sundays and holidays, of which there are a great many. No self-respecting citizen in the Latin countries would stay home on such a day. He takes his family or his sweetheart and goes to the parks, to the cafes, to the restaurants, to the concert gardens, to the country, anywhere so long that he goes. Days such as these crowd all transportation agencies to the utmost."[68]

The experience of the individual companies confirms that tramways were normally used more intensively on Sundays and holidays than on working days. At Dresden extra trailcars were always added on Sunday, and the normally inactive reserve generators of Aachen's municipal power plant were needed on Sundays and holidays. In the French cities of Nantes and Rouen this was also clearly the case.[69] The importance of recreation is also seen in the seasonal variations, since traffic was often heavier in the summer than in the winter months.

[68] McCulloch, "European Tramways," *Journal of the Western Society of Engineers* 8 (1903): 290-91. On the role of transport in the diffusion and democratization of leisure, also see Georges D'Avenel, *Le nivellement des jouissances* (Paris, 1913) and Claude Lucas, *Les transports en commun à Paris: Etude économique et sociale* (Paris, 1913), pp. 183-98.

[69] *EE* 14 (1894): 145, 210; AN, F 14, 13515.

These daily and seasonal variations in favor of holiday traffic were not at all new. Indeed, there is a good deal of evidence to suggest that travel for pleasure had produced the heaviest traffic for horse trams and that this phenomenon simply continued with electric trams. At Brussels, the tram line of 1868, first built to serve the area along the Avenue Louise, languished and faced the failure of earlier such attempts in Brussels until it was extended on out to the Cambre Woods, a favorite area of holiday walks and outings. Then the development of recreational traffic assured the line's success.[70] In the early 1880s the Brussels Tramways Company reported that the revenues of the highest month (August) were 70 percent more than the lowest (February), and that a cool and rainy summer season would sharply lower revenues and profits.[71] At roughly the same time fully one-fourth of all lines at Marseilles were "lines for outings." "On the long, beautiful days of summertime the results are wonderful there; but in winter and poor weather traffic is very much reduced."[72] At Mulhouse in the 1880s there were three trams each hour on Sundays and holidays, as opposed to two on workdays.[73]

What was new with electric trams was the scale, the organization, and the frequency of these recreational activities. There even appeared a whole series of cheap and very complete pocket-sized guides for hikes and excursions, where the only common denominator was the electric tram which made them possible. Here again Brussels and Manchester are representative of the general pattern.

Every one of the thirteen basic "beautiful and historic promenades" suggested in Michel's oft-printed guide for greater Brussels called upon the tram, as did most of the one hundred supplementary "excursions with simple itin-

[70] Jacquemyns, *Histoire Contemporaire*, pp. 177-82.
[71] AN, 65 AQ, Q 508, Annual Reports, 1880-82.
[72] AN, 65 AQ, Q 1381, Cie Générale Française, Annual Report, 1877. Also see Barker and Robbins, *London Transport*, 1: 280.
[73] *ZK* 1 (1894): 525.

eraries."[74] These itineraries called for twenty to twenty-five kilometers of travel for five or six hours, of which three or four hours were for easy walking and two were for the tramways. The basic strategy was to take the tram out to some interesting point on the outskirts, and then walk and possibly picnic through park, forest, and open country until one eventually reached another tram line. At that point the old dependable friend would carry the tired and happy hiker back to the city in comfort. It is hard to imagine—or find—a more healthful and more satisfying form of recreation.

Many English cities and counties, such as Liverpool and Yorkshire, had their "guides for tram and walking tours," as they were called. One of these, John Lingard's booklet "Where to Go by Tram around Manchester and throughout Lancashire," shows the great opportunities for tramway travel and excursions which existed by 1914 and throughout the early 1920s.[75] There were dozens of direct car routes, such as the thirty-eight-mile trip to Liverpool in four hours for 2½ shillings, or to Watergate—"30 miles on trams right to the moors of Yorkshire." Then there were numerous circular rides; many combined tram and walking tours, which might enable one to obtain "a splendid view of the surrounding country," or dine in "the fourth highest inn in England." As the compiler summed it up, "travelling by car is cheap, and it is an easy and exhilarating way of taking the air." And it was eminently egalitarian and versatile, "the nearest approach to a Motor Tour."[76] Here, incidentally, we probably see a factor in the tram's ultimate decline: as incomes rose the excursion-loving European was increasingly

[74] A. Michel, *Promenades pratiques, historiques et esthétiques aux environs de Bruxelles* (Brussels, 1911). Also, *Environs de Bruxelles: Guide de l'excursionniste* (Brussels, 1910) and Edmond Scheler, *A travers Bruxelles et ses environs* (Brussels, 1912).

[75] Reprinted by the Manchester Transport Historical Collection, Manchester Rd., Rochdale, Lancashire.

[76] *Ibid.*

unwilling to settle for what was considered second best and demanded his own automobile, which he often continues to reserve largely for weekend travel. In the years before the Great War, however, the democratization of the motorcar in Europe was scarcely conceivable. The electric tramway was the undisputed leisure-time vehicle of the masses going toward fresh air, scenic sites, amusement parks, or sporting events, as tastes and opportunities might dictate.

4. *The Tramway Workers*

Finally, on a somewhat different tack, what did electrification mean for the men who ultimately made it all possible, the street railway workers? To what extent did they profit from the new system of urban transit? Here again the point of departure must be the realities of the conditions of horsetram workers in the late 1880s.

The life of the horsetram driver and conductor in the late 1880s was a difficult one; even though the data are scattered and incomplete a fairly good "average picture" emerges. The first thing to note is the extraordinarily long work week, as the tramway worker's day tended to approximate the hours of tramway service. In British provincial cities the men generally worked seventy to eighty hours per week and received from 20 to 25 shillings for their efforts.[77] The tramway workers of Hull, for example, were scheduled to work a six-day week of about seventy-eight hours at the beginning of the decade. Sunday work was added in the mid-1880s, so that most then worked about ninety hours a week, with one day off in fourteen. This was at a time when most laborers were working a sixty-hour week, with Sundays off. In 1888 there was some improvement, when the Hull workers won one day off in every eight. Each worker

[77] D.L.G. Hunter, *Edinburgh's Transport* (Huddersfield, 1964), p. 39; Klapper, *Golden Age*, p. 133; Howe, "Municipal Ownership," pp. 53, 67-68; King, *Keighley Transport*, p. 20.

was also required to deposit £2, or about two weeks' wages, against possible fines, which were numerous and on average equaled perhaps 10 percent of the worker's wages.[78]

In the great capitals tramway employees' fairly high weekly (but not hourly) wages were won at the cost of terrible hours. On London trams in the late 1870s and early 1880s, for example, it appears that a sixteen-hour day, seven days a week, was the norm. Any leave taken was unpaid leave, and at least one worker took not a single day of rest in his five months' stint as a conductor.[79] But the relatively high daily starting pay of 5 shillings in the late 1870s, which had fallen with prices to 4s. 6d. a decade later, "never failed to produce plenty of keen recruits, primarily from the provinces," though labor turnover remained quite high.[80] Until 1889 in Vienna, and 1891 in Paris, tramway workers also averaged almost sixteen hours per day with very little time off.[81]

Beginning about 1889, the year of the famous London Dock Strike, some improvements were won, often by means of strikes. In 1889 London tramway workers received a three-hour rest period in the middle of the day; those of Berlin attained four days off per month; and Vienna workers won an average working day of twelve hours. One of the best examples of this combination of increased militancy and successful strikes was that of the Paris omnibus workers against the well-entrenched General Omnibus Company in 1891.[82]

As in Berlin before 1889, the men on the Paris omnibuses worked seven days a week in 1891. Wages were not an issue, but the very meager fringe benefits and extremely long

[78] Lee, "Tramways of Hull," 44-46.
[79] Barker and Robbins, *London Transport*, 1:282-83, based on George Lovett, *Modern Slavery: Life on the London Tramway Cars* (1877).
[80] *Ibid.*, 284-85.
[81] *La Revue Universelle des Chemins de fer*, 31 May and 7 June 1891.
[82] The company's tramway workers did not go out, and were apparently treated slightly better.

hours certainly were. (This suggests again that the weekly —though not the hourly—pay of urban transport workers was somewhat above the average for other semi-skilled employments.) Hours varied in two ways: from day to day, and as to time at the job and time actually worked there. Thus workers worked in three-day cycles of seventeen, fifteen, and thirteen hours per day, or roughly fifteen hours per day on the average and 105 hours per week. Of this time at work roughly eleven and a half, ten and a half, and nine and a half hours, or about seventy-five hours per week, would actually be spent in service on the car.[83]

With public sympathy on the side of the strikers, the Paris omnibus workers won their basic demand of twelve hours of "effective service." When this was added to another half-hour necessary for preparation of the horses, it meant an average of about twelve and a half hours per day at the job, as opposed to fifteen previously. Thus average time at the job dropped fully two and a half hours per day, although time actually worked dropped less as long periods of waiting during the day were reduced.[84] In addition, the coachmen and conductors were to receive one day of paid vacation per month and the detested fines were to be levied less severely.

This corresponds to the victory won by the tramway workers of Marseilles in 1893. There again the strike did not involve wages (4.25 to 4.50 francs per day), but rather hinged on the fact that the twelve hours of effective work were often spread over as much as sixteen or seventeen hours per day.[85] The company subsequently agreed to a limit of seventy hours per week, with a maximum of twelve hours of unbroken service per day, as well as two days of paid vacation per month.[86] The twelve-hour day with per-

[83] *Le Temps*, 27 May 1891.
[84] *Le Figaro*, 27 May 1891; France, *Statistique des grèves*, 1895, pp. 174-75.
[85] *Le Temps* and *Le Figaro*, 9 October 1893.
[86] *Le Soleil*, 11 October 1893; France, *Statistique des grèves*, 1893, p. 75.

haps two days of paid vacation each month was thus becoming the norm for French tram workers in the early 1890s. And this was apparently the general situation, at least in Western Europe. An extensive parliamentary inquiry into the conditions of British tramway workers suggested that the twelve-hour day was becoming fairly widespread by 1894, and that the average of fifteen hours at Manchester was becoming exceptional.[87]

This general improvement in the last days of the horsecar accelerated with electrification. Generally speaking, the twelve-hour day being fought for in the early 1890s was widely replaced by a ten-hour day around the turn of the century. This in turn quickly gave way to a nine-hour working day in Great Britain and many German cities in the early part of the twentieth century, although a ten-hour day seems to have been more common in France. With one day in seven free, the average work week was about fifty-four hours. There was no question that the short breaks were now on "company time." In addition, the one day off each week was invariably with pay, and fringe benefits—particularly pensions—rose significantly. Wages (and prices) increased significantly, as, for example, from an average yearly wage of 1,435 kroners in 1903 to 2,282 kroners in 1912 for employees of the Viennese municipal tramways.[88] Rather than reproducing the vexatiously incomplete data upon which these conclusions are based,[89] we shall take a closer

---

[87] HC, 1893-94, XXXIII, pp. 83, 90, 172, 525-26.

[88] Vienna, Direktion der städtischen Strassenbahnen, *Die Entwicklung der städtischen Strassenbahnen im Zehnjähriger Eigenbetriebe der Gemeinde Wien* (Vienna, 1913), p. 119.

[89] For France, see *Statistique des grèves*, 1898, p. 294; 1899, pp. 232-35; AN, F 14, 15012, "Clause relative au personnel," for material on Parisian workers; for Germany and Austria, see, in addition to Sternberg and Buchmann, *40 Jahre Essener Strassenbahnen*, pp. 82-83; Rowe, "Municipal Ownership," *AAA* 27 (1906): 59-60; *SRJ* 26 (1905): 847; for Great Britain, discussion in chapter v and Howe, "Municipal Ownership," pp. 53, 67-68; and *MTA*, 1911-12, 59-60.

look at this evolution in the key city of Berlin, as a case study of the evolving trend.

By the mid-1890s the position of Berlin streetcar workers had improved a little from the late 1880s, but not much. After 1889 the personnel had received two to four free days per month, as opposed to no paid vacation whatsoever, previously. The average workday was about fourteen hours including interruptions and preparation time, or twelve hours actually in service on the trams.[90] With electrification, beginning in 1896, there was some improvement, which was extended after the two-day strike of May 1900. By 1902 hours had been noticeably reduced: coachmen (on the omnibuses) and conductors worked an eleven-hour day on the average with twelve hours the maximum; electric motormen on the other hand worked a nine-hour day with ten hours the maximum. There was to be either no unpaid interruption, or at most one one-hour interruption, as opposed to the two one-hour interruptions previously. One day in seven was a day off with pay, and seven of these per year had to be either a Sunday or a holiday.[91]

By 1909 there was a further reduction in hours for conductors, who now averaged ten hours while motormen continued to average nine. Most important, this service was to be continuous without unpaid interruptions. In addition, numerous paid breaks, averaging twelve minutes per hour, meant that the conductors and motormen were in action roughly eight and seven and one-quarter hours per day, respectively. And of course any time spent getting in or out of the car barn was now considered part of the working day. This had not always been the case when twelve-hour days in service were the norm. Wages rose with time in service and averaged about 1,400 marks per worker in 1909, about one-third more than in 1895.[92] Health insurance, pen-

[90] Sternberg, *Das Verkehrsgewerbe Leipzigs*, p. 85; Buchmann, *Entwickelung*, p. 60.
[91] Buchmann, *Entwickelung*, pp. 60-61.
[92] Buchmann, *Entwickelung*, pp. 61-73.

sions, and death benefits were all well-developed, in accordance with the German Empire's pervasive social welfare legislation. In short, weekly wages improved moderately, while the working week was drastically reduced from roughly eighty-four hours for all horsetram workers in the early 1890s—when unpaid and often unwanted interruptions are properly included as part of the working day—to sixty and fifty-four hours for conductors and motormen respectively in 1909, when work breaks were "on company time." Surely this quite typical development represents an enormous improvement, and strongly suggests that the impact of electric traction upon streetcar workers was extremely favorable.

A brief examination of general trends, which might have caused such improvement had the clip-clop of horsecars never disappeared, suggests that this was the case. As is well-known, the years between 1900 and 1913 were a period of rising prices and very modest increases in real wages.[93] And although the data are far too imperfect to permit great certainty, it seems that tram workers conformed to the average pattern in this respect and that the increases they won were also largely nullified by inflation. The rise of one-third in nominal wages between 1895 and 1909 for Berlin workers was in line with the general trend for German wages, for example, and would have resulted in a real gain of less than 10 percent.[94]

As for the length of the working day, however, it seems that tramway workers fared considerably better than average. More specifically, they did very much better than skilled craftsmen, who had won important reductions earlier, and with whom they very largely caught up. Thus in Great Britain "that fifty-four or fifty-four and one-half-hour working week, exclusive of overtime, to which most im-

[93] C.D.H. Cole and Raymond Postgate, *The British Common People, 1746-1946* (London, 1961), pp. 455 ff., 503; Ashok V. Desai, *Real Wages in Germany, 1871-1913* (Oxford, 1968), pp. 34-37.

[94] Desai, *Real Wages*, p. 36.

portant trades had settled down in the 'seventies remained unchanged in some trades and places forty years."[95] Still, there was some modest decline to an average of about fifty to fifty-one hours in 1913. For example, this was precisely the case for printers, whose working day in 1913 "had been shortened by half an hour in forty years."[96]

In France there was apparently only a slight decline in the working day between the early 1870s and 1914, when the working day averaged slightly more than ten hours a day in the provinces and slightly less in Paris.[97] In Germany, where skilled craftsmen were working about a ten-hour day in the early 1870s, while the general norm was the twelve-hour day in industry, the fall was more noticeable.[98] By the end of the century twelve hours was considered long, eleven hours was quite usual in the majority of factories, ten hours was "firmly established in many well-organized trades," and nine hours was coming for certain others. In 1913 more than half of the organized workers still worked more than nine hours, while "perhaps even a majority of the factory workers worked longer than ten hours."[99] Thus the conclusion must be that the nine- or ten-hour day, which European tramway workers achieved by the early years of the century, represented a much better than average improvement. The causes for this improvement should therefore be sought within the industry, even if this achievement was also a graphic example of how some fortunate semi-skilled workers were able to shorten markedly their dehumanizingly long hours between 1890 and 1910.

The advent of electric traction obviously required men with different skills, but it was much less obvious to some

[95] J. H. Clapham, *An Economic History of Modern Britain*, 3 vols. (Cambridge, 1926-38), 3:477.

[96] *Ibid.*, p. 478; also, Jurgen Kuczynski, *A Short History of Labour Conditions Under Capitalism*, numerous vols. (London, 1942-45), 2:74.

[97] Kuczynski, *Labour Conditions*, 4:133, 174.

[98] *Ibid.*, 3:1, 141-44.

[99] *Ibid.*, 145; also see Gerhard Bry, *Wages in Germany, 1871-1945* (Princeton, N.J., 1960), pp. 45-46.

why they should command a higher price. Many contemporaries stated emphatically that ordinary horsecar drivers with no electric skill could quickly learn the motorman's trade.[100] It could even be argued that the new job was really easier, as an anonymous German engineer sarcastically implied in 1904. "The motormen, or rather the labor unions, suddenly discovered that there is a great difference between a motorman and a horse-car driver, although the former is not obliged to handle heavy reins and a whip while driving one or more horses and keeping a sharp lookout. This discovery resulted in wage increases and reductions from twelve to thirteen hours to eight to nine hours. Of course, conductors had to be treated likewise."[101] Why, then, the much better conditions we have established for easily learned and less physically demanding work?

Two factors seem to have been of particular importance. First, whatever management might sometimes say, it required more training and skill to be a motorman than a horsetram driver. And the economic losses caused by poor performance were much greater. One early manager told his colleagues to "see that the men running your cars are careful and capable of exercising a little judgment. A careless man will ruin your motor in a short time by forcing the whole current through it, when there is no reasonable excuse for the same; particularly in starting the cars, a little attention in this direction will amply repay you for the time and experience."[102] Even if such gross errors—or acts of sabotage—were avoided, there was still the problem of power consumption, which could vary greatly with the skill of the motorman. Because of this, after 1900 European tramways began to employ watt-meters on the cars to measure the amount of current used by their motormen. This permitted rewards for the efficient and penalties for the

---

[100] For example, *ASRA* 3 (1884-85): 132-33; *EE* 16 (1895): 369.
[101] A German Engineer, "Financial Results," *SRJ* 23 (1904): 705.
[102] *SRJ* 5 (1890): 341.

inept, and helped workers understand how their efficiency could be raised.[103]

The need for greater skill and judgment is also seen in the training of motormen. The experience of Hamburg Tramways was typical. The company found that the best men to train as motormen were the former horsecar drivers, who were already well acquainted with streetcar traffic. For a few days the candidate would accompany an experienced motorman, who would point out the general features of electric operation. A head motorman or his assistant would then take the candidate on scheduled trips and progressively let him operate the car. This would go on for three weeks, at which time the candidate would be thoroughly tested. "If after three weeks the candidate exhibits no aptness for the position, no more time is wasted on him, and he is sent away, because it has been found that if a man does not grasp the problem in three weeks he probably never will."[104] Therefore horsecar drivers were required to up-grade their skills, and not all could meet the challenge.

This might not have led to improved conditions if total employment on street railways had been declining: a worker might have needed to up-grade his skills just to keep his job. But of course the demand for motormen was rising very rapidly with electrification. This second factor meant that the horsecar drivers, who had the great asset of being already experienced in traffic matters, and who could also master the new techniques, found themselves in a very favorable bargaining position. The Great Berlin Street Railway Company, for example, "in the midst of the change from animal to electric traction, with the accompanying traffic increase and line construction, needed more personnel. The employees saw this as the right moment to achieve

[103] *SRJ* 21 (1903): 668-69; Hermes, *Finanzierung*, p. 53; Vienna, Direktion der städtischen Strassenbahnen, *Die Entwicklung der städtischen Strassenbahnen im Zehnjähriger Eigenbetriebe der Gemeinde Wien* (Vienna, 1913), p. 92.
[104] Vellguth, "Hamburg," *SRJ* 19 (1902): 10.

their well-known demands for higher wages and shorter hours by means of force."[105] Thus with the very effective strike of 1900, motormen gained a nine-hour day, but horsecar drivers only succeeded in winning an eleven-hour day.

The combination of increased skills and expanding demand leaves out a third possible factor often mentioned by contemporaries—the more enlightened labor policies of municipal ownership. As we have seen in chapter v, the desire to improve working conditions was an important factor in municipalization in Great Britain, and this is true of municipalization elsewhere as well. And of course British workers on municipal electric tramways did fare much better than those who had toiled for the horsecar companies. Yet in France and in Germany private companies also improved, or were forced to improve, conditions notably, mainly for the reasons mentioned above. And major private companies in Germany generally, like those in Berlin and Hamburg, offered their workers conditions similar to those found under German municipal operation. It would seem therefore that municipal ownership may have reinforced the basic trend of sharply improved working conditions, but that it was not a primary factor.

[105] Buchmann, *Die Entwickelung*, p. 60.

VII. Conclusions

In spite of the transformation of European cities throughout the nineteenth century because of industrialization and population growth, urban public transportation developed slowly and cautiously until the very last decade of the century. Urban omnibuses did grow out of the short stagecoach in the course of the first half of the century. But these infrequent, uncomfortable, and relatively expensive coaches concentrated on serving a middle-class clientele and were of marginal significance except in the largest agglomerations. Horse tramways catered to a larger section of the population, and they spread across Europe and experienced rapid expansion in the 1870s.

Yet within a decade the slow-moving, inelastic, horse-drawn trams had ceased to expand. They were clearly unable to satisfy either the enormous latent demand for improved public transportation or to alleviate the concentration and unhealthy overcrowding of European cities. And so despite countless efforts to achieve satisfactory mechanical traction, the traditional horse labored on: the technological alternatives, such as steam trams, either failed to meet demands for clean, inoffensive techniques or they failed to offer clear economic advantages over existing methods. In the broad social and economic perspective such alternatives were little more than mechanical curiosities, adding color to the urban scene.

It was within this context that the European-conceived and American-executed innovation of dependable overhead electric traction for street railways marked a revolutionary breakthrough, a breakthrough which swept across the United States after 1888 and was then diffused throughout Europe and the rest of the world. The overhead electric method meant not only an enormous improvement in the quality of transit—most notably because of its increased speed, extension of area served, and lower fares—but also in the quality of the good which streetcar companies could and did provide in the face of great consumer acceptance. The result was a revolution in European urban public transportation.

The use of the term "revolution" is no flight into scholastic hyperbole. Total passengers carried on European tramways—judging by data on Austria-Hungary, France, Germany, and Great Britain—increased more than seven-fold in the course of a generation, from 1886 to 1910, while per capita usage for city dwellers increased roughly four-fold in the same period. Traffic patterns of different European cities also showed a sharp, "revolutionary" discontinuity coinciding with streetcar electrification. Passengers carried normally doubled or tripled in two to five years, depending upon how rapidly all the lines of a given network were transformed and extended.

The rapid rate of European growth becomes clearer when it is contrasted with that in the United States of America. Long the world leader in the technical and commercial development of urban public transit, the United States was far in advance of Europe in 1890. By 1910 Europe's much more rapid growth—American per capita usage increased about 50 percent in this period—had closed the gap, and Europe was on the verge of taking an indisputable lead in urban public transport. By that time the European electric tramway industry was firmly established and steadily expanding. Portents of the industry's decline, a decline which all nations would subsequently share, although in vastly different proportions, were scarcely visible. An investigation of the factors in that very uneven pattern of decline (and revival) of electric street railways across the face of Europe—an important if neglected topic in its own right—would clearly begin with World War I and its consequences. Before 1914 the trolley, like monarchy, still reigned.

There is another important point to note here, a point

sometimes made its connection with the usefulness of the concept of the Industrial Revolution. The change from an essentially agricultural to an essentially industrial economy and society has occurred in different countries only once, argue proponents of the concept. After that revolutionary, once-and-for-all change it is only the specific content of industrial output that is modified, as old industries evolve and new industries arise to maintain the growth already launched.

Within the same framework, I would argue that the change from animate-powered transport of the age of walking cities and horse-drawn vehicles, including tramways, to inanimate, mechanized, mass-produced, and mass-oriented urban public transportation has occurred only once. For Europe, that once was with electric streetcars. Thereafter urban public transportation has evolved with buses, high-speed trains, express subways, etc., or even declined where the harmful consequences of basing urban civilization upon the private automobile have been grossly underestimated, as in the United States. But it has not been revolutionized.

The revolutionary significance of the new mode of transport was also reflected in its impact on society. In the first place, public transport simply became a much more important factor in the lives of European urban populations. This increased importance was particularly noticeable for those of modest means, who received extra consideration and special cheap tickets. Here, incidentally, is a graphic example of the textbook cliché about the rise of mass society at the end of the nineteenth century, as millions of people anonymously climbed onto the electric tram together. Second, and there is more to do here, electric tramways had an impact on public welfare and urban form. I have tried to show that suburban expansion was facilitated by electric streetcars, which promoted a reasonable diffusion of population without, however, blowing the city apart. Similarly, if less dramatically, electric streetcars played a definite if heretofore unnoticed role in excursions and expanding leisure-time activities. Finally, the transformation of transport facilitated, and to a considerable extent caused, the marked improvement in the working conditions of tramway workers, who had previously toiled in extremely difficult conditions.

If the speed and content of the electric streetcar transformation was revolutionary, the process itself also had extremely interesting aspects. These aspects shed light on the question of development, diffusion, and management of major technological innovations that are public by their very nature.

There can be no question that the initiative for change originated with private entrepreneurs, who sought to profit from the economic advantages of cost-reducing, supply-increasing electric traction. Thus in city after city the local tramway company petitioned the appropriate officials for permission to install the new overhead traction. Yet a closer look shows that a very few leading electric producers, who held the necessary techniques and engineering capacity, were behind the vast majority of such petitions, after buying or allying themselves with local tramway companies. These electrical manufacturers were less interested in substantial future profits for operating companies than in large and immediate entrepreneurial profits from the sale of equipment and expertise.

Had the small number of producers effectively combined to divide up the market, they might conceivably have impeded the spread of electric traction, as they tried to force tramway companies and municipalities to accept unfavorable conditions. Yet until at least 1901, when tramway electrification was largely completed, these few firms engaged in aggressive oligopolistic competition and developed to the utmost (or even overdeveloped) the new economic opportunity. This enabled municipalities to drive good bargains for the public in negotiations over electrification. This effective functioning of late nineteenth-century capitalism was seen in detail in the case of France. There the pioneering entrepreneurship of the principal firm, the French Thomson-Houston Company, encouraged followers and competitors who overbuilt and overspeculated before the collapse of the European tramway boom.

Electric tramway development in France also points up an important factor often omitted in discussion of entrepreneurship within a given economy—the foreign entrepreneur. Certainly differences in entrepreneurial capacity, resting in large part on differences in technical capacity, exist in all sorts of categories—by nation, by region, by culture, by sector, etc.—and they must not be ignored. At the same time foreign enterprise has historically provided the means to reduce such differences, often so effectively that the original differences are themselves obscured and the "foreigner" is assimilated into the dominant group. So it was with American entrepreneurship in French tramway electrification: foreign entrepreneurship substituted for domestic business leadership, to the extent that such a substitution was necessary.

This is related to problems of comparative economic history. On the one hand, electric street railways support rather traditional views concerning the strengths and weaknesses of the different European economies in this period. Nor is this surprising: electric traction was closely related to the new electrical manufacturing industry, which contemporary observers often used to measure a country's standing in the international economic competition. The United States and Germany undeniably led the pack with an impressive combination of technological innovation, rapid domestic development, and foreign investment in advanced nations. France and Belgium, and Italy and Austria-Hungary, for that matter, were not far behind in adopting electric traction. Yet with the possible exception of Belgium they were clearly followers and not leaders in almost every area of the new industry. Great Britain was a laggard, a laggard who had actually pioneered in horse tramways in many a continental city in the 1870s. Russia (and southeastern Europe) was largely dependent upon foreign enterprise and technology for her electric tramways, which nonetheless served all of her large and medium cities. This was an order that might have been expected.

Yet the differences between the participants in the course of street railway transformation were not tremendous, and it would be a mistake to focus only on them. Technical ability and rates of adoption varied, to be sure, but all the major countries finished the race and all reached the same destination. They all mastered the new system and participated fully in the rise of urban mass transport. (To a considerable extent this was also the case in the larger cities of the colonial and underdeveloped world in these years.)

This final equality in electric tramways is at least as remarkable as the transitory differences. It would seem that foreign entrepreneurship was a crucial factor, as in the case of France. Loosely speaking, we may conclude that what American enterprise was to France and Great Britain, German and French enterprise was to the countries of the Mediterranean. And what Belgian entrepreneurs were to Eastern Europe and the Middle East, their British counterparts were to the colonies and Latin America. Thus foreign enterprise smoothed out differences between countries and areas. Perhaps the lesson here is that gaps between nations in new industries and problems of inadequate domestic enterprise in certain areas can be solved to a considerable extent, at least within capitalist economies, by such international flows and substitutions.

Whatever the source of entrepreneurship within Europe, it had to work within the framework of strict public regulation of urban transportation. Within that framework technical and economic factors drew certain general boundary lines regarding what was possible, but the process of negotiation and adoption was strongly influenced by non-technical and non-economic factors. Specifically, the cultural perceptions of Europeans rejected or impeded the diffusion of the new American techno-economic system because of the aesthetic damage—the "visual pollution"—it seemed to entail, just as they had earlier rejected dirty, noisy steam tramways. What was accepted, happily or otherwise, in the American environment was unacceptable in the European one.

This led to attempts both to supersede and to adapt the American innovation to meet these non-economic and non-technical criticisms. These efforts were successful in that they produced a variety of technical combinations and technological alternatives for the consideration of society and its policy makers. This was a key step in the adoption of a large portion of the basic innovation of overhead traction, because the technological alternatives expanded the range of possible outcomes. These outcomes were less satisfactory from the techno-economic point of view, but they offered marked cultural and aesthetic improvements. Society and its decision-makers could then find acceptable trade-offs between conflicting demands and values.

It is important to note that aesthetic concerns were constrained by other cultural values, especially the ideal of social improvement and increased welfare for poorer classes. This ideal sought to limit both the added expense of less efficient, "luxury" methods, as well as the portion of the gains going to private owners and entrepreneurs. It facilitated reappraisal of the initial hostility toward overhead traction, and helped win support for the European modification, with its more handsome poles and less obtrusive wires. It also helps explain the appeal of municipal ownership in Great Britain, which was seen in part as a necessary institutional innovation for the best utilization of the new urban technology.

The significance of the process of development, modification, and adoption we have examined in detail in relationship to the electric streetcar revolution in Europe is, I think, by no means limited to that case alone. Increasingly, we realize that the major technological thrusts and movements which have vast consequences for society cannot be allowed to run wildly on the basis of what is presently cheapest and most dependable, without proper regard for long-term costs and related negative consequences. Indeed, in certain academic circles the catchword "technology assessment" is increasingly uttered with that hushed solemnity associated with the latest big race for big money. And we hear of enormously complicated and of course enormously expensive systems approaches which will model and calculate the innumerable pluses and minuses of major technological developments. Let us hope that some of this work will bear good fruit. Yet, given previous problems in this field, it would seem that investigators need humility and the public and its representatives need a healthy skepticism.

But they need optimism as well, for much can be done with good common sense. They need to take to heart the lesson of the electric streetcar revolution in Europe. They should see it as an excellent, well-documented, early example of the successful control and management of fundamental technological innovation by an advanced society and its officials. This control, this management of technology, which seems likely to continue to spread to ever larger portions of the economies of highly developed nations, demanded at least three forces.

First, it required a substantial block of the public to be willing to look beyond immediate technical expediency and economic costs, a public willing to refuse unsatisfactory solutions even when they had no good alternative. Second, it required flexible technologists and resourceful private enterprise capable of designing their systems so as to meet cultural and social demands, while still retaining and perfecting the essence of their techno-economic improvements. Third, it required competent and impartial public authority to weigh alternative solutions and negotiate acceptable outcomes, including that of sending plans back to the drawing boards. With such actors it was possible to manage one major case of inexorable technological change, so that that change harmonized with society's broad needs and evolving aspriations. Is that not one of the challenges of our time?

Bibliography

When I began examining European urban public transportation at the end of the nineteenth century, I was both pleased and chagrined to find that there was no good discussion of relevant sources and bibliography. Pleased because it confirmed my belief that the subject had been very inadequately studied; chagrined because everything was to do and lacunae would therefore be inevitable. This being the case and given the fact that all the basic sources have been thoroughly cited, it seems best to mention briefly the quality and quantity of the materials themselves, as well as list the most important of them.

1. *Public and Private Archives*

The basic archival sources for this study were French. They allowed many insights into the process of government regulation and private entrepreneurship which could not have been obtained from published sources. At the Archives Nationales (AN), Paris, the F 14 series of the Ministry of Public Works regarding all tramways in Paris and the provinces was used (dossiers 13507-30 and 14999-15032). So was the enormous 65 AQ series, which is organized by corporations, and which allowed me to cull information on a multitude of tramway and electrical companies all over Europe from the contemporary financial press. Weak on Germany and Great Britain, this series is not only important for France and Belgium but also for Latin and Eastern Europe, as well as for colonial areas. These materials were complemented by invaluable studies on individual firms and general conditions in the private archives of the Crédit Lyonnais (CL), as well as by the smaller amount of tramway material at the Banque de l'Union Parisienne (BUP), both in Paris.

In England, I examined those manuscript sources relating to British tramway companies which are held by the British Transport Commission Historical Office (66 Porchester Road, Bayswater, London). Unfortunately, I found very little there which was not in technical periodicals.

2. *Periodicals, Associations, and Handbooks*

Technical and professional journals and proceedings dealing with aspects of street railway development were the most important single source for this study, a source which runs to tens of thousands of pages. Since much of this information is repetitious and often very technical, I chose to concentrate on four periodicals which seemed most useful, each having unique virtues as to coverage, area, and viewpoint. These were: *The Electrical Engineer (EE)*, London; *L'Industrie Electrique (IE)*, Paris; *Street Railway Journal (SRJ)*, New York; and the difficult-to-locate *Zeitschrift für Kleinbahnen (ZK)*, published from 1894 by the Prussian Ministerium der offenlichen Arbeiten, which I found in the Staatsbibliothek in Munich. In addition to countless short reports and many long articles, these journals quote and summarize innumerable other materials: papers before professional groups, findings of committees and city engineers, articles in other journals, local newspaper accounts, etc. *ZK*, in particular, provides an extensive review of the literature on street railways in each issue, which allows the researcher to pinpoint important and non-repetitive articles in a host of journals. The most useful of these for me were: *Deutsche Zeitschrift für Elektrotechnik*, Halle; *Electrician*, London; *L'Electricien*, Paris; *Electric Railway and Tramway Journal (ERTJ)*, London; *Elektrotechnische Zeitschrift (EZ)*, Berlin; *Le Génie Civil*, Paris; *Revue Générale des Chemins de fer et des Tramways*, Paris; *Traction and Transmission*, London; *Verkehrstechnische Woche und Eisenbahntechnische Zeitschrift*, Berlin; *Zeitschrift des Oesterreichischen Ingenieur- und Architekten-*

Vereines (ZOIAV), Vienna; *Zeitschrift des Vereines deutscher Ingenieure (ZVDI)*, Berlin; *Zeitschrift für das gesamte Local- und Strassenbahn-Wesen (ZGLSW)*, Wiesbaden; and *Zeitschrift für Transportwesen und Strassenbau (ZTS)*, Berlin. As the foregoing suggests, the many railroad journals were of little use.

Tramway industry organizations were another good source. Both the American Street Railway Association *(ASRA)* and the Municipal Tramways Association of Great Britain *(MTA)* published annual *Proceedings*. The important Union Internationale Permanente des Tramways, founded [1887?] and headquartered in Brussels, had annual or biannual meetings in various cities, which attracted members from all over Europe. To my knowledge, however, the Union did not publish its proceedings, with the exception of the 1900 meetings in Paris: *Congrès International des Tramways, Paris, Septembre 1900: Comptes-Rendus détaillés* (Brussels, 1900). Here again, these and similar proceedings dealing with street railway questions, such as those of the (British) Tramway Institute, may be followed through reports and excerpts in the technical journals. This valuable source has been thoroughly utilized. The Union des Tramways de France published the *Annuaire Général des Tramways de France* (Paris, 1901), Edouard Fuster, ed., as well as a journal from 1906. All French tramways companies and certain vital statistics for each of them are in the 1901 publication, as are German tramways for all years after 1896 in the financial handbook for Germany, *Die deutschen Elektrischen Strassenbahnen* ... (Berlin, 1896—).

Other particularly useful contemporary periodicals were the *Annals of the American Academy of Political and Social Sciences (AAA)*, *Municipal Affairs (MA)*, New York; and the *Municipal Year Book of the United Kingdom*, which contained a handy summary of official statistics. Also useful for this study were the important *Journal of Transport History (JTH)*, Leicester; *Transport History (TH)*; and two publications of the Light Railway Transport League: *Tramway Review*, "an historical record of tramways in the British Isles"; and *Modern Tramway and Light Railway Review*, published by Ian Allen, Shepperton, Middlesex, a leading publisher in transportation and tramway history (along with the Advertiser Press of Huddersfield). One of the great values of these publications is that numerous advertisements and reviews enable one to keep track of the widely scattered literature of tramway enthusiasts. Similar publications, such as *Der Deutsche Verkehrs-Amateur, Rail et Traction*, and *Der Stadtverkehr*, which deal mainly with contemporary developments, were not consulted.

3. Selected Documents, Monographs, and Secondary Works

Although there is no integrated study of European transit electrification, a number of works in transportation, urban, and economic history were most helpful. This was particularly true of old monographs on the transport of individual cities (Buchmann, Grossmann, Haselmann, Martin, and Sternberg), provisional syntheses at the national level (mainly Handlmeier, Klapper, von Lindheim, and Weil), and a few recent monographs of excellent quality (such as Barker and Robbins, Kellett, Passer, and Warner), which provided both insights and inspiration.

Allgemeine Elektricitäts-Gesellschaft, Berlin. No title. Berlin, n.d. [1899?]. This work is in the John Crerar Library, Chicago.

Arrivetz, Jean. *Histoire des transports à Lyon*. Lyon, 1966.

Austria. Eisenbahn Ministerium. *Oesterreichische Eisenbahnstatistik für das Jahr—*. Vienna, annual publication.

Barbillion, Louis, and Griffisch, G. J. *Traité pratique de traction électrique*. 2 vols. Paris, 1903-04.

Barker, T. C., and Robbins, Michael. *A History of London Transport: Passenger Travel and the Development of the Metropolis*, vol. 1, *The Nineteenth Century*. London, 1963.

Bett, Wingate H., and Gillham, John C. *Great British Tramways Networks.* 3d. ed. London, 1957.
Boshart, August. *Strassenbahnen.* Berlin, 1920.
Brook, Roy. *The Tramways of Huddersfield: A History of Huddersfield Corporation Tramways, 1883-1940.* Huddersfield, 1959.
Buchmann, Eduard. *Die Entwickelung der Grossen Berliner Strassenbahn und ihre Bedeutung für die Verkehrsentwikelung Berlins.* Berlin, 1910.
Burrows, V. E. *Tramways in Metropolitan Essex.* Huddersfield, 1967.
Bussy, André. *La municipalisation des tramways: Ses résultats financiers à l'étranger.* Paris, 1908.
Cadoux, Gaston. *La vie des grandes capitales: Etudes comparatives sur Londres, Paris, Berlin.* Paris, 1908.
Carver, Humphrey. *Cities in the Suburbs.* Toronto, 1962.
Chaumeil, Louis. *Les omnibus et les tramways à Paris.* Paris, 1913.
Clark, D. Kinnear. *Tramways: Their Construction and Working.* 2d. ed. London, 1894.
Colson, C. *Abrégé de la législation des chemins de fer et tramways.* 2d. ed. Paris, 1905.
Cormack, Ian L. "1894 and All That." Glasgow, 1968. (This author has a number of short works published by the Scottish Tramway Museum Society, Glasgow.)
Creighton, Roger L. *Urban Transportation Planning.* Urbana, Ill., 1970.
Crosby, Oscar T., and Bell, Louis. *The Electric Street Railway in Theory and Practice.* New York, 1892.
Dickinson, Robert E. *The West European City: A Geographical Interpretation.* London, 1951.
Dollfus, Charles, and Geoffroy, Edgar de. *Histoire de la locomotion terrestre: Les Chemins de fer.* Paris, 1935.
Doolittle, F. W. *Studies in the Cost of Urban Transportation Service.* New York, 1916.
Dupuy, Paul. *La traction électrique.* Paris, 1897.
Dyos, H. J. *Victorian Suburb: A Study of the Growth of Camberwell.* Leicester, 1961.

Dyos, H. J., and Aldcroft, D. H. *British Transport: An Economic Survey from the Seventeenth Century to the Twentieth.* Leicester, 1969.

[Essen]. *40 Jahre Essener Strassenbahnen, 1893-1933.* Essen, 1933.

Fasolt, Friedrich. *Die sieben gröszten deutschen Elektricitätsgesellschaften, ihre Entwicklung und Unternehmertägkeit.* Dresden, 1904.

Fitzgerald, John E., and Howes, Osborne Jr. *Reports on Systems of Transportation in some European Cities.* Boston, 1891.

France. Ministère des Travaux Publics. Direction des Chemins de Fer. *Statistique des Chemins de Fer.* Paris, annual publication.

[Frankfurt am Main.] *60 Jahre städtische elektrische Strassenbahn in Frankfurt am Main.* N.p. [Frankfurt am Main?], 1959.

George, Pierre. *Le fait urbain à travers le monde.* Paris, 1952.

Germany. Statistisches Reichsamt. *Statistisches Jahrbuch für das Deutsche Reich.* Berlin, annual publication.

Gragt, F. Van der. *Europe's Greatest Tramway Network: Tramways in the Rhein-Ruhr Area of Germany.* Leiden, 1968.

Great Britain. House of Commons. Board of Trade. *Returns for Street and Road Tramways.* Annual publication.

Die Grosse Berliner Strassenbahn, 1871-1902: Denkschrift aus Anlasz der vollstandigen Durchführung des elektromotorischen Betriebes. Berlin, 1902.

Grossmann, Hermann. *Die kommunale Bedeutung des Strassenbahnwesen beleuchtet am Werdegange der Dresdner Strassenbahnen.* Dresden, 1903.

Gunther, Arthur. *Die kommunalen Strassenbahnen.* Jena, 1913.

Haselmann, Alfred. *Die Aachener Kleinbahnen.* Jena, 1909.

Hendlmeier, Wolfgang. *Von der Pferde-Eisenbahn zur Schnell-Strassenbahn: Überblick über die Entwicklung des deutschen Strassenbahn- und Obuswesens unter besonderer Berücksichtigung der westdeutschen Betriebe.* Munich, 1968.

Hermes, Friedrich. *Finanzierung und Rentabilität deutscher Strassenbahnen.* Jena, 1909.

Howe, Frederic C. *European Cities at Work.* New York, 1913.

———. "Municipal Ownership in Great Britain," *Bulletin of the Bureau of Labor,* No. 62 (January 1906): 1-123.

Howes, Osborne Jr. *Report on the Transportation of Passengers in and around the Cities of Europe.* Boston, 1891.

Hunter, D.L.G. *Edinburgh's Transport.* Huddersfield, 1964.

Jackson, Alan A., and Croome, Desmond F. *Rails Through the Clay: A History of London's Tube Railways.* London, 1962.

Jackson-Stevens, E. *British Electric Tramways.* Newton Abbot, Devon, 1971.

Joyce, James. *Tramways of the World.* London, 1965.

Kellett, John R. *The Impact of Railways on Victorian Cities.* London, 1969.

King, J. S. *Keighley Corporation Transport.* Huddersfield, 1964.

Klapper, Charles. *The Golden Age of Tramways.* London, 1961.

Klein-Bader, C. *75 Jahre Münchner Strassenbahn, 1876-1951.* Munich, 1951.

Lee, G. A. "The Tramways of Kingston-upon-Hull: A Study of Municipal Enterprise." Ph.D. thesis, Sheffield University, 1968.

Lindheim, Wilhelm von. *Strassenbahnen in Belgien, Deutschland, Grossbritannien und Irland, Frankreich, Italien, Oesterreich Ungarn, den Niederlanden, Niederländisch-Indien, der Schweiz und den verschiedenen Staaten von Amerika: Statistisches und Finanzielles unter besonderer Berücksichtigung der Wiener Verhältnisse.* Vienna, 1888.

Lotz, Walter. *Verkehrsentwicklung in Deutschland, 1800-1900.* Leipzig, 1900.
Manchester. Tramways Department. *The Passenger Transportation Problem: Report of the Special Subcommittee.* Manchester, 1914.
Martin, Alfred. *Etude historique et statistique sur les moyens de transport dans Paris.* Paris, 1894.
Mason, E. S. *The Street Railway in Massachusetts.* Cambridge, Mass., 1932.
Massachusetts. Legislature. Special Committee on Street Railways. *Report on the Relations between Cities and Towns and Street Railway Companies.* Boston, 1898. (House Doc. 475.)
Miller, John Anderson. *Fares, Please!: From Horse-cars to Streamliners.* New York, 1941.
Neefe, M., ed. *Statistisches Jahrbuch deutscher Städte.* Breslau, 1890—.
Passer, Harold C. *The Electrical Manufacturers, 1875-1900: A Study in Competition, Entrepreneurship, Technical Change, and Economic Growth.* Cambridge, Mass., 1953.
Pinner, Felix. *Emil Rathenau und das elektrotechnische Zeitalter.* Leipzig, 1918.
Prasuhn, P. H. *Chronik der Strassenbahn.* Hanover, 1969.
Robert, Jean. *Les tramways parisiens.* Paris, 1959.
Rowsome, Frank Jr. *Trolley Car Treasury: A Century of American Streetcars—Horsecars, Cable Cars, Interurbans, and Trolleys.* New York, 1956.
Sarafon, E. *Les tramways.* 4th. ed. Paris, 1898.
Schiemann, Max. *Bau und Betrieb elektrischer Bahnen.* 2 vols. Leipzig, 1898.
Siemens, Georg. *Geschichte des Hauses Siemens.* 3 vols. Munich, 1947-52.
Sternberg, Wilhelm. *Das Verkehrsgewerbe Leipzigs.* Jena, 1904.
Union Elektricitäts-Gesellschaft. *Elektrische Strassenbahnen, Système Thomson-Houston.* Berlin, 1895.

United States. Department of the Interior. Census Office. *Report on Transportation Business in the United States, 1890.* Part I. *Transportation by Land.* Washington, D.C., 1895.

Vienna. Direktion der städtischen Strassenbahnen. *Die Entwicklung der städtischen Strassenbahnen im zehnjährigen Eigenbetriebe der Gemeinde Wien.* Vienna, 1913.

Villars, A. *Les tramways électriques à Amiens.* Amiens, 1896.

Warner, Sam B. Jr. *Streetcar Suburbs: The Process of Growth in Boston, 1870-1900.* Cambridge, Mass, 1962.

Weber, Adna. *The Growth of Cities in the Nineteenth Century: A Study in Statistics.* New York, 1899.

Weil, Julius. *Die Entstehung und Entwicklung unserer elektrischen Strassenbahnen: In gemeinfasslicher Darstellung.* Leipzig, 1899.

Whitcombe, H. A. *History of the Steam Tram.* South Godstone, Surrey, 1954.

Wilson, Delos F. *Municipal Franchises.* 2 vols. New York, 1911.

Index

Aachen, 208
Adams, Charles Francis, 92
A.E.G. *See* Allgemeine Elektricitäts-Gesellschaft
aesthetic considerations in urban transportation, 83, 165, 244-46; in Berlin, 121-24; and overhead conductors, 48-49, 84-95; in Paris, 160-61; and steam tramways, 30-31, 34. *See also* overhead conductors; specific cities; specific countries
Albany, 92
Algerian Tramways Company, 142
Algiers, 142
Allgemeine Elektricitäts-Gesellschaft, 43, 77-78, 100, 111, 115-16
Altrincham, 218-19
America. *See* United States
"American railroads," 15-16, 19
American Street-Railway Association, 45
Amiens, 142
Anderson and Munro Company, 170
Angers, 153n
Anglobank, 111
Ashton-under-Lyne, 218-19
Auderghem, 212, 215
Austria, 71-72, 82. *See also* Austria-Hungary
Austria-Hungary, 22, 81, 87, 240, 243
automobile, 18, 190, 228-29
Avignon, 153n, 154

Baltimore, 11, 195
Baltimore and Ohio Railroad, 36
Banque de l'Afrique du Sud, 145
Banque de l'Union Parisienne, 81
Banque Française et Italienne, 17
Banque Henrotte, 144
Banque Internationale de Paris, 144n, 145, 149, 151-52
Barking Road Line, 165
Basel, 89
battery cars, 39-40, 74-76, 96-97, 106-07, 119, 165-67
Baudry (retired army officer), 10
Beaumont engines, 29
Becker and Company, 115
Belgium, 22, 72, 144-45, 158, 208, 243-44. *See also* Brussels
Bentley, Edward, 44-45
Bentley-Knight Electric Railway Company, 45
Bercroft, Henry, 164
Berlin, 6, 11, 17-18, 117, 209, 220; conditions of tramway workers in, 230, 233-34; early efforts of Siemens in, 37-38, 44; electric tramways of, 80-81, 86, 121, 123-24, 194-98; horse tramways of, 24-25; "mixed" systems of electric traction in, 99-100, 103. *See also* Great Berlin Street Railway Company
Berlin Industrial Exposition of 1879, 37
Berlin Stock Exchange, 80
Bessbrook and Newry Tramway Company, 70, 164, 170
Bessbrook Spinning Company, 164
Billy, Edouard de, 153
Birmingham, 7-9, 85, 171, 187, 193
Birmingham Tramways Company, 179
Blackpool, 39, 70
Blackwell, R. W., and Company, 185
Boendall, 212, 215
Boisfort, 212, 215-16

257

Bordeaux, 11, 100, 130, 146, 152, 178; electrification of tramways in, 138-141
Bordeaux Tramways and Omnibus Company, 140-41
Bordeaux Tramways and Omnibus Company Ltd., 138-39
Boston, 11, 51, 195, 197, 224
Bourges, 154
Bower, Abraham, 10
bow trolley, 79
brackets, use of, 102, 106, 182
Bradford, 193
Brandenburg Gate, 124
Bremen, 17, 77, 109, 194
Bremen Tramways Company, 77
Breslau, 17, 103, 194
Brighton, 38, 70
Brill, J. G. Company, 183
British Insulated Wire Company, 185
British Thomson-Houston Company, 170, 171, 183, 185
British Westinghouse Electric Company, 182, 185
Bruges, 3
Brush Electrical Engineering Company, 185
Brussels, 18, 86-87, 96, 145; Avenue Louise in, 210, 227; Cambre Woods of, 210, 214-15, 227; communes of, 212; electric tramways and the growth of, 209-16; excursions from, 227-28; Leopold Quarter of, 210, 214; map of, 211; population of, 210-13
Brussels Tramways Company, 29-30, 96, 214-16, 227
Buchmann, Eduard, 209
Budapest, 100
Buffalo, 92, 195
Burrell engines, 31
Byatt, I.C.R., 185

cable cars, 40-41
Caen, 152
Camberwell, 13
Cannes, 154

Canning Town Line, 166-67
capitalism, 162
Cette, 154
Châlons-sur-Marne, 152
Chamberlain, Joseph, 171
Chamon, G., 128
Charles Bridge, at Prague, 99
Chaudoir, Georges, 144
Chemnitz, 194
Chicago, 197, 199-201
Chicago Railway Exposition of 1883, 42
cities: congestion of, in Europe, 6-9, 18, 37-38, 206-08; in France, 7-8, 18, 86, 101, 154-55; in Germany, 11, 39, 44, 78-80, 194-96; in Great Britain, 7-9, 163-64, 187, 193, 195, 198, 228; medieval and baroque, 3-4; and suburban expansion, 8-9, 55, 114, 205-19; in the United States, 11, 14-15
City and South London Railway, 170
Claret, J., 132, 142n
Claret-Vuilleumier contact system, 150
Clermont-Ferrand, 132
Cleveland, 44
coaches, 4-5
Coffin, Charles A., 128
Cologne, 17, 70, 96, 194, 197
concessions, 89n; and comparison of American and European pattern, 91-94; competition for, 138-40, 149-50, 153-54; early pattern of, in Europe, 19-21; in Great Britain, 168-69; and private entrepreneurs, 111-12; renegotiation of, in Europe, 89-91, 115, 107-24, 134, 139-40; and workmen's fares, 116-17. See also specific cities; specific countries
conduit system, 106-07
Continental Metropolitan Tramways Company, 146n
corruption, 94
Coutant, Jules, 146n

Crédit Lyonnais, 131, 137, 141-42

Dalrymple, James, 200-01
Danzig, 17, 86
Davenport, Thomas, 35
Davidson, Robert, 36
Denver, 195
Diatto surface contact system, 150, 158
Dickinson Company, 138
Dickinson, Robert E., 6-7, 208
Dick, Kerr and Company, 185
Dortmund, 194
Douai, 153n
Dreiser, Theodore, 199
Dresden, 6, 11, 17, 79, 86, 110, 226; rides per capita at, 194, 197
Dublin, 170
Dublin United Tramways Company, 170, 179
Duisberg, 65, 194
"dummy" locomotive, 27-29
Dunne, Edward, 199-201
Dusseldorf, 17, 194
dynamo, 36

East Cleveland Company, 45
East Paris Tramways Company, 146, 148-49, 160
Edison Electric Light Company, 48
Edison General Electric Company, 127-28. *See also* General Electric Company
Edison, Thomas A., 42-45, 48, 147
Eisenbahnkonsortium für Handel und Industrie Hermann Bachstein, 204-05
Electric Construction Corporation, 170, 185
electric lighting, 169
Electrical Engineer, 96n, 169, 168, 173
electrical manufacturers, 61-62, 91, 242-44; in France, 109, 160-62; in Germany, 77-80, 109, 125-26; in Great Britain, 109, 169-70, 185-86. *See also* entrepreneurship; specific firms

Electrician, 186n
elevated railways, 38, 44, 224
Empain group, 149
entrepreneurship: in Europe and United States, 73-74, 126-30, 144-45, 162, 242-44; of general contractors, 20-21. *See also* electrical producers; specific countries; specific firms
environmental requirements. *See* aesthetic considerations
Essen, 194, 203-05
Etablissements Postel-Vinay, 130
Europe: and comparisons with United States, 68, 70-71, 84-85, 195-201; national differences in tramway electrification within, 73-74; and public policy on tramways, 244-46; recreational travel in, 226-29; and spread of electric tramways, 67-83. *See also* specific countries and cities
Eu to Tréport Tramway Company, 148, 152
excursions, 227-229
Exploration Company of London, 145, 151-52

fares. *See* tramways, fares of
feeders, 62, 102, 134-35, 182
Field, S. D., 42
Fives-Lille Company, 153
Foiret, A., 128
Fontainebleau, 154
Forest, 212, 215-16
France: 22, 72-74, 76, 81-82, 126-62; and aesthetic considerations, 86-87, 101-02; competition for concessions in, 17, 138-40, 153-54; conditions of tramway workers in, 140, 231-32, 238; early tramways in, 17-18; electrical manufacturers of, 109, 126-44; and electric tramways after 1900, 154-62, 191; entrepreneurship in, 74, 242-44; fares in, 113-14, 116-17; investment in electric tramways in, 66-69; profits of tramways in,

France *(cont.)*
131, 158; regulation of tramways in, 89, 94, 142; riders on tramways in, 59-61, 80-82, 240; and tramway law of 11th of June 1880, 19-21, 94, 133. *See also* specific cities franchises. *See* concessions
Francq, Léon, 33
Frankfurt-Offenbach Tramway Company, 39, 46
Frankfurt on the Main, 17, 108, 179, 194, 223
French Thomson-Houston Company (La Compagnie Française pour l'Exploitation des procédés Thomson-Houston): 100, 126-44, 156-57, 161-62, 173, 243; accomplishments of, 149; begins manufacturing and financing equipment, 130-31; at Bordeaux, 138-41; comparison of, with British Thomson-Houston Company, 171; and competition with other firms, 146, 153; and dividends paid, 143; and electric tramways at Rouen, 133-38; and increases of capital, 128-30; origins of, 127-130; profits of, 132-33, 142-44; and financial return on its tramway shares, 141; at Rouen, 133-38

General Electric Company, 127-29, 157, 170-71, 183
General Electric Power and Traction Company, 165-67, 179
General French Tramways Company, 17, 134, 143; and early experiments with mechanical traction, 32-33; financial problems of, 131-32; after 1900, 158-59
General Omnibus Company, 12-13, 16, 146-47, 157, 159, 161, 230
General Paris Tramways Company, 81, 146, 159, 161
General Traction Company, 144-55; criticized as monopoly, 146; financial difficulties of, 151-53; inflated capital of, 148, 159; and resignation of founders, 152; suburban concessions of, 146-47
Genoa, 56, 225
Gera, 78
Germany: 22, 53, 67, 240, 243-44; and acceptance of overhead wires, 108-09; conditions of tramway workers in, 230, 232-38; development of electric tramways in, 75-82; early tramways of, 17; electrical manufacturers of, 125-26; entrepreneurship in, 73-74; fares in, 113, 115-16, 120, 123; increase of riders in, 80-82; and investment in electric tramways, 67; profits of operating companies in, 80; rides per capita in, 193-98
Gesellschaft für elektrischen Unternehmungen, 115
Ghent, 96-97
Glasgow: 9, 166, 199-200; Common Good Fund of, 183; fares at, 177, 183; leadership of, in Great Britain, 173-84, 187, 190; and manufacturing facilities at Coplawhill, 176, 183; municipalization of tramways in, 175-76; profits of municipal tramways at, 178, 183; riders on tramways in, 183-84, 193, 197; struggle of city with tramways company, 174-77; suburban expansion of, 183-84
Glasgow Corporation. *See* Glasgow
Glasgow Corporation Tramways. *See* Glasgow
Glasgow Herald, 180
Glasgow Tramways and Omnibus Company, 173-77, 179
Glasgow Tramways Committee, 176, 178-79, 190
Gould, Jay, 48
Great Berlin Horse Railway Company. *See* Great Berlin Street Railway Company

Great Berlin Street Railway Company, 29, 121, 237-38
Great Britain: concessions for tramways in, 20, 111, 168-69; condition of tramway workers in, 229-30, 232, 234-35, 238; conservatism of, 95; double-deckers in, 53; electrical producers in, 185-86; entrepreneurship in, 73-74, 243-44; foreign investment of, 133, 243-44; horse tramways in, 16-17, 22, 163n; hostility toward horse tramways companies in, 169, 174-75; inadequate depreciation for tramways in, 188-191; and investment in electric tramways, 66-69; management of municipal tramways in, 186-91; municipal enterprise in, 171-91; number of cities with municipal tramways in, 184-85; and opposition to overhead conductors, 109, 163-65, 168; regulation in, 19-21, 167, 173; riders on tramways in, 59-61, 80-83, 240; spread of electric tramways in, 71-73, 76, 168-73; and standardization of tramway equipment, 185-86; and State Carriage Act of 1832, 20; steam tramways in, 29-31; and Tramways Act of 1870, 20, 168-69, 172, 174, 184; and Use of Mechanical Power on Tramways Act of 1879, 30-31; and workmen's fares, 116. *See also* individual cities
Greater Leipzig Tramways Company, 114-15
Gross-Lichterfelde line, 38, 44
Guillain, F., 156
Gulich and Company, 203
Gunzburg, Baron, 145

hackney carriages, 5
Halle, 57, 65, 77
Halle Tramway Company, 77-78
Hallidie, Andrew, 40

Hamburg, 17, 31, 70, 96, 117, 119-22, 194
Hamburg Street Railway Company, 119-21, 237
Hanover, 11, 17, 79, 96, 194
Harding, Palmer, 21, 27, 133-34, 146n
Hartmann (tramway director), 222
Hendlmeier, Wolfgang, 209
Holland, 22
Holy Roman Empire, 3
Hopkinson, Edward, 164, 170
horses, 62, 87-88, 99; and hygiene, 26, 107-08; traction with, 9-10. *See also* tramways, horse; individual cities and companies
housing. *See* lower classes, housing
Howe, Frederic, 198
Hüber battery cars, 119
Huddersfield, 173
Hungary, 81n. *See also* Austria-Hungary

incandescent lamp, 43, 78
Indianapolis, 195
industrialization, 6-8, 241
L'Industrie Electrique, 71, 75
Institute of Civil Engineers, 164
Institution of Electrical Engineers, 168
International Congress of Tramways, 222
investment: American, in France, 126-30; in electric tramways, 61-69; foreign, 127-28; 144-45; in tramways, by public, 148-49, 151-52, 155-56
Italy, 72, 243

Jacobi, H. M., 36
Johnson, E. H., 47
Julien battery cars, 96

Kansas City, 195
Karlsruhe, 17
Keighley Tramways Company, 26
Kellett, John R., 9
Kiel, 194

Kiev, 54, 56
Kindleberger, Charles P., 126n
Kingston-upon-Hull, 7-8, 15, 229
Kitson engines, 31
Knight, Walter, 44-45
Konigsberg, 194
Krummer Company, 79
Krupp of Essen, 203-04

La Compagnie pour la fabrication des compteurs et matériel d'usines à gaz, 128-29
Lamm, Emile, 33
Lampard, Eric, 52
Latin America, 244
leases for tramways. *See* concessions
Le Creusot, 154
Leeds, 116, 193; Roundhay Park line for, 167, 170, 180
Left Bank Tramways Company, 146, 150-51, 159n, 160
Le Havre, 17, 134
Leipzig, 11, 31, 94; development of electric tramways in, 114-17, 194, 197; horse tramways in, 17, 24-25
Leipzig Electrical Tramway Company, 115. *See also* Greater Leipzig Tramways Company
Le Mans, 153n
Liège, 144
Lille, 7-8, 33
Lille-Roubaix-Tourcoing "Electric" Company, 224
Lindheim, Wilhelm von, 193, 196
Lingard, John, 228
Liverpool, 7, 9, 17, 193, 197, 228
London: 187, 197, 224, 230; early public transportation in, 4-6; omnibus service in, 9-10, 12-13, 23
London County Council, 166
London Crystal Palace Exhibition of 1882, 47
London General Omnibus Company Ltd., 12
London underground, 47, 145, 164n
Loubat, Alphonse, 14-16
lower classes, housing of, 206-08, 219, 221-23
Lyons, 11, 33, 81, 98, 110, 153
Lyons Tramways Omnium Company, 153-56, 225

Macartney, McElroy and Company, 182, 185
Manchester: riders on tramways at, 193, 197, 217-18
Mannesmann Pipe Works, and its poles for tramways, 101-05, 120
Marseilles: 17, 100, 227; conditions of tramway workers in, 231-32; renegotiation of concession at, 110, 118
Martin, Albro, 198
Martin, Alfred, 6
Maruéjouls, Emile, 150, 152
Mason, John, 14
Massachusetts, 92-93
Massachusetts Street Railway Commission, 93
Mather and Platt Company, 164, 170, 185
Mechanical Tramways for the Suburbs of Paris Company, 146, 152
Mekarski compressed-air engines, 29-30, 33-34
Merryweather and Sons of London, 27, 29
Metropolitan Company, of Paris. *See* Paris, underground railway
Metz, 17
Mézières, 152
Michel, A., 227
Middle East, 244
Milan, 110, 130
Milwaukee, 195
Minneapolis, 195
"mixed" systems of electric traction, 75-76, 99-100, 106-07
Montauban, 154
Montluçon, 154
Montpellier, 152
Morgan, J. P. 127
Morison, Fynes, 4

INDEX   263

Moscow, 225
Mulhouse, 81, 227
Munich, 11, 17, 84, 109-11, 112, 117-18, 194, 209
Municipal Electrical Association, 186
municipal enterprise, 171-91, 238
Municipal Tramways Association, 186-88
Murphy (tramway manager), 179

Nagelmackers, Jules, 144
Nancy, 17, 85
Nantes, 10, 33, 226
Nantes Tramways Company, 34
Naples, 225
Napoleon Bonaparte, 209
Newark, 195
New Orleans, 33
New Vienna Tramway Company, 111
New York, 10-11, 15, 38, 92, 195-97, 224
New York and Harlem Railroad Company, 14
Neyrand, Louis, 153
Northern Pacific Railroad, 42
North Metropolitan Tramways Company, of London, 29, 96, 165-67, 179
North Paris Tramways Company, 30
North-South subway line, of Paris, 154, 225
Nottingham, 193
Nuremberg, 194, 223-24

Oerlikon Works, 79, 132
Oldham, 217-18
Omaha, 195
Omnes (hatmaker), 10
omnibuses, 10 13, 18, 22-23. See also individual cities
Oran, 153n
Orléans, 17
overhead conductors, 39, 44, 74-76, 135, 163, 239; agreement to remove, 117-18; at Bordeaux, 139-40; cost of, 62-63; defense of, 107-09; development of, 45-51; at Glasgow, 180-82; in Great Britain, 187; opposition to, in Europe, 84-95; at Paris, 150, 160-61; safety of, 87-88; and Siemens and Halske, 132; and Sprague, 48-51. See also specific cities; specific countries; tramways, electric
overhead electric system. See overhead conductors

Page motor, 36
Paris: 25, 30, 96, 99-100, 220, 230-31, 235; concessions at, 94, 146-47; early public transportation in, 4-6; and General Omnibus Company, 146-47; omnibuses and horse tramways in, 10-13, 15-18, 23; and overhead wires, 86, 150; reorganization of public transport in, 157-61; and steam tramways, 27-28, 31; suburban tramways for, 33-34, 146-50, 155, 209; tramways riders in, 81, 161; and underground railway, the Metropolitan Company, 146-47, 149, 159, 161, 225; workmen's tramways at, 116-17
Paris and Department of the Seine Tramways Company, 114
Paris Exposition of 1881, 39, 46
Paris Exposition of 1900, 158
Pascal, Blaise, 5, 10
Passer, Harold C., 36, 41n, 42-43
Paton, Walter, 181
Pau, 154
paving requirement, 26
peasants, 208
Philadelphia, 11, 197
Philippart, Faure and Reynier, 99
Poitiers, 154
poles, 84-85, 87-88, 101-07, 120-21, 182
pollution problems, on London underground, 47
Porter, Robert P., 199
Portrush to Bushmills tramway, 39, 70

Portugal, 128
power stations, 62
Prussian Ministry of Public Works, 124
Purrey locomotives, 29

railroads, 8-9, 13, 22, 42, 44, 198n
rails, 13-16, 20, 63, 120n, 134
Rathenau Emil, 43, 78
regulation of tramways: in Europe, 88-94; in France after 1900, 157-62; in Paris, 146-47; in United States, 91-94. *See also* specific cities; specific countries, tramways
Reims Tramways Company, 23
Reise (engineer), 108
Remscheid, 54
Renard (engineer), 144
Rennes, 153n
Rice, E. W., 128
Richebourg Baths Coach, 10
Richmond, 47, 49-50, 70
rides per capita, comparison of Europe and the United States, 195-98. *See also* tramways, rides on
"ring streets," 18
Rochefort, 154
Rochester, 195
Rogers, J. H., 189
Rome, 110
Roubaix, 33, 153n
Rouen: 21, 59, 117-18, 146, 226; electrification of tramways at, 133-38; tramway riders at, 135-37
Rouen Tramways Company, 133, 138
Roundhay Park Line. *See* Leeds
Rowan, W. R., 29, 109-10
Russia, 53, 72, 127, 145n, 243-44
Ryde Pier, 39, 70

Saint-Nazaire, 154
St. Paul, 195
St. Peter Port, Guernsey, 170
St. Petersburg, 111
Saint-Quentin, 154

San Francisco, 195
Schukert and Company, 79, 99, 111
Scientific American, 58-59
sedan chair, 6
Serpollet locomotives, 29
Sheffield, 193
Siemens, Werner von, and the development of electric traction, 37-41, 43-45
Siemens and Halske Company, 78-79, 111, 170
Siemens Brothers, 185
Siemens equipment, 89, 154; and "mixed" systems of, 99-100, 124
Singer Company, 79
Siry, E., 128
snowplow cars, 55
Société Alsacienne de Constructions Mécaniques, 154
Société Generale (of France), 151, 155
South Africa, 145
South Bend, 46
South Paris Tramways Company, 27, 146n
Spain, 72, 128
Sprague, Frank J., 127-28; and the development of electric traction, 47-50, 70
Sprague equipment, 74
Stewart, J. E., 186
Stettin, 194
stock-market break of 1900, 151
Stockport, 217-19
Street Railway Journal, 51, 70, 96n
street railways. *See* tramways
streets: congestion in, 37-38, 224-25; management of, for tramways, 102, 106, 108, 172; quality of, and urban transport, 11-12, 14-15, 41, 49; rebuilding of, for electric tramways, 222-24
Stuttgart, 17, 56, 194
surface-conduit conductors, 74-76, 98-99
surface-contact system, 98-99
Swiss Engineering Works of Winterthur, 29, 119

INDEX 265

Switzerland, 22, 72

technological alternatives, 83, 112-13, 245-46; development of, 74-77, 95-107; in Europe and America, 74-75. *See also* specific cities, countries, firms; tramways, electric
technology, gains from, 63, 90-91. *See also* tramways, electric
telephone and telegraph lines, 87-88
Terbueren, 216
Thomson-Houston Electric Company, 45, 47, 50, 126-29. *See also* British Thomson-Houston Company; French Thomson-Houston Company; Union Elektricitäts-Gesellschaft
Thomson-Houston equipment, 74, 110; in Germany, 54, 77-78, 109, 116, 119, 123; in Great Britain, 167, 170. For France, *see* French Thomson-Houston Company
Thomson-Houston International Company, 127-28
Thury system of overhead traction, 132
Toronto, 87
Toronto Exhibition of 1884, 45
Toulouse, 155
Tours, 17
trailer cars, 53-54, 63
Train, George Francis, 16
tramways, electric: advantages of, 51-67; at Bordeaux, 138-41; capital requirements of, 61-63; and central business district, 220; diffusion of, in Europe, 67-83, 239-46; early European lead in, 40, 70; early experiments with, 35-46; on experimental basis for certain lines, 109-10, 167; fares of, 58, 113-14, 135-37, 139-140, 149-50; and growth of Brussels, 209-16; and housing for poorer classes, 55, 114, 205-17; and impact on society, 192-238; and increases in fares, 160-61; investment in, 61-69; and land values, 220-22; at Leipzig, 114-16; limitations of, 224-25; and lower classes, 202-05, 226, 241; in Manchester, 197, 216-19; operating costs of, 58-61; profits of, 136-37; and recreation, 225-29, 241-42; riders on, 80-83, 135-37, 140, 193-203; at Rouen, 133-38; and suburban expansion, 114, 205-25, 241; and tramway workers, 117, 232-38, 242; and urban planning, 222-24; workmen's tickets on, 116-17, 138. *See also* aesthetic considerations; France; Germany; Great Britain; overhead conductors; specific cities; United States
tramways, horse: compared with electric tramways, 52-55, 58-59; continued use of, 29-32; development of, 14-18, 21-22; disadvantages of, 25-27; fares of, 22-25; origins of, 13-14; and private enterprise, 18-21; profits of, 80, 131; and recreation, 227; regulation of, 18-21; riders on, 22-25; at Rouen, 133-34. *See also* France; Germany; Great Britain; specific cities; tramways, electric
tramways, steam, 27-34, 40, 50
Tramways of Paris and the Department of the Seine Company, 146, 149, 157, 159
transportation, public: and antipollution considerations, 30-34, 84-95; development of technological alternatives for, 95-107; development of, in Europe with electric tramways, 66-83, 192-205; early developments in, 3-12; and early European experiments with electric traction, 35-40; and horse tramways, 13-25; increased use of, 192-205; and industrialization, 6-8; and municipal enterprise,

transportation (cont.)
66; regulation of, 19-21, 89-95, 107-24; revolution in, 239-42. See also cities; concessions; France; Germany; Great Britain; tramways, electric; tramways, horse
trolley wheel, 46. See also overhead conductors
Trouvé battery car, 39
Tsaritsyn, 155
Tudor-Hagen Company, 79

Uccle, 212, 214-15
U.E.G. See Union Elektricitäts-Gesellschaft
Uetersen, 17
underground railways, 224-25. See also London underground; Paris, underground railway
Union Elektricitäts-Gesellschaft, 78-79, 116, 127
Union of French Tramways, 207
United Kingdom. See Great Britain
United States, 26, 53, 84-85, 190-91, 220, 239-41, 243-44; cable cars in, 50; and comparison with Europe, 70-71, 90-95, 195-201; development of electric traction in, 44-51; electrical manufacturers in, 127; regulation in, 91-94; rides per capita in, 195-98; steam tramways in, 30, 41, 50; street railways in, after 1900, 198-202

Vals-les-Bains, 153n
Van Depoele, Charles, 45-50
Vanves to Paris (Champ de Mars) Tramway, 157-58
Vienna, 18, 24, 54, 86, 100, 111, 225, 230
Vienna Streetcar Company, 24
Villard, Henry, 42
Vilvorde, 216
Volk, Magnus, 38-39

waiting pavillions, 121-22
Warner, Sam B. Jr., 7
Watermael, 212, 215
West Brighton and Shoreham Tramway Company, 165
West Ham Corporation, 166-67
Westinghouse equipment, 74, 182
West Paris Tramways Company, 146, 149-50, 160
Wiener Bankverein, 111
Wiesbaden, 17
Wigam Tramway Company, 166
Wilkinson steam trams, 29
Winterthur steam locomotives, 119
workers on tramways, 117, 172-78, 229-238. See also specific cities
working class usage. See tramways, riders on
workmen's fares, 116-17, 138
Wuppertal, 17

Yerkes, Charles T., 145, 199
Young, John, 181-82, 190

zone system, 113-14, 137-38

Library of Congress Cataloging in Publication Data

McKay, John P
    Tramways and trolleys.

    Bibliography: p.
    Includes index.
    1. Street-railroads—Europe—History. 2. Urban transportation—Europe—History. I. Title.
HE3812.M33   1976   388.4′094   76-3261
ISBN 0-691-05240-9